The rise of the Rustbelt

The rise of the Rustbelt

EDITED BY

Philip Cooke
University of Wales, Cardiff

First published in 1995 by UCL Press.

UCL Press Limited
University College London
Gower Street
London WC1E 6BT

The name of University College London (UCL) is a registered
trade mark used by UCL Press with the consent of the owner.

ISBNs:1-85728-419-4 HB
        1-85728-420-8 PB

British Library Cataloguing in Publication Data
A catalogue record for this book is available from the British Library.

Typeset in Palatino.
Printed and bound by
Biddles Ltd, Guildford and King's Lynn, England.

Contents

Preface

In October 1992 I had the honour of presenting a lecture on the subject of "European experiences of regional economic development" at a conference held by European Dialogue, a UK organizing committee for the Prague-based Helsinki Citizens' Assembly. The conference, held in Manchester (UK), was jointly organized by the Friedrich Ebert Foundation in association with Charter 88, the Centre for Local Economic Strategies, Helsinki Citizens' Association (Scotland) and the New Economics Foundation.

The conference proceedings were subsequently published by European Dialogue (11 Goodwin St, London N4 3HQ) under the conference title of *Power to the people? Economic self-determination and the regions*. Among the contributors are Will Hutton, then Economics Editor of *The Guardian*, Paatricia Hewitt, Deputy Director of the Institute for Public Policy Research, the Chairs of the Scottish and Welsh Assembly Campaigns, Isobel Lindsay and John Osmond, and the Co-Chair of the Helsinki Citizens' Assembly, Mary Kaldor.

The conference explored the case for increased regional economic and political self-determination in the UK, drawing on experiences from other European countries and, to a lesser extent, North America. That the conference became committed to the goal of increased regional autonomy in the UK was testified to by the founding of Regional Dialogue, a campaigning network of organizations dedicated to decentralization and democratic renewal. Coincidentally, the conference took place as the mass closure programme was announced for the British coal industry, preparatory to its privatization. The question of regional economic renewal from within was thus a live issue in the political context of the day.

Alive to the exceptional difficulties of endogenous renewal faced by regions in process of losing their economic rationale, Klaus Funken, Director of the London office of the Ebert Foundation suggested I organize a joint conference between the authorities responsible for the Ruhr district of Germany and industrial South Wales in the UK. The Ebert Foundation kindly agreed to be a main co-funder of such an event, to be held in Cardiff during the following year. With the support of other co-funders, the conference duly took place in September, 1993. That was the origin of this book.

To the name of the Friedrich Ebert Foundation were subsequently added the co-sponsorships of the Anglo–German Foundation for the Study of Industrial Society, thanks to the support of its Projects Director, Dr Ray Cunningham, the Welsh Development Agency, through its then Head of Marketing Research, Penny Mitchell, and the International Labour Office,Geneva, through its Industrial Activities Branch Chief, Gabriele Stoikov, and the Head of the New Industrial Organization Programme of the International Institute for Labour Studies, Dr Werner Sengenberger. Each of these supporters deserves the fullest acknowledgement and grateful thanks for enabling the conference to take place, bringing experts from Germany and beyond, to succeed. As noted later in this book, a further conference, hosted by the government of North-Rhine–Westphalia, then took place in October 1994.

By the 1994 conference, the scope had grown to include reports of regional renewal strategies from North America too. This offered a useful opportunity to bring such stories to even wider academic, business and policy communities than the original Europe-only concept. In collecting proceedings from the Cardiff conference, I took the opportunity of commissioning three new contributions from friends in older industrial regions of Canada and the USA. The result is as presented. I take pleasure in thanking Roger Jones, Publisher and Chief Executive of UCL Press Limited for his excellent stewardship of this project from the outset. It has truly been a joint effort. I wish also to thank colleagues at the Centre for Advanced Studies, especially Jean Rees and George Karyotakis, for helping enormously and quickly with Roger Jones' IT demands.

The book itself seeks to show the possibilities and some of the limits, pitfalls even, of policy efforts made by business and government to bring about the renewal of badly hit regional economies, whose dependence on industries of the earlier phases of industrialization left them vulnerable to deindustrialization in the final quarter of the twentieth century. The findings of the book give some grounds for hope that increased regional autonomy over industrial policies can often be associated with success in the restructuring of older industrial economies. Of central importance is an institutional structure capable of consolidating regional interests to enable global and local economic forces to be integrated at the regional level. Successful regional economies have often shown this capacity in the past. Now there is evidence that some recently less successful regions have learnt lessons enabling them to develop the foundations for economic success in the future.

Phil Cooke, Centre for Advanced Studies, University of Wales, Cardiff
May, 1995

Contributors

Bob Beauregard, Professor at the Graduate School of Public and International Affairs, University of Pittsburgh.

Gerhard Bosch is a Professor and Director of the Labour Market division of the Institute of Work and Technology, Gelsenkirchen.

Phil Cooke is a Professor and Director of the Centre for Advanced Studies in the Social Sciences, University of Wales, Cardiff.

Sara Davies is a Researcher at the Department of City & Regional Planning, University of Wales, Cardiff.

Sabina Deitrick is Assistant Professor at the Graduate School of Public and International Affairs, University of Pittsburgh.

Richard Florida is a Professor and Director of the Centre for Economic Development, H. John Heinz III School of Public Policy and Management, Carnegie–Mellon University, Pittsburgh.

Meric Gertler is a Professor and Director, Program in Planning, Department of Geography, University of Toronto.

Rob Huggins is a Researcher at the Centre for Advanced Studies in the Social Sciences, University of Wales, Cardiff.

Heiderose Kilper is a Senior Researcher at the Institute of Work & Technology, Gelsenkirchen.

Jon Morris is Professor of Management at the Business School, University of Glamorgan.

Rolf Plake is a Senior Consultant with ISA Consult, Hamburg.

Dieter Rehfeld is a Senior Researcher at the Institute of Work and Technology, Gelsenkirchen.

Reinhard Thomalla is the Chief Officer of the Ministry of Economics, Government of North-Rhine–Westphalia.

Richard Watson is an independent consultant, specializing in energy and environmental matters.

Gerald Wood is a Lecturer in the Department of Geography, University of Duisburg.

CHAPTER ONE

Introduction

Phil Cooke

This book has been prompted by a remarkable turnaround in the economic fortunes of what were, only a decade ago in the early 1980s, all too easily dismissed as the redundant "Rustbelt" regions of Europe and North America. Terms such as the "Sunbelt" or, more prosaically, "the South" were ranged against "Snowbelt", "Frostbelt", or equally prosaically, "the North", as markers of economic dynamism and economic collapse respectively (Perry & Watkins 1978, Sawers & Tabb 1984). Now, in the 1990s, the tables appear to be turning once again, with huge question marks hovering over the defence industries, which contributed massively to Sunbelt success in the USA and European high technology sectors, and signs of successful restructuring in some "sunset" industries and regions.

The origin of the chapters on the UK and German subunits of Wales and North-Rhine–Westphalia lay in a conference, held in October 1993 in Cardiff, which sought to explore, compare and contrast the apparently successful restructuring strategies adopted by their industry and regional development authorities. The conference was entitled "Revitalising Older Industrial Regions" and it brought together an interesting mix of business, policy and academic personnel from the two countries. They spoke on four main themes that remain well represented in the book: regional and urban *economic policies, business strategies,* vocational and further *training initiatives,* and *environmental policies.* This matrix of themes and professional groupings was deemed such a successful way of examining the questions posed that a second, larger conference was held in Oberhausen, in the heart of the Ruhr district, in October 1994. This conference, funded by the North-Rhine–Westphalian government through its research institutes at Düsseldorf, Gelsenkirchen and Wuppertal, was entitled "Regiovision: Roads To Sustainability."

1

In the latter conference, the scope of representation was extended to include reports from other regions in process of restructuring, notably from both the US "Sunbelt" and "Frostbelt", and from southern and central Europe: Catalonia in Spain and Upper Silesia in Poland. In part this echoed the sentiment that more evidence was needed to establish how justified and generalizable the suspicion was that the Rustbelt might be reviving, especially from North America. Hence, for this book, invitations were issued to researchers working on the older industrial regions of the USA and Canada to contribute their findings, keeping within the broad thematic perspectives that had framed the conference proceedings. To keep an already complex project under control, the book's focus was restricted to UK (Wales), Germany (North-Rhine–Westphalia) and North America (Great Lakes Region) in geographical terms (but, for example, for southern Europe see Garofoli 1992; for Central and Eastern Europe, see Gorzelak & Kuklinski 1992 and Gorzelak & Jalowiecki 1993).

Remarkably, what had occurred in the 1990s in the two older European industrial regions, based on coal and steel production, appeared also to be the case for the North American Great Lakes Region. That is, by dint of industrial restructuring supported by regional economic development policies of various kinds, there were strong signs of regional economic recovery, especially economically down stream of these traditional staple industries in engineering and services of many kinds. What is most intriguing in terms of regional economic development theory is the common observation, which can be made from each region, that the revival of heavy industry regions occurs through a shift to higher skilled, higher value-added *engineering* industry rather than – as many policy experts advised in the early 1980s – seeking to leapfrog into wholly new, often high technology sectors.

In none of the cases to be presented in depth in this book could successful restructuring be said to have taken place following a sustained policy of seeking to attract conventionally understood high tech industry (e.g. semiconductors, computers, advanced telecoms, software, aeronautics, biotechnology, etc.). Importantly, though, that is emphatically *not* to say that a technology policy has been absent from the rebuilding process initiated and pursued by regional and federal or central government administrations during the late 1980s and early 1990s. In each case a heightened place for technology support has been found, most notably in North-Rhine–Westphalia, but that support has been aimed more or less universally at assisting innovation not in traditional, nor in high tech, industries, but in *modern developments* of twentieth-century products, notably *auto-*

motive and *electronics* industries or innovative uses for traditional engineering technologies, classically in the development of the *environmental technologies* cluster in North-Rhine–Westphalia. In reporting these developments, the book will seek to account for this phenomenon of *regeneration of mature technologies* in theoretical and empirical terms. In doing so, attention will focus particularly on three interrelated categories that crop up repeatedly: regions, clusters, and innovation networks.

Regions, clusters and innovation networks

In an era when the power of the largest multinational corporations to operate on a global canvas has become even more entrenched, it may be thought that economic or administrative organization at anything less than the traditional nation State level would be too weak to exert significant influence over their locational and other investment decisions. However, such an assumption would be misplaced. By the late 1980s Sony and Honda, two of Japan's leading multinationals, were using the rhetoric of "global localization" in their advertising material; by the 1990s, aspects of the strategy were being implemented (Cooke et al. 1992).

"Global localization", as defined by Sony and Honda, and subsequently emulated by other Japanese corporate giants such as Mitsubishi, involves structuring corporate organization with the aim of having the complete range of corporate business functions in each of the three "Triad" markets of the global economy – Europe, North America and Southeast Asia (Ohmae 1985). Global localization involves establishing overseas marketing offices, increasing local content ratios in production, building up overseas financing functions, and establishing local research and development (R&D) facilities. Then, within this functional framework, locals are promoted to managerial positions, they gain increasing autonomy from head office, seek quotations on local stock markets and diversify the business according to local demand (Cooke et al. 1992).

Actions speak louder than words and, until recently, the acid tests of management autonomy and the export of R&D showed Sony, Honda, Mitsubishi and Fujitsu, the strongest proponents, to be some way from fulfilling the aspiration. However, Sony's European Technology Centre at Stuttgart shows far more interest in developing factory automation than might be anticipated from a consumer electronics company. Similarly, Sharp, with R&D based at Oxford, has local product development author-

3

ity for consumer products. According to official figures, Japanese companies claim at least 264 "R&D facilities" in Europe as a whole, 83 in the UK, 53 in Germany. However, of these only 19 and 18 respectively can be classed as independent, non-factory–based facilities. In fact only Canon, with two companies on the Surrey University technology park, comes close to behaving in the way suggested by the "global localization" rhetoric. Both Canon Audio and Criterion Software have complete, localized innovation and commercialization, but not, as yet, stock flotation (Lorenz 1994).

In contrast, US companies increased by ninefold the amount of R&D expenditure abroad in the 1985–91 period in support of US overseas capital investment that expanded significantly in the 1970s. Three forces are perceived to underpin this process. First, *globalization*, which means there is more R&D activity in each of the Triad economies originating from other Triad areas. Secondly, knowledge production itself has become more geographically spread, no longer being the preserve of the USA, as it was for much of the post-war period during which US research came to predominate. Thirdly, foreign researchers are cheaper than American. Thus, whereas R&D investment by US firms stagnated in the USA from 1985 to 1991, it practically doubled abroad, reaching US$8.7 billion in 1991, with 75 per cent in Europe, and only 6 per cent in Japan (Shapley 1994).

Importantly, this kind of investment by Japan and the USA, whether in independent R&D, or more factory-linked, is geographically focused at the micro-regional as well as the macro-regional level. Thus, Sharp have their European R&D centre at Oxford, and Toshiba and Hitachi both have basic research centres at Cambridge, the former at the Cavendish laboratory where in 1994 a breakthrough in "quantum effect integrated circuits" built on that centre's pedigree in atomic research and promises to revolutionize micro-electronics technology in the next decade (Cookson 1994). It has already been noted that Sony's European R&D centre is at Fellbach, near Stuttgart, in the heart of the Baden–Württemberg mechanical and electronics cluster. The reason for choosing that location was to access the large pools of highly qualified "mechatronics" postgraduates and to interact with the large numbers of subcontractor and user-firms in the manufacturing systems industry found locally (Cooke et al. 1993).

REGIONS

These observations lead to a reflection on recent research published by the OECD (de Vet 1993). In a detailed study of the interaction effects of globalization and location processes at the local level, de Vet (1993) found that the development of global networks of interlinked firms and the globalization of factors of production was accompanied by the reinforcement of *regional* production clusters. The reasons offered in explanation of this phenomenon are as follows. First, globalization expresses the effect of a weakening of the economic sovereignty of the nation State (see also Held 1991). That is, until the emergence of supranational economic associations such as the European Union, the advanced countries operated national economic policies, often supporting "national champion" industries or firms behind preferential trade barriers. Common markets make that impossible when, as after the Single Europe Act of 1992, these barriers are removed, such removal having already been discounted by key multinationals years earlier. The decline in regulatory influence by national governments over competitiveness in the domestic economy means its weaker parts ultimately go to the wall – coal, steel and textiles being classic instances, as testified by the content of this book. However, the corollary is that the internationally competitive parts of the economy, possibly just as regionalized as the declining sectors, seek competitive advantage by attempting to mobilize all their assets. National governments find it impossible overtly to champion strong, regionalized and competitive parts of the economy while being powerless to save uncompetitive parts. But regional administrations, where such exist, have no such qualms. Rather, they can be seen, and may see themselves, as having precisely such a "neo-mercantilist" remit in relation to their regions' economy and society.

Hence, mobilizing all a region's assets can mean including governmental and para-governmental agencies in promoting the strengths of the regional economy as a whole on an international canvas. This process can be further supported by the judicious adoption of regional industrial policies to smooth technology transfer, give grants to innovative start-ups or for establishment of R&D units in medium-size firms, as happened in the 1980s in some German, Italian and Spanish regions (Cooke et al. 1993, Körfer & Latniak 1994a). These processes of external promotion and internal support by regional authorities lead to enhanced regional specialization in competitive economic activities. This, in turn, makes such regions attractive to foreign direct investment, precisely one of the promotional aims of such regional activity. The region thus becomes more specialized in its strengths, and more and more of a global force in those areas of specialization. In a study of foreign direct investment in seven OECD countries de Vet (1993) found a strong tendency for globalization (measured in terms of

5

foreign direct investment) to reinforce regional specialization in the manner anticipated by the theory in question. In policy terms, the obvious recommendation is that regional economic competitiveness in the 1990s rests on successfully interlinking regional networks with global networks of innovation and production.

This is a different and more powerful analysis and argument than that which is associated with the often vacuous slogan of a "Europe of the Regions" (for a critique see Amin & Tomaney 1994, Meegan 1994). The latter aspiration, originating from the Strasbourg-based Council of Europe (1986), has mixed appeal, mainly to politicians and administrators involved in supranational governance in the European Union. But, as Harvie (1994) shows, quite convincingly, despite those origins, which converge around the widespread sense among EU politicians and administrators that the old nation States are often the main obstacle to progress, it is beginning to echo the emergence of phenomena such as those noted by de Vet (1993).

Whereas the Council of Europe line expressed a politico-administrative interest in eroding nation State sovereignty, its appeal was often to cultural regionalists from the suppressed nations embodied in the nineteenth-century nation States that came to prominence in the age of imperialism. But in the 1980s there emerged a new, more powerful, because more economically self-assured, phenomenon in Europe, which Harvie (1994) terms *"bourgeois regionalism"*. This is associated with, in some cases, historic "national regions" such as Catalonia or even Lombardy (where a particularly ungenerous regionalist backlash, originating in the Lombard League entered the Berlusconi government of Italy in 1994 as the geographically broader Northern League). But it is equally promoted by relatively new "regions" such as Baden–Württemberg and Rhône–Alpes. Together, these four formed the "Four Motors for Europe" partnership in 1987 as self-perceived "motor-regions" of their respective States, confident in their economic power and frustrated at their inability to act without reference to Paris, Rome, Madrid and Bonn.

Frustration of this kind was summed up by the President of Rhône–Alpes as follows:

"the European single market will only work on the back of co-operation between regions, irrespective of what passes between national capitals. Ironically, the creation of a single market is encouraging the region, like many of its European neighbours, to try to pull more decision-making power from a central government which it has always felt has interfered too much in local affairs." (Dawkins 1990)

6

Such sentiment led ultimately to the establishment under the Maastricht Treaty of the European Union's Committee of the Regions. The doctrine embodied in the Treaty envisages that two of the three "pillars" of the European Union, the EU institutions and the regions, will become more important, whereas the third, the States, will not. Already, dissatisfaction at the inadequate servicing of the new Committee of the Regions (it shares a secretariat with the Economic and Social Committee of the EU) and the fact that *local* authorities are represented (because the States are suspicious of the regions) mean that it is presently under review. For the 1996 revision of the Maastricht Treaty, these two problems are on the agenda of the review committee under the rapporteurship of the powerful Catalan President, Jordi Pujol. His view is that the Committee should get its own secretariat and that local government should be separated from the regions in the equivalent of a "lower house" of the committee. It remains to be seen whether this will be achieved, but the absolute centrality of the regional dimension to EU thinking is testified by the attention being given to the definition of regions by new members, hitherto relatively unregionalized, such as Sweden and Finland (Pujol 1994).

This resonates with recent findings from research conducted in the UK into the impact of the Single Market upon economic development, particularly in respect of the present and future role of industrial policy (Begg & Mayes 1993; see also NIEC 1994). A key conclusion drawn from this research is that the strict monetary and budgetary criteria being deployed within the exchange rate mechanism, and the trend towards economic and monetary union within the European Union, mean that central governments, influenced by their central banks, are extremely reluctant to commit themselves to strategic industrial policies that might incur major public expenditure. However, at regional level, many of Europe's most successful economies had implemented judicious, often customized, financial, technological and skills-related programmes of the kind identified in de Vet's (1993) work, and for the same reasons. Moreover, such programmes were often inclusive of institutions outside the confines of government itself. Thus, chambers of commerce, private technology-transfer agencies, local authorities, universities and research institutes were often to be seen operating in partnership to promote economic development in a regional setting. As will be seen, the initiatives taken by the *Land* government and others in North-Rhine–Westphalia to upgrade the competitiveness of the economy are a case in point, as ably described by Huggins & Thomalla in Chapter 2 and Bosch & Davies in Chapters 8 and 9 of this book.

Further support for the advancement of regions, as economic actors with enhanced influence during this era of globalization, has been advanced by Ohmae (1993). Building on his earlier analyses of the emergence of the Triad powers (ibid. 1985) and of the implications of this for the economic worth of national frontiers in an increasingly "borderless world" (ibid. 1990), he has turned his attention to the corollary in the "global–local" couplet. Ohmae foresees the rise of what he calls the "region State". He selects as exemplars of the process such "bourgeois regions" (Harvie 1994) as Baden–Württemberg, Catalonia and Alsace–Lorraine but also Wales (less a bourgeois than a historic non-State nation as Nairn 1977 sees it) and the aforementioned northern Italy. To these he adds interesting examples of cross-border economic regions such as San Diego–Tijuana, Hong Kong–Canton and Singapore–Indonesia. These are the natural economic zones of the borderless world, not the nation States whose borders are often economically meaningless, argues Ohmae.

Interestingly, Ohmae contrasts the success and size of the European Single Market and the North American Free Trade Area of Canada, Mexico and the USA, with the position in Asia and Japan, whose combined economies lag behind by some US$2 trillion. For Asia to keep pace with the EU and NAFTA, it needs to develop roughly a further 20 "region States", the aggregate of which, were they each to be the equivalent of a Singapore, would make up the deficit. China is the obvious source of these new region State economies. Fourteen new economic zones, one of which at Yunnan is a cross-border development with Laos and Vietnam, are under development. Vietnam itself, and the governments of Indonesia, Malaysia and Thailand (at the Straits of Malacca) are also developing such special economic zones. The key point about such economic regions, and older ones such as the American Midwest, and even the Sunbelt, is that their primary economic linkages are with other regions in the global economy rather than within their host nations.

It is in North America, especially since the signing of NAFTA, that the most significant new regionalisms have emerged. Quebec is clearly very close to being economically and politically autonomous although still within the Canadian federation. The 1994 election produced a solid vote in favour of independence and, clearly, the chances that Quebec may leave Canada altogether have to be seriously entertained. This has forced other Canadian provinces to look anew at their own relationships with the outside world. One of them, Ontario, has formed an economic partnership with the Four Motor Regions, along with Wales, which signed such an agreement in 1990. Ontario, as will be shown in Chapter 7, has experienced severe job-loss and restructuring consequent upon Canada's sign-ing of the NAFTA agreement, and it needs to globalize its trading practices rapidly. Such agreements are a means to doing this (see also Drache & Gertler 1991, Drache 1992).

But the most serious regionalist backlash in the NAFTA area occurred in the Chiapas region of Mexico. A neglected region in the south, with a large pre-Columbian population, Chiapas quickly began to experience both loss of domestic food markets and penetration of local markets by more effi-cient food producers from farther north. This in turn fomented a violent ethno-regional backlash and underground guerilla-based political move-ment, which has given the Mexican government pause to think about the impact of its globalization strategy as it affects its own people. Regrettably, repression rather than redistribution has been the initial response.

Thus, globalization is not without its tensions. Interestingly, whether these are primarily political or economic, they are increasingly being played out at the regional level. Economic forces of globalization, under conditions of deregulation of national economies and liberal free-trade policy at the international level, are causing regions to try to improve com-petitiveness. Where regional governance structures exist, these are joining forces with business to assist. Where they succeed, the regions in question attract further new investment from overseas. The old nation States are relatively powerless either to support declining industries or to redistrib-ute income because of the constraints imposed by the ideology of global monetarism. The key question to emerge from this analysis is whether or not "region States" can discover ways in which they can collaborate as well as compete (and not just as "clubs" of rich regions) to assist in the interregional equalization process without which, in some extreme cases, interregional competition may descend into war?

CLUSTERS

Since Porter (1990) applied the word "cluster" to the nineteenth-century idea of the *industrial district* – developed by Marshall (1927) to describe geographically concentrated groupings of firms, large and small, that interact with each other via subcontracting, joint venture or other collabo-rative means, gaining external economies of scale in so doing – the term has become popular with policy-makers, if less so with academics. Some of the latter have taken a snobbish view that here is yet another piece of corporate graffiti to emanate from Harvard Business School to enhance the marketing potential of the School rather than the firms it professes to advise. Other more leftward-leaning criticisms have stressed the emphasis on *"competitive advantage"* and seen Porter as an apologist for neoclassical economic theory masquerading as practical business advice, (see Lazonick 1992, Harrison 1994).

But Porter's work, which is mainly a synthesis of earlier research on modern industrial districts conducted in Italy (e.g. Brusco 1982, 1992, Becattini 1990) allied to his earlier derivation of successful business or corporate strategy from Chandler (1990), is neither of these caricatures. As Harrison (1994) notes, global competitive advantage for the firm or region rests upon four key economic characteristics:

- factor conditions: quality of labour force, infrastructure and finance for business
- demand conditions: scale and quality of the market at home and abroad
- supplier industries: globally competitive suppliers, specialized business services, including finance and innovation
- business strategy: rivalry between local firms but willingness to co-operate in research, sales & marketing.

These four conditions are perceived as essential to the development of clusters of densely networked firms capable of global reach but deriving their strength from regional markets. Krugman (1991) has noted a similar phenomenon in arguing that such clusters generate secondary demand for capital equipment, thus becoming important domestic markets in support industries outside the initial specialism, be it textiles or automotive components.

Porter's thesis emphasizes competitiveness and competition, but embedded in it is an interesting recognition of the relevance of co-operation to competitive advantage. This is spotted by Lazonick (1992) and others (e.g. Boekholt 1994), who note how Porter's own cases reveal the importance of interfirm co-operation to economic success. These include "government-supported technical institutes", "ties through the scientific community", "professional associations" and "family ties", as well as "links to other industries", "industry clubs" and "closely knit social–cultural links", to mention but a few. In truth, much of the source of Porter's theory of competitive advantage rests upon *co-operative* behaviour between firms, and between firms and institutions.

It is this hidden dimension of *co-operation* that helps give clusters their competitive advantage. Moreover, by underestimating the importance of co-operation, as eventually Porter (1990) himself does, there is a danger of failing to understand a key dimension of economic success, and one that may come to be a defining feature of the post-Keynesian economy. The key lineaments of the co-operative side of economic organization are shown adjacent to the more familiar competitive ones in Table 1.1.

Table 1.1 Co-operative and competitive economic co-ordination.

Co-operative	Competitive
(i) Through reciprocal agreements	(i) Rational cost–benefit comparison
(ii) Based on custom	(ii) Substitution of production factors
(iii)Sustained by reputation	(iii)Non-price competition
(iv) Provoked by competition	(iv) Enhanced by collaboration
(v) Integrated by trust	(v) Extended by user-involvement

Source: after Dei Ottati (1994).

Clusters are thus aggregates of firms and non-firm institutions that supply external economies of scale through their capacity for optimization of learning practices by co-operative as well as competitive economic relations and interactions.

When studies of clusters are done in detail, as is the case in Rehfeld's analysis of the old and new clusters in the Ruhr area (Ch. 6), it is evident that the linkage structures thereby mapped out represent the lines of co-operative force that facilitate the coalescence of the cluster. Some of these co-operative force-lines may be destructive, as, for instance, where they descend into cartels. Others are constructive, as when trusted partners exchange know-how, facilitate learning and help improve the performance of the regional economy as a whole.

Another good example of this is Boekholt's (1994) anatomy of the Dutch cut-flower industry, centred upon Amsterdam. This world-leader industry depends on the collective provision of vocational training, the development of basic research at universities and plant-breeding stations, and the existence of regional technical and other demonstration centres. Equally, it depends on competitive institutions such as the flower auction at Aalsmeer, and other auctions, or the highly competitive greenhouse suppliers or specialized logistics companies and retail outlets. These are expressions of an "associative" culture of economic activity (e.g. Casson 1993, Hirst 1994).

We receive a clear idea of the associative approach to public policy in the chapters by Huggins & Thomalla (Ch. 2) and Kilper & Wood (Ch. 10), who, in different ways, describe the partnerships that are a normal and long-established part of the economic development process in North-Rhine–Westphalia. Their emergence elsewhere is described for Wales in Chapter 3 and by Florida, Gertler and Deitrick/Beauregard for North America. In North-Rhine–Westphalia associative consortia and partnerships reinforce intraregional and subregional cluster formation, not only around regional technology development programmes such as PlaNet Ruhr but also econo-environmental regeneration strategies that are tasked with environmental recovery, economic renewal and cultural revaluation, such as that of the IBA Emscher Park.

In such a context, the co-operative dimension is to the forefront. Reciprocal agreements have to be established based on customary practice or the reputation of the forum members. At the heart of such processes must be the factor of mutual self-regard and, above all else, trust, the key element of the associative mode of co-ordination (on this, see Sabel 1992). To be sure, such associative behaviour and the policy networks (Marin & Mayntz 1991) that underpin them have competitive intent, to ensure their industry or district survives and prospers by becoming increasingly competitive. Cleaning up the Ruhr is not meant to turn it into a rural idyll by driving the inhabitants away; it is to make the area a more attractive place to live and work for both existing residents and those that might be attracted in as new firms and foreign firms conceivably become established as a result of the competitive success of the programme.

Interestingly, there are pronounced signs in Wales (Ch. 3), and the different parts of the North American Rustbelt that associative thinking, partnership building and encouragement of policy networks to facilitate the emergence of new industrial clusters are developing. The MAIN networks in Pennsylvania, as also described in Coy (1992) and Sabel (1992), are modelled on European ideas of cluster facilitation and policies in support of them. The Ontario provincial government has adopted an experimental policy of cluster-building from below, notably through community enterprise to regenerate such older industrial communities as Hamilton, where the steel industry is being restructured, by adopting an innovative strategy of building up the culture industries in connection directly and indirectly with the university and its associated arts and cultural capacity. This policy shows strong signs of learning from the developmental experience of Stratford, Ontario, a former railway town that has become world famous as a centre for the arts, especially theatre. And in Wales, the policies of the Welsh Office and Welsh Development Agency have sought to build partnerships to effect the urban renewal and face-lifting of former heavy-industry towns. Moreover, the partnership, associational, "club" or "forum" building process has been extended into industry through the Supplier Development Programme, which knits indigenous and inward-investing firms together in supply chains for the automotive, electronics, office-supply and medical technology industries.

In other words, in an era when stand-alone mass production on Fordist lines is no longer a source of competitive advantage (Lipietz 1987), the regional and subregional focus of policy networks and business predispositions coalesces around a common interest in optimizing the efficient functioning of an increasingly complex, externalized system of economic co-ordination. For the moment the cluster constitutes competitive advantage and the regional State is its facilitator.

INNOVATION NETWORKS

Mention has been made of networks in discussing the associative links between firms and non-firm agencies and institutions that comprise the cluster, or *milieu* as Maillat (1991) calls it. Networks are the nodes and linkages that constitute a cluster. But, crucially, we are reminded once again that these can be global as well as regional. Virtual "districts" of researchers no doubt exist, operating in cybertime over cyberspace, just as in Prato (Dei Ottati 1994) or Carpi (Brusco 1992) in northern Italy, entrepreneurs, politicians and the officers of local authorities or chambers of commerce interact in the local restaurant, wine bar or on the way to church.

Networks are often contrasted with *markets* on the one hand, and *hierarchies,* on the other. The distinctions are neatly drawn by Powell (1990):

> . . . In network modes of resource allocation, transactions occur neither through discrete exchanges (markets) nor by administrative fiat (hierarchies), but through networks of individuals or institutions engaged in reciprocal, preferential, mutually supportive actions. (Powell 1990: 78; parentheses added)

Powell provides the key to understanding of the essential ingredients of successful *networking* as a practical activity.

In the global economic context of today, with the nation State losing much of its ability to promote the economic wellbeing of its citizens, regions are gaining in importance, as we have seen. One reason for this, having to do with networking, is that they are of a suitable scale for networking within the milieu of the cluster. Accordingly, co-ordinated efforts can be meaningfully undertaken to promote wealth-creating economic activities. In mobilizing all their assets to position themselves favourably within global markets, thereby strengthening sector-specific industrial clusters, they benefit from the double advantage of clustering, as discussed, *and* relatively close geographical co-location. This means important face-to-face interaction can occur, as well as more remote electronic networking. The importance of this, according to Chesnais (1988) and Johanson (1991), who have examined the *innovative* functions of networks, is as follows:

> . . . Dealing with practical, production-related issues, such as designing software or making product adjustments or applications tend to be geographically clustering phenomena. Trust is built between lower managers, and the networks they build are kept going for as long as possible . . . (quoted in Harrison 1994: 75).

Networking is more efficient than *markets* (where trust is at a minimum and key information may remain undisclosed) or *hierarchies* (where knowledge is power) in realizing the potential for creating and diffusing economically exploitable knowledge as the key to competitive success.

A network form of innovation *architecture* is based on flow-processes (echoing Castells' notion of a "space of flows" in the informational city; Castells 1989) rather than on the more prosaic basic–specific competences of administrative institutions. It goes beyond the static supply of services to individual firms and implies a collective setting of direction. Successful networking requires:

- an initial predisposition to *exchange* information
- *trust* in the *reliability* of the other participants
- a recognition that best practice is transferable through *learning*
- a willingness to keep key reciprocal relationships *preferential*
- inclusion and active participation through *empowerment* in the flow-processes of the network.

In other words, networks involve relationships of mutual dependence but provide gains from the pooling of competences. A significant amount of "*social capital*" (Putnam 1993) has to be invested, which is always vulnerable to changes in institutional position of the different network members. To some extent they may also constrain members' capacity to act (unlike, say, markets, where contracts can be terminated) where dependence becomes too one-sided.

One of the most important spheres in which networks assist wealth-creation and regional competitiveness is *innovation.* This is the process whereby new knowledge, patented as an invention, is moved to the stage of commercialization. Clearly, this is a point in the knowledge-exploitation process where the often academic originators of the patented knowledge are likely to come into contact with research, engineering and marketing personnel of firms seeking to reap commercial advantage from the exploitation opportunity. All the aspects of networking discussed above come into play when interactions of this kind take place. It is different from the hierarchical process of knowledge generation inside the large firm and different from the often lateral networking that occurs between researchers in universities or institutes. Different competences with equal validity come into play where the marketer or the design engineer wrestle with the constraints of helping transform an invention into a product or service with market appeal.

Many regional administrations, particularly in the European Union, have either adapted a pre-existing presence of universities and research institutes into an innovation architecture more capable of engaging in the commercialization process, or have sought to establish it where it either did not exist or was unsuitable, perhaps because of being associated with a declining industrial sector. North-Rhine–Westphalia is a paradigmatic case of the rapid build-up of a new innovation architecture to meet perceived requirements for developing successful competitive advantage, as Huggins & Thomalla make clear in Chapter 2. It is a remarkable fact of Westphalia's historic existence under the Prussian State that no universities were allowed in the Ruhr for fear that the coalminers and steelworkers and their families would become too educated and thereby, potentially, revolutionary.

More recently, and from a less-deprived academic infrastructure, quite successful attempts have been made to integrate the research and training systems further with the innovative requirements of business in Wales and the diverse parts of the Great Lakes Region of North America. In Pennsylvania, Carnegie–Mellon University has always had a close innovative partnership posture towards business, and attempts were made in the 1980s to extend such relationships even to the community colleges, with the aid of the Ben Franklin Partnership. This is a network-inducing State financing institution meant to help small and medium-size businesses to restructure (often in traditional industries such as plastics, tool-and-die and clothing industries).

In Wales, especially industrial South Wales, a plethora of innovation support initiatives have come to fruition, many backed by European Union financial packages. A Regional Technology Plan (RTP) is being developed in a partnership between the University of Wales, Cardiff (UWC), and the Welsh Development Agency (WDA). In South Wales a technopole is being developed, uniquely, to serve the innovation needs of the region rather than the more conventional city-focus of the French and Japanese concept. A pilot project involving Cardiff University's Centre for

15

Advanced Studies, the WDA, TECs, a Quality Centre, three software and network management firms, and a dozen "guinea-pig" manufacturing firms in the former coalfield, is developing an innovation network based on the Internet and World Wide Web. This aims to supply innovation information to businesses and, crucially, to enable them to present themselves to each other and beyond, on the global scale, whether as potential buyers, suppliers or seekers or providers of solutions to innovation-related problems.

Hence, networking is being actively perceived as having an important contribution to make to the attempts by traditional firms to develop innovation competences in new fields. It is equally favourable to efforts to encourage new firms to develop by taking advantage of opportunities in these new fields themselves, and to enable existing or newer small firms to meet the often exacting requirements of larger customer firms, especially, for example, the Japanese and Germans, for local suppliers in a cluster setting focused on the regional scale.

Conclusions: the future of older industrial regions

In the early 1980s, it could easily appear that older industrial regions – the "Rustbelts" of North America and Europe – were effectively finished as serious contributors to the general economic welfare. They would be recipients of a "begging-bowl" form of support from the social security budgets of their central governments, from the regional aid budgets and the retraining agencies. The most likely expectation to be fulfilled would be accelerating population loss, continued environmental degradation and relatively little new enterprise formation, although some low-wage branch-plant inward investment by multinationals might be anticipated. By and large, many of these expectations have been fulfilled, but there have been unexpected developments too, at least in the cases to be analyzed in more depth in this book.

Fundamentally, if older industrial regions, dependent on too-narrow a base in declining industries such as coalmining, steelmaking, shipbuilding or textiles, are to survive and prosper, they must diversify, either vertically or laterally, and preferably both. *Vertical* diversification means two things:

- Firms can diversify into new products in the same branch. The classic instance is where a steel firm that traditionally specialized in bulk steel production diversifies into special steels, such as stainless steel or one or more of the variants of anodised steel, or even into steel alloys. This is a relatively narrow form of vertical diversification, but one that has been pursued by German, British and American steel and textiles firms in the past.

- Another, broader form of vertical diversification is where such a firm (let us take steelmaking as our example once again) diversifies into the production of a processed product that embodies steel but was not hitherto produced by the company. This will almost certainly occur through acquisition. An example would be the German steel company Hoesch, which in the 1980s entered the car-door manufacturing process. The company thus found a customer for its own steel as well as developing in a higher value-added market. Hoesch later extended overseas by acquiring the UK automotive firm Camford Pressings, which makes other car-body panels as well as doors. However, getting into such a broader vertical diversification strategy, the firm is also becoming involved in a vertical *integration* strategy, with costs as well as benefits. In Hoesch's case, producing car doors required expertise in automotive electronics, since doors contain electronic locks, windows and hi-fi systems. The firm acquired Rafi, an automotive electronics firm, to supply some of this equipment, but the ramifications of automotive electronics supply-chains proved difficult to manage. In the early 1990s Krupp, another larger German steel producer, acquired Hoesch and sought to minimize the move into the electronics field in line with a more traditional "stick to the knitting" philosophy.

Lateral diversification is the even broader extension of a firm's activities away from its basic origins. US Steel or USX as it became known, once the USA's largest steel producer, founded by Andrew Carnegie, had ceased producing steel altogether by the early 1980s, by which time it had become, in effect, a bank. In Germany, Ruhr-based steel producer Mannesmann made a similar move out of steel production and, through its subsidiary Rexroth, became an industrial machinery producer and, through an even larger leap from one branch to another, a major producer of telecommunications equipment. Equally, the fact that Ruhrkohle, the coal mining company and steel companies such as Hoesch, Mannesmann, Thyssen, Klöckner and Krupp, have diversified into automotive recycling, waste removal, packaging and plastics recycling or incineration in North-Rhine–Westphalia, is a sign that quite major lateral diversification can indeed assist as a survival strategy for firms in traditional industries in established industrial regions.

17

Each of these moves is interesting because they represent diversification moves *within* firms. In the UK this is very unusual, although in the USA, as we have seen, it is less so. The answer to the diversification problem in the older industrial regions of the UK, of which South Wales is a prime example, is to do little or nothing to arrest the rundown of the industry in question, whether coal, steel, textiles or shipbuilding, or even, in the Thatcher years, to encourage it. Accordingly, labour pools are created, wage expectations are driven down and an active policy of encouraging inward investment is pursued. Frequently, the new jobs are in light automotive or electronic engineering; they tend to employ women rather than redundant coalminers or steelworkers; but they may, in certain settings and through the judicious application of regional industrial support policies, lead to the development of supply-chain clusters. These may be in indigenous or even medium-size inward-investing supply firms, where the skill requirements can be high and men have a better chance of employment if they have trained or retrained appropriately.

As key features of a restructuring strategy for a region, the question of training and retraining is tackled by Bosch in Chapter 8 and Davies in Chapter 9. Bosch argues that the internal diversification approach in the Ruhr has, in principle, created opportunities for redeployed workers to retrain to fit into the newly diversified firm's activities, without redundancy and within the firm. Davies contrasts the relatively well financed retraining packages in Germany with the apparently reasonably financed but inadequately managed system that has operated in the UK. Finally, in comparison with the *internal diversification* strategy for coal and steel in Germany, an *external diversification* strategy is more typical of the Anglo–American neo-liberal approach. The UK passion for "creative destruction" (Schumpeter 1943) as a restructuring strategy is testified yet again in the energy production field, where Watson (Ch. 11) demonstrates the questionable nature of the decision-making that resulted in the newly privatized electricity supply companies constructing their own gas-fired power stations in preference to buying coal-generated power. The fact that an environmental justification has sometimes been used for this practice merely adds insult to injury.

The chapters that follow will trace the processes, problems and prospects for older industrial regions on the basis of detailed knowledge of events over the 1980s and 1990s in four countries in two continents. In general, there are grounds for optimism for the future of older industrial regions if some of the lessons recounted here can be taken on board, suitably adapted, elsewhere. However, there is no magic recipe for restructuring in such difficult circumstances, merely some possibly generalizable advice about the importance of a regional focus, partnership in policy-making, and a willingness by regional and business administrations to try to seek the most appropriate industrial diversification strategy at the earliest opportunity.

CHAPTER TWO

Promoting innovation through technology networks in North-Rhine–Westphalia

Robert Huggins & Reinhard Thomalla

Introduction

TECHNOLOGY POLICY IN NORTH-RHINE – WESTPHALIA

For the past 30 years the State of North-Rhine–Westphalia (NRW) has been confronted with structural problems as a direct result of the decline of its traditional industries: coal, steel and textiles. The industrial heartland of this region, the Ruhr area, which was traditionally dominated by the coal and steel industries, has been plunged into a period of fundamental structural change that is still far from over. Nevertheless, North-Rhine–Westphalia has maintained its position as one of Europe's economic front-runners and is set to play a leading role in the European Single Market, thanks to its dynamic and innovative economy.

The modernization and diversification of traditional industries and the establishment of new sectors geared to the products and services of the future bear witness to the continuing process of structural change. The need to adapt to constantly changing national and international demands fosters creativity and mobilizes growth potential. Research and development are an important part of this process and 25000 scientists are employed in 50 universities and polytechnics, 3 major research institutes and a variety of other research establishments in North-Rhine–Westphalia. Covering research into a wide variety of fields, these organizations are a source of economic stimulus in the region. Several technology-based intermediary organizations have been set up to make the results available to the corporate sector (Cooke & Davies 1993).

Zukunftsinitiative für die Regionen Nordrhein–Westfalens (ZIN) – "future initiative for coal and steel regions" – is the name given to the initiative/programme introduced by the State of NRW to foster enthusiasm and creativity among regional policy-makers by giving them more responsibility. The main action areas of the programme consist of the following:

- innovation and technology stimulation
- qualification/skills of employees
- creation and protection of jobs
- extension and modernization of infrastructure
- improvement of the environmental and energy situation (Hassink 1992).

Moreover, all groups that have a stake in the regional society must agree on the proposals, and regional negotiating tables have to build a sound consensus. Also the regional consensus approach has to lay the basis for a sensible ranking of location factors ensuring the most important have priority so that cross-purposes are avoided. Thus, the initiative is built upon three basic principles (Jochimsen 1990, Hassink 1992):

- regionalization (more decision-making power to the region)
- co-operation (broad consensus in the regions)
- co-ordination (between the region and State).

The programme has generally been well received and widely applauded; also, because of the co-operation of all relevant bodies in the region, the psychological value has been great. Technology policy as part of the Land's ZIN industrial policy offers aid to self-help groups to strengthen the technology base of SMEs in particular, and it comprises:

- organization of links between science and industry by building up a comprehensive technology transfer network
- the provision of advisory services for SMEs to eliminate technological obstacles
- encouragement of industry's communal institutions in R&D
- assistance of technology centres to boost the technological potential in the regions and to support the establishment of innovative companies
- assistance of joint and individual company projects to enable them to develop, launch and distribute new, highly complex, high-risk products and processes
- promotion of technology-orientated staff training
- stimulation and support of future-orientated industrial programmes and technology agencies

21

- interlinking of individual technology and structural tools to create a technology infrastructure network and to offer primarily SMEs the chance to get ahead in the continual process of industrial and technological change.

Precisely how important NRW's role is in the area of technology in Germany is proven by two separate facts. For the years 1991 to 1994, the German Ministry of Research and Technology (BMFT) has allocated assistance amounting to roughly DM120 million annually, 60 per cent of which is destined for NRW. In addition to this, it is the home of the largest collaborative research project on neural networks, in which the six provincial universities of Bielefeld, Paderborn, Bochum, Duisburg, Bonn and Düsseldorf all participate.

A TECHNOLOGY TRANSFER INFRASTRUCTURE

The development of technology is increasingly characterized by exponential growth of knowledge, that leads to shorter and shorter product lifecycles. Therefore, close attention must be paid to the effectiveness of the organization of technology transfer. This organization must be based on effective co-operation between the different transfer partners and agents, and therefore orientated to transfer services relevant to application in products and methods in industry (Alemann 1990).

Since the early 1980s, an extensive technology transfer network has been built up in NRW, embracing a wide range of organizations. In the Ruhr area of NRW, all universities and polytechnics have been building up technology transfer offices since 1985. Also, since 1989, some transfer offices of institutions of higher education, such as the Technology Transfer Office of the Dortmund University and Polytechnic, have also developed regional functions, establishing branches in small cities that do not possess public research centres. Transfer offices at institutions of higher education offer a whole range of services to SMEs in the region. Not only are the institutions of higher education equipped with technology transfer offices, but many chambers of commerce and trade unions also have their own transfer offices. The Trade Union Office of Oberhausen, for example, is particularly involved in supporting employees in the use and development of new technologies.

Such technology transfer offices have facilitated the development of a knowledge infrastructure, which has become increasingly important, particularly for innovative firms. This knowledge infrastructure is significant in terms of the supply of highly qualified employees and the stimulation of business start-ups by spin-offs, as well as stimulating technology transfer to regional firms. The knowledge infrastructure of NRW has strongly improved during the past two decades. The situation has improved with regard to both universities and non-academic research institutions. The knowledge infrastructure is progressively considered as an important tool to support the regional economy and to accelerate the restructuring of the economy (Hassink 1992).

NRW government policy is based on the following key assumptions:

- Manufacturing quality products requires ever closer relations between manufacturers and suppliers, as well as between manufacturers and customers. For this, employees must be fairly highly qualified.
- Development and manufacture of high tech products or procedures, and the commercial development of new fields of innovation, capitalize on close co-operation between industry and research establishments. Employees are therefore expected to be highly qualified and ready to co-operate.
- The manufacture of standard products, implementing manufacturing procedures of a simple structure, does not require a "feel" for the customer nor any extensive co-operation, and employees need not be particularly skilled.

The consequences of these developments are clear. First, there will be more and more locations where the manufacture of standard products is possible; cheaper locations will prevail. Also, to an ever-increasing degree, the manufacture of quality and high tech products will depend on the skills of personnel and on efficient locational co-operation structures. NRW's economic policy is focusing on strengthening its location in a quality-orientated competition.

Locational co-operation structures are established by the exchange of information on market trends, technologies and technological developments in related industries, thus concentrating the activities of the enterprises involved on certain markets and market segments; eventually, the location will have certain specializing characteristics (Thomalla 1993). These contacts within the corporate sector will be reinforced with a variety of co-operative schemes involving research institutions, the public sector and relevant groups in society. The results are qualitative locational advantages that will not be easily copied.

NRW economic policy supports the creation of new co-operation structures – as well as the fostering of those already existing – chiefly by the very comprehensive technology-orientated infrastructural network. The network was established through initiatives by interested parties in the various regions, towns and cities, industries and non-governmental organizations; it is maintained by its work, consensus and co-operation, which lends persistence and predictability to the individual institutions, helping them overcome the frequent problems that arise during the initial stages.

The main players in the NRW technology network

THE FOUR PILLARS OF NRW NETWORKING STRATEGY

Through its technology policy, NRW has created a strategy of innovating through networking, which draws on the benefits of both central government strategy-making, and regional and local policies. Rather than imposing too high a level of institutional and hierarchical co-ordination on its technological infrastructure, NRW appears to have accepted that, at its present stage of development, overlapping technological networks are the most efficient way of promoting innovative activity. The State of NRW has adopted an interventionist approach by creating a public infrastructure of technology institutions that provide a range of services for industry, particularly via intermediary bodies that serve as linkage-points from universities and research centres to SMEs. Within these intermediary bodies/ initiatives there are four main support organizations, or what might be termed pillars of the innovation/technology network in NRW:

- industry's 31 R&D centres operated jointly, as at Moers, for example, where a Mechatronics Institute is run by the Chamber of Commerce, the Society for Research and Testing, a group of Duisburg University professors, a private company and West LB, the NRW State bank
- Technology Transfer Offices/Stations for promotion of co-operation between science and business (50 offices in NRW)
- Technology Centres for support of young, innovative companies in the setting-up phase, under one roof with common use of infrastructure facilities; in many cases sector-orientated concentration (48 Centres in NRW)
- Technology Agencies/Initiatives supporting co-operation of specialized businesses in technological and business innovations (26 in NRW).

These four primary instruments of the technology network seek to maintain and strengthen the competitive position of firms, mainly SMEs, which in NRW represent about 95 per cent of the industrial firms and more than

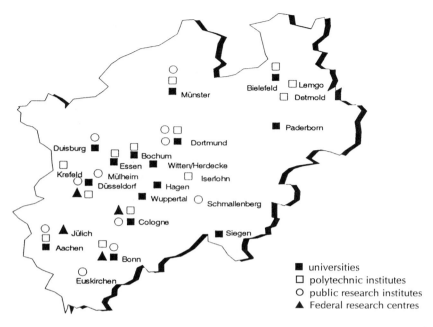

Figure 2.1   Science institutions in NRW (*Source:* Economic Development Corporation of North-Rhine–Westphalia).

60 per cent of all employees in the technology-based sector of the economy. As intermediaries they act as the gateways of the knowledge network between firms and NRW's 50 higher education institutes, 40 An-Institutes (privately-owned application orientated research centres), 31 research and development institutes and also the ZENIT organization – NRW's Centre of Innovation and Technology. Together these organizations form a dense network of public and private science orientated organizations (as shown in Figs 2.1, 2.2). The extent of the intermediary transfer institutions' operations corresponds with the research institutes' collaboration with SMEs, and some commentators have suggested that they will become even more important as research institutes reduce the activities of their own transfer departments (Davies 1994). This suggests that intermediaries will inevitably become ever more integrated into the regional economy.

The transformation of the NRW infrastructure into an effective network support system has not been determined by the mere number of institutions providing innovative services. It is when these institutions are linked together that their individual information supplies and problem-solving capacities add up to a support infrastructure with a high level of connectivity (Grabher 1993a). The formation of new regional institutions and the

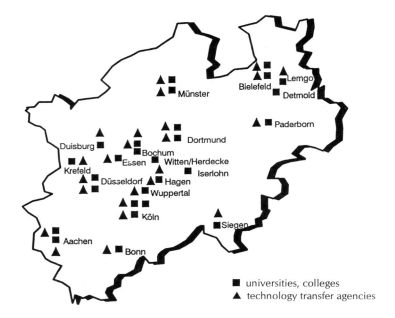

Figure 2.2 Scientific transfer in NRW (*Source:* Economic Development Corporation of North-Rhine–Westphalia).

thickening of the regional infrastructure have cast some doubts on its efficiency, but one of the key advantages of "organic" networks is their ability to disseminate and interpret new information. Also, information passed through networks is often "thicker" than information obtained in the market, and "freer" than information communicated in a hierarchy. As Herrigel (1993) has argued, streamlining the infrastructure according to a confined logic of economic efficiency may have counterproductive effects because:

> the fragmented, overlapping and seemingly redundant character of the public and private institutional network . . . is, paradoxically, the most efficient way to provide services to decentralized production. (Herrigel 1993: 232)

Grabher (1991, 1993a) views NRW as consisting of loosely coupled networks creating opportunities for sharing the learning experience of cooperating partners that results from their exchange relations with third parties. The loose coupling of the following institutions thus increases the learning capacity of networks.

26

R&D CENTRES

Until the 1980s, NRW had few research centres such as institutes of Germany's Max Planck Gesellschaft (which undertakes basic research projects) and the Fraunhofer Gesellschaft (which undertakes applied research for firms and has 45 centres throughout Germany). The Max Planck Gesellschaft has set up eleven institutes in NRW since 1984, with a further six Fraunhofer institutes in the region.

NRW also has an array of An-Institutes, which are private bodies founded jointly by professors and an association of firms or a chamber of commerce and industry, and which can use the facilities of the technical colleges. NRW is one of three States in Germany that regulate the creation and activity of An-Institutes, following legislation in 1992; NRW also allocates partial funding to the setting-up of such bodies.

TECHNOLOGY TRANSFER STATIONS/OFFICES

Research institutions by themselves cannot upgrade a region's innovative capacity; they require a technological infrastructure to diffuse innovation. In NRW each higher education institute has a Technology Transfer Station to provide information on and access to research capacities, as well as details of grants available from the State of NRW, the German Federal State and EU technology projects. Further technology transfer agencies have been developed by the chambers of commerce and industry, professional associations and craft chambers.

NRW is currently the only German State that funds the Deutscher Gewerkschaftbund's Technologieberatungsstelle – the German trade union council's technological advice service (DGB TBS) which was set up in 1987 and has 6 offices with 24 technical workers. It aims to advise trade unions and workers representatives on works councils concerning technology, for example, to offer evaluations of the impact of technological changes on the shop floor and to draw up worker-friendly alternatives (Davies 1994).

TECHNOLOGY-SPECIFIC AGENCIES/INITIATIVES

Sector-specific programmes have been initiated over several years by the State of NRW, through its economic development corporation. They seek to promote co-operation between specialized businesses with regard to both technological and economic innovation, offering technical advice to SMEs. There are the following agencies within NRW:

27

- fuzzy logic technology
- software for education
- informatics
- computer integrated manufacturing (CIM)
- telecommunications
- media technology
- product design technology
- environmental technology
- biotechnology
- laser technology
- ceramics (auto suppliers)
- wood technology (furniture industry)
- plastics
- solar energy
- machine tools
- iron and steel
- aerospace
- cross-sector training.

ZENIT – CENTRE FOR INNOVATION AND TECHNOLOGY

ZENIT was founded as a limited company in 1984 to promote innovation and to perform technology transfer, in particular for SMEs in the manufacturing sectors. The model chosen was a public–private partnership combining the interests of three shareholders:

- industry via a support association with about 100 SMEs distributed all over NRW (main interest: practical relevance of the transfer services)
- State of NRW via the Ministry of Economics, Industry and Technology (main interest: integration of the transfer process into the technology infrastructure of the State)
- the financial sector via the State bank West LB (main interest: integration of technology-orientated transfer know-how into the assessment of projects to be financed within the Federal State subsidy programme.

ZENIT is located in Mulheim-an-der-Ruhr, significantly a town with no higher education institutes, and therefore draws upon a regional network of links with universities, research institutes, firms, associations, local authorities, credit institutes, chambers of commerce and industry, advisory and technology transfer services. ZENIT was set-up by the State of NRW as the pivotal player in the processes of technological change and economic modernization, and was the key element of the ZIN technology policy. Initially ZENIT was aimed at promoting the use of advanced technology in eight industries dominated by SMEs – environmental and energy technologies, microelectronics, measuring, information and communications technologies (ICT), biotechnology, human technology and materials technology. The role of ZENIT has altered somewhat since its creation, so that today it specializes in environmental technology and environmental management, production technology, the European internal market, and the marketing of technology. It also still provides information on other technologies, for example, micro-technologies, sensors, biotechnology, laser technology and new materials. As funding from the State and banks has gradually decreased, ZENIT has become entirely self-financing. The three main objectives of ZENIT within the sphere of the promotion of innovation and technology are:

- competent partner of industrial firms
- link between firms, and university institutes and firms
- think-tank to improve transfer processes and structural changes in industry in NRW (Cooke & Davies 1993).

The ZENIT team currently consists of about 50 people operating within the NRW technology network. ZENIT is highly aware that technology transfer must not only be directed to technology alone, but must be integrated into a company's visions, strategies and different activities and functions. Therefore, ZENIT is involved in management, financing, qualifications, co-operation and also market research and technology marketing. ZENIT is an integral part of the NRW network and it provides advisory and consultancy services mainly to industrial enterprises. The aim is to show companies how they can use technical innovation in future-orientated fields of technology. The technical and economic problems, which are often closely related, are solved by a team of experts competent in wide array of sectors. ZENIT has come in for some criticism from time to time, particularly from the chambers of commerce and technology advisory services in NRW, who fear there is too much of an overlap with regard to their respective functions.

DECENTRALIZED NETWORKING IN NRW

Within NRW most networks exist as decentralized forms, either within cities, municipalities or counties, which are perceived as the most effective way of raising innovative and productive capacity. Moreover, local/regional action is perceived as more cost-effective, in that networking arrangements maximize resources that are otherwise wasted on futile competition, and also enable smaller towns to benefit from the resources enjoyed by larger populated areas, for example, higher education institutes, research centres, technology transfer services and possibly the attraction of inward investment. However, a decentralized networking strategy does have certain weaknesses as the "regions" of NRW conform to the areas of the chambers of commerce and industry, which do not always form "natural entities". The strategy has been criticized by some people for allowing larger cities to dominate smaller towns, which lose out rather than benefit from the regional emphasis. Other commentators, however, argue that such networks have thrived because of the strong tradition for local administration in NRW allowing each "region" to build up its own unique set of resources (Fürst & Kilper 1995).

The role of technology centres

THE THEORY

Technology centres form an important part of the innovation network in NRW, with the underlying idea being to concentrate innovative potential on specific sites, achieving synergies that subsequently resonate throughout the region. Technology centres usually provide inexpensive premises and a variety of services to help creative new companies get off to a good start. The background to each technology centre is different, depending on local infrastructure and potential. Consequently, each centre focuses on different fields of business, and rent structures and services vary from centre to centre. There are currently 48 technology centres in North-Rhine–Westphalia.

The State of North-Rhine–Westphalia provides assistance in the establishment of technology centres as part of its technology programme; however, all centres have to be local initiatives. They are generally started and operated as collaborative ventures involving local chambers of commerce, guilds of trades, higher education establishments, research institutes, banks, companies and local councils. The technology centres are a good example of partnership between the public and private sectors (Fromhold-Eisebith 1992).

Technology centres are particularly geared towards assisting SMEs, which are often vulnerable to delays in their development stages which can have dramatic effects on the entire product life-cycle. Technology centres in NRW usually offer a total care package for technology-based start-ups and firms with R&D projects; producer service firms as well as manufacturing firms are perceived as important forces for innovation. The technology centre management systematically organizes co-operative endeavour between universities, research institutes and companies, thus actively supporting the process of technology transfer, differentiating the processes of technology centres from other initiatives. The technology centres build up networks within their regions and with organizations outside the region enabling firms to access the entire technology support infrastructure that exists in NRW. The centres are distinguished by the following characteristics:

- firms are technology-based, not simply start-ups
- takes care of a firm until its project has been fully developed, if possible
- provides floorspace on flexible terms
- provides a common infrastructure
- provides business advice
- works in close co-operation with universities and other research institutes
- promotes a culture of co-operation
- offers most of its services to other firms within the region.

Technology centres are seen to act as crystallization points that construct stable structures between research centres, innovative firms, start-ups and the actors involved in economic development. The centres also provide a means of organizing co-operation between basic research, applied research and production on a local/regional level. They link research expertise to the needs of firms, and can speed up the process of technology transfer. The centres may also improve a region's ability to attract other innovative firms. Examples of this in NRW are Ericsson in Herzogengrath, Mitsubishi in Alsdorf, and Elmos in Dortmund.

THE REALITY

Along with technology centres, science & technology parks have over the past 15 years facilitated the emergence of a technology transfer network involving many institutions and covering almost the whole of Germany. These institutions seek to develop and optimize the transfer of know-how and technology. In essence, the principal functions of the technology centres and science parks are to disclose and transfer information on their own services, as well as on those provided by the research and higher education sector to firms indigenous to the area.

On the whole, NRW has a dense network of transfer and counselling/consultancy agencies. However, it is worth noting that there are differences in quality and efficiency between agencies, not least because the organizational integration and design of the technology centres is left to the individual universities. It is also evident that certain technology centres are having to grapple with acceptance problems, as they have only recently become an institutionalized part of the research and higher education sector. Although the transfer services of the research and higher education sector do play a significant part in the innovative behaviour of small business, this does not always mean that technology centres have been integrated in the process. Much of the information transfer behaviour exhibited by innovative small firms in technology centres still reveals a dominance of informal, personal communication with customers, suppliers and competitors. In this context the transfer processes of the technology centres can be effective only if long-standing personal contacts exist that have been renewed on many occasions, thus establishing and cementing a relationship of confidence and understanding conducive to information transfer (Staudt et al. 1994).

Case studies: networks in action

THE AACHEN TECHNOLOGY NETWORK

The Aachen region on the border with Holland and Belgium in the west of NRW, with a population of 1.51 million, has restructured itself in ten years from a declining coal and textile area to into a dynamic high tech region. The success of Aachen is a story of the utilization of resources that already existed, the most important of which is the massive Jülich Research Centre, along with the Technical University and Chamber of Commerce and Industry.

Since 1983, Aachen has developed an innovation network involving almost 400 scientific institutes. Aachen has one of the largest technical universities in Europe, and also one of the largest research centres at Jülich, with over 4500 employees and 800 scientific staff. The region's academic strength is evident from the fact that approximately 25 per cent of engineers in Germany with a PhD obtained it from an institution in Aachen.

Aachen managed successfully the support for vertical technology transfer from the prestigious Rheinisch–Westfälische Technische Hochschule (technical university, RWTH) – to the local economy by establishing the economic development body Aachener Gesellschaft für Innovation und Technologietransfer (AGIT). The technology potential of Aachen has developed rapidly since, with many spin-offs for surrounding local authorities. Aachen has managed its structural crisis of the 1980s successfully, mainly by integrating the RWTH into the local economy. The main initiator in this process was the Chamber of Commerce and Industry, through a co-operation agreement with RWTH, leading to the creation of the Innovation and Technology Centre, which is operated by AGIT. AGIT acts as the focal point for the regional network that involves not only universities and technology-based institutions but also banks, the employment department, and insurance companies (Fig. 2.3). The banks, in particular, were very receptive during the initiation stages of AGIT (see also Kooistra 1991).

The Aachen Technology Centre, which was established in 1984, has had an impact far beyond the Aachen area. It was the first German centre of its kind and it remains one of Germany's most successful centres, attracting new small firms in future growth fields. Before a new enterprise moves into the Technology Centre, AGIT and the Chamber, along with a team of experts, offer advice to the management, particularly of a financial nature,

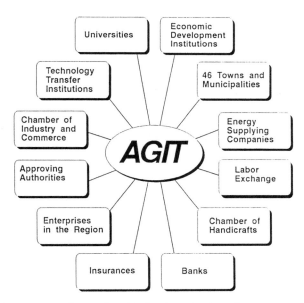

Figure 2.3 The Aachen Technology Region (*Source:* AGIT).

focusing on providing assistance in applying for public grants and subsidies, innovation credits and venture capital. The shareholders of AGIT include the local chamber of commerce and industry, the municipal and county councils, the Aachen University, and representatives of local industry (see Fig. 2.4). This broad shareholding facilitates a high degree of consensus as to the direction of technology policy.

AGIT now manages three innovation centres, including a medical centre, as well as advising the following seven centres spread throughout the Aachen region:

Corporate Meeting

Municipality of Aachen	Aachen District and WFG of Aachen District	Heinsberg District and WFG of Heinsberg District	Euskirchen District	Düren District	Chamber of Industry and Commerce

Chamber of Crafts and Trade	RHEGIT e.V.	ZAR e.V.	Aachener und Münchener Versicherung AG	Saving banks of the Aachen Region

Supervisory Board
26 members

Management

Department I	Department II	Department III
Management of three technology centers in the City of Aachen • Canvassing, counselling and support for the founding of innovative enterprises • Serving and advising of the TC's in the region	Realisation of projects in applied research and development • Support of innovation and technology transfer in medium-sized industries in NRW	Technology oriented promotion of business and location publicity for the AACHEN TECHNOLOGY REGION • Public relations • Office of the Regional Conference Aachen

Figure 2.4 The Aachen Society for Innovation and Technology Transfer (AGIT).

- Jülich Technology Centre
- Huckelhoven Incubator and Service Centre
- Herzogengrath Technology Park
- Gellenkirchen Euro Service Centre
- Eschweiler Business Technology Centre
- Baesweiler International Transfer and Service Centre
- Alsdorf Trade and Industrial estate.

AGIT also facilitates technology transfer for SMEs, as well as undertaking technology-orientated economic development. Although most of the firms in the innovation centres are start-ups, the Ford Motor Company has a small research facility at one of the centres. Although employing only four people at present, Ford is hoping to expand rapidly within the Aachen area. As well as the classic activities of innovation centres, AGIT is also able to offer services through a local network of lawyers, accountants and patent experts, as well as scientific and technical experts.

Realizing the comprehensive and constantly expanding supply of research results and innovative technologies in the Aachen region, AGIT set up its Technology Transfer Department 1986, operating as a link between research and industrial applications (see Fig. 2.5). AGIT aims to upgrade the technological capability of local firms through the rapid introduction

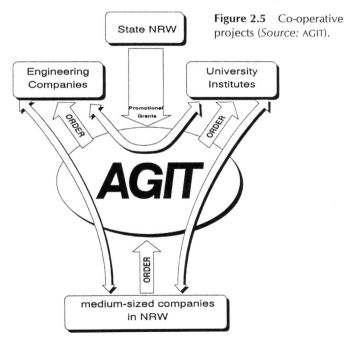

Figure 2.5 Co-operative projects (*Source:* AGIT).

and application of new technologies, processes and organization to secure competitiveness for SMEs. Incorporated into this technology transfer network are two Fraunhofer Institutes and many R&D sections of large companies, as well as 1000 consulting and software houses. AGIT also acts as an intermediary to obtain funding for firms and universities, undertakes feasibility and evaluation of projects, evaluation of marketing, and brings together complementary firms into mini-clusters. These mini-clusters have so far taken the form of industry clubs and know-how networks, and the development of sector-specific new projects. The most successful network is the informatics/software club, which has been very active in the production of joint venture software.

Despite its success, the Aachen system does have weaknesses. Although it is a good example of innovation networking, the region is slightly insular, with most of the networking being parochial. SMEs, in particular, are prone to return to their old adversarial ways unless they continually see the advantage of network arrangements. This has meant that AGIT and the Chamber are constantly developing new initiatives to promote networking awareness among firms, involving considerable levels of human and financial resources.

THE DORTMUND TECHNOPOLE

The Dortmund Technology Park, which was created in 1988 to foster technology and innovation developed at the university and local research institutes, has expanded rapidly to become the focus of technology-based activities in the Dortmund area. There are currently 150 firms in the Park involved in the development and manufacture of high tech products or in support for those firms. Within the Park and its vicinity there are many R&D institutes other than the university, for instance, Fraunhofer Institute for Logistics (transport technology and distribution), Institute for Robotics and two Max Planck Institutes. Including these institutes, the following bodies form the core nodes of the Dortmund information network:
- Chamber of Commerce and Industry
- Dortmund's Office of Economic Development
- university and polytechnic
- research institutes
- financial institutions and venture capital firms
- Chamber of Craftsmen
- consultants.

The Dortmund Technology Centre – located in the middle of the Park –

is the hub of innovative R&D within the "technopole". Although it started life as a technology transfer station, it has now become an important cluster for software and computer engineering firms, which have previously existed on a large scale only in southern Germany. These have come to be regarded as vital for the development of Dortmund's economy, in that the jobs created are usually highly skilled. The Centre is not an incubator as such, but aims to act as interface between research institutions and existing firms. The Park's International Centre primarily supports American technology companies in their quest to penetrate European markets. The Centre offers many of the administrative features associated with a technology centre, but is geared towards the needs of non-German speakers.

The Park also has the following Centres:
• Centre for Micro-structural Development
• Centre for Quality Assurance and Testing
• Centre for Technology Transfer
• Centre for Environmental Technology and Services
• Software Support Centre.

Research in the Dortmund area is concentrated predominantly on computer science and engineering (electrical, mechanical, chemical). In addition, many projects are conducted in environmental technology and special materials. In total there are 28 scientific research institutes employing around 3500 scientists and engineers.

These institutes are able to take advantage of the NRW Patent and Innovation Agency that was established within the Park in 1992. PINA NRW is a private company that has received assistance from the State of NRW during its initial stages and has developed a service package for investors and innovators from science and industry. This is geared to evaluating, safeguarding, developing and launching new products and processes with a view to commercial potential. It also co-finances national and, where appropriate, international protection of intellectual property through the acquisition of commercial rights. In certain cases PINA NRW finances the construction of working models and prototypes, and detailed market research surveys. Currently PINA NRW holds the marketing rights to almost 500 national and international patents in NRW and is involved with many international technology transfer organizations.

Dortmund's many research institutions have allowed the area to develop as one of Germany's most prolific areas with regard to technical collaboration, co-operation and networking. The Dortmund Consensus of Chamber of Commerce and Industry, City Council, banks, university and Economic Development Agency have strategically planned the technological developments that have taken place within the vicinity of the university. A whole range of new institutions has now developed in this area, along with several large firms. Although the Chamber of Commerce and Industry is not as active as it is in Aachen, Dortmund appears to have more activity from large industry and, for example, the Hoesch Corporation still plays an important part in the regional network through funding, subcontracting and outsourcing to developing firms.

THE COLOGNE TELECOMMUNICATIONS CLUSTER

The necessity for technological infrastructure and networking has been understood in Cologne for some years. Technology round-tables and technology circles in particular are a common feature of the research institutes, university and the Technology Centre. Although in the past the area has been best known for its automotive industry, the economy has become increasingly service orientated, with approximately 66 per cent of new developments being in that service sector. Most initiatives are now public–private partnerships involving:

- the university
- technical colleges
- German Aerospace Research Establishment
- German Space Agency
- Max Planck Institutes
- City of Cologne
- Cologne Technology Centre
- Cologne Teleport Media Park.

The Cologne Technology Centre is owned by the City of Cologne, the Cologne Savings Bank and Telenorma, a telecommunications subsidiary of the Bosch Group. There are currently 24 companies working in the Centre (18 others have now grown large enough to become established outside the Centre), which focuses on the following areas:

- communications technology
- manufacturing technology
- production of equipment and appliances
- microelectronics
- environmental technology.

The Centre co-operates with all the major R&D institutes in the area, particularly Cologne University, Cologne Polytechnic, the Rhineland Technical Control Association and the German National Aerospace Research Establishment.

Growth in the media sector has been explosive, with more than 50 per cent of media firms in NRW being founded from 1981 onwards. Cologne is one of Germany's largest media and communication centres, with 1500 companies and 43000 people working in the industry. Cologne has a long tradition as a media city, with many newspapers, magazines and printing houses having had their headquarters in the city for many years.

In recent years more and more companies from the innovative electronic media sector have also been setting up facilities in the area, particularly at the Cologne Teleport Media Park. Such firms have been attracted by an infrastructure that includes the Institute for Radio Economics and the Centre for Interactive Media. The Teleport Media Park, which is a combination of telecommunications and entertainment companies, is a joint venture partnership of Deutsche Bundespost Telekom (DBT, which owns 51%), Intercai Teleconsult (a Netherlands-based company), and Media Park Cologne.

DBT is being privatized and deregulated, thus facing an influx of competition. By 1998, Germans will have a choice of three carriers for international calls, and private carriers will be able to operate their own networks and supply value-added services. The Media Park is hoping that there will be sufficient interest in locating in the Park by such private investors and international carriers. DBT will still provide lines into and out of buildings, but other carriers can operate the internal network and value added services. The teleport company plans broad band connections, plus an internal fibre-based wide area network that will allow video conferencing and audiovisual telecommunication. It is hoped that the Media Park will be the first of several teleport projects in Germany, creating a national network that will be connected internationally by satellite links. Ultimately, the teleports are seen as serving globally operating companies through a worldwide communications network. DBT, for example, is planning special telecom services for the Japanese. With NRW housing the largest colony of Japanese in Europe, Japanese businessmen will benefit from a broadband ISDN connection for voice, data, text and image communication between Düsseldorf, Cologne, Bonn and Berlin which will be re-transmitted to Japan by satellite.

Concluding remarks

The technology policy followed consistently for several years by the State of NRW is now reaping its rewards. More than 800000 workers are already employed in technology sectors such as robotics, microelectronics, laser technology, opto-electronics, biotechnology and environmental science. The innovation network has been very effective in developing small R&D-based firms, and revenue figures for start-ups in the technology centres are impressive. Despite there being a wide array of agencies, initiatives and institutions, the network structure gives it a transparency allowing easy access. It still remains to be seen whether or not too many institutions and initiatives have been introduced over too short a time-period and if there will be a market for all their services in the long term. In some areas of NRW, such as east of Dortmund, there are suggestions that there are already too many technology centres giving the possibility of overlap.

The innovation network has yet to establish much electronic networking, despite the fact that many of those involved are spread over a wide geographical area. Steps are now being undertaken to put the relevant infrastructure in place. Easy access information databases are increasingly being promoted by the Chambers of Commerce and Industry. The involvement of the regional banking system in the innovation network is an important plus point, and venture capital is a very important issue in NRW. Most of the actors involved in the network are encouraged to become stakeholders in the technology centres. Many of the innovation projects in the region – particularly those involving the EU – involve a cluster of firms from the same sector in the region.

It has taken over ten years to create the infrastructure for the innovation network and one of the most important results of the focus on innovation policy has been the requirement for new educational schemes to be developed. Such schemes train students early in their education to co-operate with partners from other disciplines and to assimilate some basic knowledge about these fields. Also, emphasis has been given to interdisciplinary teamwork, and the need for industry to improve its awareness of interdisciplinary co-operation. Together, this emphasis on technology transfer and training capture the essence of the NRW (and broader German) approach to promoting a more knowledge-intensive economic development strategy than prevailed hitherto, one in which technology networks are seen to be of key importance.

CHAPTER THREE

New wave regional and urban revitalization strategies in Wales

Phil Cooke

Introduction

The 1980s witnessed dramatic changes in urban and regional policies in the UK in general and Wales in particular. In the urban field, there was a significant decline in the relative autonomy of local government to manage the urban development process, as *central* government sought to curtail costs, partly by curbing powers. Thus, as urban policy-analyst Lawless (1991) noted, there was a move to both *liberalize* and *deregulate* urban policy. *Liberalization* included opening up the policy-making and, particularly, the policy implementation phases to the private sector (Stockbridge Village, near Liverpool, and Birmingham Heartlands are instances at different urban scales of both policy formation and implementation beyond direct local government purview). *Deregulation* has been even more far-reaching and has involved reducing or removing land-use control powers from local government planning authorities through Enterprise Zones, Simplified Planning Zones and in the areas covered by the Urban Development Corporations.

The National Audit Office report (1989) – *Regenerating the cities* – showed, perhaps not that surprisingly but certainly dramatically, how the then projected Urban Programme budget composition changed from 1984 to 1993. At the beginning, only 25 per cent of the £500 million spent was allocated to Urban Development Grants and Corporations, the other 75 per cent being spent on Urban Programme, much of which had directly social (not only private) gain written into it. By 1993 (the end of the period) Urban Programme had dwindled to 40 per cent, Urban Development

41

Grants and Corporations were now accounting for 60 per cent of total spend, which in 1989 prices was only a little higher (£530 million), although it had reached closer to £800 million in 1991. In that year Urban Programme dropped to less than one-third of expenditure. Hence, it is clear that there has been a massive shift of resources towards policy initiatives that work initially to the advantage of the private developer, at the expense of initiatives that benefit less well-off urban residents.

There is no disputing this observation, and government Ministers would not only *not* wish to challenge it but would actively applaud it as a sign that policy was working, urban riots, soaring crime rates and racist backlashes notwithstanding. Over £2000 million of public investment has been made in the British Urban Development Corporations since they were launched in 1981. Most of that money has been spent in London Docklands. For example, the Centre for Local Economic Strategies (CLES 1990) report showed that London Docklands Development Corporation received £813 million, whereas the other ten UDCs received £600 million in government allocation between 1989 and 1992. Meanwhile, Urban Programme received, in real terms and for the whole country, some £620 million.

The clear conclusion to be drawn from these expenditure patterns is as follows: *as urban policy expenditure in Britain has been moved towards direct support for the private sector it has also moved geographically away from the regions and towards London.*

An interesting question that arises in connection with this preliminary but rather incontestable deduction is whether this is coincidence or part of a pattern also affecting the other main element of government expenditure of a territorial kind, namely regional expenditure?

The first thing to note is that, as shown in *Hansard* (18/12/91: the UK Parliament's official record), overall government expenditure on Regional Assistance fell from £1236 million in 1981 to £461 million in 1991 (and £101 million in 1995). If these figures are deflated for comparability in the same way those for Urban Programme were, the real reduction is from some £2163 million in 1981 to £369 million in 1991 (at constant 1989 prices). There can be no question that this is *a staggering reduction* in real financial assistance to the economically deprived regions of the UK. This easily absorbs the extra expenditure incurred by the advent of the Urban Development Corporations and still allows real repayments to the Treasury. So, in financial terms we see that UK government policy for cities and regions since 1979 or so has been to boost financial assistance to London and to reduce it relatively and, in many cases, absolutely, in most other areas previously deemed to be in need.

So much has the policy bias towards London and the South East of England now become that, in the new 1993 map of Regional Assistance, large areas of the traditionally assisted areas were downgraded in favour of some localities in South East England. The rationale for this was a rapid increase in unemployment there and a high but stable level in the older industrial areas, such as Wales. Indeed, the unemployment level in Wales had dipped below the UK average in March 1992 for the first time since 1924 – a sign of the longevity of the restructuring process in the Welsh economy.

Nevertheless, it could not truthfully be said that the economic problems that had beset Wales for so long had been solved simply from a reading of its relative unemployment position in relation to the UK. Rather, for the first time in the twentieth century, the whole of the UK had suffered a severe recession, particularly the South East. By late 1993, unemployment figures showed the South East once again falling below the UK average, whereas Wales, for example, reverted to the average, still staying on or near it in 1995. As the UK moved glacier-like out of recession, it could be anticipated that the South East, normally the UK's wealthiest and least unemployment-prone region, would return to a below-average unemployment rate. Meanwhile, much of the subsidy warranted by processes of industrial change in the maturer industrial regions had been lost.

Dealing with regional financial retrenchment

Wales is better equipped to deal with the kind of financial retrenchment described than are, for example, the regions of England. The only other part of Great Britain equally if not better equipped is Scotland. Both have territorial ministries of the UK State at Cabinet level, whose incumbents can, in theory, speak for their domains in the highest council in the land. Whether the Ministers *do* very much or not in their own right is largely a matter of presumption; some do more than others. However, some find they have the ear of government in presenting political opinion from the majorities of the electorate in both Wales and Scotland, who are not supporters of the Conservative government. This *difference* means that, not infrequently, policies pursued at UK level are *transmuted* into something else in the two territories.

In Wales, the best example of this is the Land Authority for Wales, established in 1975 under the Community Land Act, a piece of legislation that scarcely survived the first year of the 1979 Thatcher administration. How-

43

ever, the Land Authority does still exist in Wales, where it was, in any case, set up institutionally in a way different from that in England. There, the role of acquiring and disposing of development land, especially in situations of market failure, was allocated to local government. But in Wales, as in some other older industrial areas of the UK, local government had, under Labour Party control, become corrupt in places, and was not entirely trusted, even by the same party in government. Although the whole of local government in England could not be treated as corrupt and refused the right democratically to manage the land development process, the same was not to be the case in Wales. The non-elected governmental agency (or QUANGO, as the phenomenon is more popularly known) survives in Wales long after its democratically elected form has disappeared elsewhere.

This is merely the most curious case, not necessarily the most important. That accolade belongs to the Welsh Development Agency (WDA), another QUANGO legally established in 1975 by the Labour government of the day (the Scottish Development Agency was established at the same time, but was replaced by the decentralized Scottish Enterprise in April 1991). Like the Land Authority for Wales, the Welsh Development Agency survives, although no longer unscathed by the vagaries of privatization, deregulation, liberalization or *quasi-markets* (Le Grand 1990). Hence, these bodies have demonstrated, like a multitude of others from the Welsh Office, through the Welsh Arts Council and Wales Tourist Board, to the Countryside Council for Wales and *Cadw* (Ancient Monuments) that *as long as they remain unelected they are safe*.

It is this very characteristic, *survivability*, which gives the *quasi-governmental*, if not the newer, quasi-market, institutions such as the Health Trusts, Housing Trusts, Educational Trusts and so on, added importance *during a period of very considerable economic, social and technological change*.

In the sphere of economic development within Wales, The Welsh Development Agency, assisted by the powers, albeit diminished, of the Welsh Office on Regional Assistance, has played an almost continental European role as *animateur* or orchestrator of some remarkably *innovative* initiatives to regenerate key elements in the Welsh economy. Among the most important of these elements have been the attraction of "blue-chip" overseas firms, promoting innovative training packages, improving the quality of manufacturing suppliers, and environmental upgrading. The days when the WDA was known as a builder of "sheds" and Europe's largest industrial property-owner have gone, as the Agency has been forced to sell off its property holdings (to the value of £85 million in 1993/4).

Hence, the WDA, as the main economic development institution in

Wales, has not been immune from the influence of government controls on public expenditure. As well as property sales, occasioning reductions in *rental* income, the Agency's core budget (a direct Treasury subvention), cut to £60 million in 1993, and set to decline to £25 million by 1996, is plainly in decline. These are the two fundamental sources of Agency income, and their attenuation has caused the WDA to rethink its *modus operandi*. At the head of the new agenda is full acceptance of Conservative government insistence that public expenditure should, wherever possible, be subject to the *quasi-market* discipline of the *public–private partnership* (on this, see also Osborne & Gaebler 1992).

We shall see later how this operates for WDA urban policy, one of the Agency's most rapidly growing activities, but for the moment I will look at some examples of the *partnership* ethic as it applies in the field of economic and industrial regeneration.

Regional and urban revitalization

The regional development initiatives pursued following the economic crisis of the early 1980s, when Wales lost over 100000 jobs in coalmining, steelmaking and metal manufacturing, have sought to *diversify* the industrial base and enhance the financial and other private services industries. A substantial proportion of new manufacturing investment has been attracted from overseas, particularly during the late 1980s and early 1990s. Now, there are 44 Japanese plants in Wales and 54 from Germany, joining the 130 mostly longer-established North American ones. A few foreign finance houses such as Chemical Bank, BNP, Allied Irish, Bank of Ireland, axa (France), DAS (Germany), NCM (Netherlands), Zurich Insurance and Société Générale now have a presence, mostly in South Wales. It is claimed by the Welsh Office and the WDA that Wales received as much as 20 per cent of UK foreign investment, a figure that reached £1000 million per year by the late 1980s. This is certainly marketing hyperbole, but even a more sober assessment, reduced to a more realistic proportion of some 13 per cent, demonstrates a remarkable achievement for a part of the UK with only a 5 per cent share of GDP.

Thus, Wales has become more of a manufacturing economy than it was, and more so than the rest of the UK. By 1993 the share of manufacturing in GDP in Wales was 28 per cent, compared to 23 per cent for the UK. Banking, finance and insurance employment rose from 50000 to 90000 between

45

1981 and 1991. This was achieved by the relatively straightforward and traditional methods of hard-sell, regional assistance and property rental packages. Moreover, the fact that Welsh labour costs in manufacturing are only some 90 per cent of the UK's and 50 per cent of Germany's has been a factor. But now in the 1990s and the aftermath of recession in Europe, with the rush to be in the Single Market before inauguration day, and the new imperatives of *lean management and production* causing firms to focus more on the need to restructure *in situ,* the picture has changed somewhat (Cooke 1993, Cooke et al. 1993).

Developing the *partnership* model to a greater extent than hitherto, particularly by working with firms and staying longer with inward investors, through providing more "aftercare", the main development bodies in Wales have engaged in a quality drive to complement the previous jobs-imperative of quantity. Among some of the more innovative partnership arrangements have been the following:

SOURCE WALES

Source Wales is a supplier development programme in which suppliers are put together with potential customers to form *clusters,* in the sense described by Porter (1990). The innovative features of this initiative are that it raises standards among *indigenous* firms, it encourages SMEs to see some of the virtues of co-operation as against stand-alone competition, and it requires that they become tutors to each other. Now, there are at least twenty "clubs" of supplier firms feeding into larger customers. Development agencies from overseas send missions to observe this phenomenon.

EUROPEAN INITIATIVES

Among the most imaginative of the European initiatives is Eurolink, which has put together over 130 firms in Wales and its partner regions of Baden–Württemberg, Catalonia, Lombardy and Rhône–Alpes (Cooke 1992). Through the networks, SMEs are put in partnership with complementary overseas firms with whom they might engage in marketing, technology exchange or product development activities. Other European initiatives, and the important economic partnering already noted, include establishing in Brussels in 1992 the Wales European Centre, a partnership between most of the key central and local government economic development bodies, Training and Enterprise Councils and university colleges. Other initiatives include; Contact Europe (partnerships outside the "partner regions"), Fit for Europe (readiness by SMEs for Single Market), Europartenariat (SME Trade Fair), Euro Info Centre (databases), and European Training Initiatives (e.g. COMETT). The variety of primarily SME-focused European initiatives takes advantage of the research insight that it is SMEs in export markets that grow fastest and flourish most (Storey & Johnson 1987).

INNOVATION INITIATIVES

Innovation initiatives are some of the most interesting and exciting activities currently being conducted mainly, but not exclusively, by the WDA. The Welsh Office, for example, commissioned research to identify the nature and extent of the "soft infrastructure" of innovation support institutions and the advanced technologies available in firms and universities in Wales. Together with the WDA they have successfully established a *Relay Centre,* a means of conveying information to firms about EC-funded science and technology exploitation opportunities. Several EC STRIDE Technology Audits have been conducted by the WDA's Technology office, an Integrated Innovation Programme for the IT industries has been in place for nearly two years, and Innovative Training partnerships exist for the engineering industries. In November 1993 The Engineering Centre was officially launched by the Secretary of State for Wales. This is a partnership between, *inter alia,* the Welsh Office, the WDA, local government, TECs, firms, colleges, the UK Engineering Council, the Royal Academy of Engineering, and many other bodies, aimed at boosting the number of recruits to the engineering profession.

Most recently, work has begun on establishing two technopoles, one in North Wales – the Snowdonia Technopole – with an emphasis on biotechnology and medical diagnostics, the other being the South Wales Technopole, which will aim to boost innovation in the all-important engineering industries, especially IT, automotive and new materials. Both are funded in large part by the EU (DG 13 and 16 respectively). Also to be funded by the EC is RTP, a pilot Regional Technology Plan in which Wales is one of four Euro-regions, along with Limburg, Lorraine and Saxony, to have the chance to develop an integrated innovation strategy for the whole of its territory.

All of these initiatives are based on networks and partnerships of some kind, usually involving the main public agencies, but increasingly extending to include the private sector as well. They are evident signs of a new, perhaps leaner, more cost-effective way of conducting economic development activity in the more complex and less predictable conditions of the *fin de siècle* era.

New wave urban policy initiatives

Within the context of these efforts to knit together a new regional economy, capable of surviving better the vagaries of a more competitive and innovative world than the industrial dinosaurs of the previous age, the question of environmental quality is paramount.

Older industrial areas inherit a despoiled landscape and, in this respect, industrial Wales, both North and South, is no different from the Ruhrgebiet in North-Rhine–Westphalia, except that in some respects the Ruhrgebiet may now be more environmentally revitalized because of initiatives such as the Emscher Park International Building Exhibition (Danielzyk & Wood 1993). For some years in the 1960s and 1970s, Wales was a mecca for government bodies wishing to see best practice in the reclamation of land poisoned by toxic waste. The Lower Swansea Valley project was pathbreaking in showing that land devastated by heavy-metals smelting activity could be returned to a condition in which a rich tree and grassland cover could thrive. Since then, much of the worst industrial dereliction associated with the coal industry and, to a lesser extent, steel manufacture has been restored. Coal tips have been removed or landscaped, water courses improved and biocover planted. To a large extent, the goals of land reclamation, as set for the fledgling WDA in 1975 by its enabling legislation, have been achieved. But those were set to the standards of the early 1970s; we are now twenty years on and expectations are higher, customers being more discerning than before.

The WDA has become an increasingly important player in the environmental upgrading business in urban and industrial Wales. As local government powers and resources were circumscribed during the era of Conservative government, so the WDA accrued a larger role in urban regeneration. This part of the WDA's activities grew to an expenditure level of £30 million from virtually zero. It pioneered the *Urban Joint Venture*, a partnership system involving itself as broker and part-funder, the local authority as customer and the private development company as provider of urban environmental upgrading.

The philosophy was simple. Wales is a *market* for inward investors and other investors; its quality of life is the unique sales proposition. However, in many Welsh towns, industrial dereliction and deindustrialization have left a legacy of low-grade urban industrial environments. This is where the jobs are needed, but investors may be put off by a poor urban environment and inadequate amenities. Local authorities have neither the finance to upgrade these places themselves nor the influence to attract private property developers to do it for them. The WDA is in the marketing business, has finance, and therefore is the logical agent to fill the gap.

Interestingly though, there is a further dimension to the philosophy, which involves a notion of urban hierarchy. Decisions regarding the kind of urban joint venture a town will have are conditioned by the view of that town's position in the WDA's vision of the future urban hierarchy of Wales. Inevitably, some towns gain and others lose in such a scenario. Thus, Merthyr Tydfil is conceived as having the possibility to be *the* service centre for the South Wales Valleys. Even though Pontypridd's residents might think it has a better chance to perform that function, they are not offered the option. The Cynon Valley is seen as having potential as a *higher value-added niche*, although quite why is unclear, given that it is presently one of the most deprived of communities in Wales.

Ammanford, at the western end of the Valleys area, has been the recipient of £64 million of much-needed urban investment, of which in the first five years £6 million will be public, the rest a mix of public and private. Farther west in industrial South Wales, Llanelli is the beneficiary of even more. These are sizeable sums for investment-deprived localities. But some important communities do not receive such sums. The most notorious case is that of the Rhondda Valley, with a comparable population and deprivation-rating to any. But Rhondda councillors were unwilling to fall into step with the WDA view of its future position in the Welsh urban hierarchy, not as a services or high-value–added centre but as a dormitory town with a few tourist attractions (Cooke & Jones 1993).

The new wave of urban policy-making in Wales, as elsewhere in Britain, is that of "whoever pays the piper, calls the tune". It is present in the principle by which what remains of Urban Programme funding in Wales is allocated not to the community in greatest need but to the ones in some need who show the greatest enthusiasm for fitting in with government privatization or quasi-market principles. It is based on partnership and networking, but the strength of networks can be their capacity to *exclude* those who do not conveniently fit in with others' expectations.

A footnote to this caveat regarding the relative diminution of communities' capabilities to influence their destinies, except insofar as they go along with someone else's dream, concerns the present popularity of the *forum* as a mechanism for policy-making in the urban arena. This too is a sign of the contemporary feebleness of democratic institutions at the local level. There has been something of an epidemic of them in Wales recently, as there has in North-Rhine–Westphalia and other parts of continental Europe. Some of the Welsh ones are Clwyd Economic Forum, Valleys

Forum, Cardiff Economic Forum, Rural Wales Forum, Cardiff Bay Forum and Swansea Partnership, and no doubt there are others. In some ways they are valuable in bringing experts who would not normally be involved in local policy-making into that activity. But they are experts, not representatives. They are probably harmless since, if I am right and local government is seriously enfeebled, any of the bright ideas to emerge will likely evaporate as the morning dew. If they are acting as local government's present-day unpaid "think-tank", then things may be far worse than many may have suspected.

Conclusions

I have argued in this chapter that both urban and regional policy are in transition in the UK and that Wales is not immune, although it is sometimes able to mould the impact of change because of its quite strong institutional individuality.

It was shown how UK government expenditure in urban policy had stagnated and regional spending had declined colossally in real terms during the 1980s and 1990s. Not only that, there has been a massive switch away from assisting the older industrial regions towards supporting the temporarily depressed London and South East England, traditionally the UK's richest region. As if that were not enough of a shift, it was shown that an increased proportion of an enlarged urban policy expenditure was being used directly to support the private property development industry. Surprisingly, such conclusions seem not to be politically contentious in the UK of today.

The chapter then went on to explore how, in this new colder climate for public expenditure, the key economic development institutions in Wales had been responding. Much, although by no means all, of this focused on Wales' premier development body, the Welsh Development Agency.

The key and overriding conclusion is that policy has unquestionably shifted in its operational methods, towards *partnership* rather than stand-alone policy action of an earlier era, of a kind that could be vulnerable to coming unstuck. Beyond that, however, strong signs were evident that, as budgets diminished and economic conditions became more difficult and more competitive, policy was turning towards assisting home-grown businesses. The aim was to enable the most receptive to benefit from integrating their activities with the inward-investment successes of the 1980s.

In the regional industrial field, where, hitherto, political involvement at local level had not been strong, this approach has every appearance of being successful, although the real test of success is the quality of the outcomes rather than inputs, and it is too early to judge the outputs from this "new wave" of policy-making.

At the urban level, where local government has been traditionally much more active, the picture is less easily described as a resounding success. To be sure, many Urban Joint Ventures have been formed and town centres have been improved. Whether that in itself has been responsible for assisting inward investors to locate or not remains to be seen. However, to the extent that a policy exists of rewarding some localities with a privileged place in a putative new urban hierarchy, in which clustering of economic activity by high and low value-added activity is a main policy discriminator, it is certainly "new wave". It is also contentious and it points up one of the hidden negatives of the new partnership and networking arrangements. On the surface they appear, and indeed are, superior to the technocratic or bureaucratic elitism of old-style government decision-making, but they are just as capable of excluding the awkward, determined or simply non-compliant party. However, in Wales and the UK in the 1990s, there is no possibility that the independent-minded town council can pursue its own democratically accountable destiny: it is too impoverished to do so. In a competitive world economy, where every asset, it is thought, must be mobilized if older industrial towns are not to die, this has the appearance of the ultimate insult.

Acknowledgements

The research on which this chapter is based derives from research sponsored by the Economic and Social Research Council in a project entitled "Networking, training and technology transfer: regional innovation in Europe", and the European Commission in a project entitled "Local development strategies in economically disintegrated areas". I wish to thank the sponsors and all those in Wales who gave their time to respond to the research questions.

CHAPTER FOUR

From front-runner to also-ran – the transformation of a once-dominant industrial region: Pennsylvania, USA

Sabina Deitrick & Robert A. Beauregard

The State of Pennsylvania, one of the 13 original colonies that seceded from Great Britain, played a pivotal role in the industrialization of the USA. From the colonial period to the industrial age, Philadelphia, the State's largest city, was a financial and commercial centre for an expanding nation. The region itself was a major producer of food and timber. Spurred by an abundance of natural resources, large-scale immigration, and willing financiers, and supported by an extensive transportation network of canals and, by mid-century, railroads, the State "gained a national supremacy in heavy industry that lasted until the end of the 19th century" (Cochran 1978: 66). In shipbuilding, textiles, oil extraction, iron & steel, and coal mining, Pennsylvania led the way to the twentieth century.

The continued westward expansion of the country dispersed the manufacturing activity concentrated in Pennsylvania and other northeast States. Nevertheless, until the end of Second World War, Pennsylvania grew at a rate comparable to the country as a whole. However, in the past 50 years there has been serious economic restructuring leading to the deindustrialization of the State and decades of stagnant economic and demographic growth. Key industries – steel, coal, apparel, textiles, shipbuilding – were decimated, and tens of thousands lost their jobs. In response, local and State governments, often devising their own economic development programs, have attempted to bolster economic activity, and in doing so have generally abandoned those industries that once were the mainstays of their economies.[1]

The story of Pennsylvania's deindustrialization and of the State government's policy responses to promote growth constitute the themes of this chapter. We begin by reviewing the post-war restructuring of the Pennsylvania economy and then focus specifically on four subregions: the metropolitan areas of Allentown–Bethlehem–Easton (hereafter Allentown), Philadelphia, Pittsburgh, and Scranton–Wilkes-Barre–Hazelton (hereafter Scranton). These subregions, centred around the State's major cities, were the primary sites of nineteenth century industrialization. Subsequently, we explore various responses to deindustrialization, giving particular emphasis to the role of the State government. The chapter ends with an assessment of the impact of these programs on reindustrialization and with speculative comments about the region's likely future.

Pennsylvania's story does not have a happy ending. The State lost its heavy industry and since that time has had modest population and employment growth. It has not developed new, propulsive industries, nor has it enjoyed in the past 40 years the economic prosperity that earlier propulsive industries had spawned. Rather, Pennsylvania is a slow-growth region with an ageing population, an economy only slightly more diversified than it had been in its industrializing past, and employment growth in regional activities such as health services and education rather than national activities such as steel production.

The region is no longer situated at the cutting edge of the national economy. With the collapse of many of its major industries, the State's leaders are searching for new and innovative industrial sectors that will spur exports, new capital investment, job growth and the in-migration of young households.

Post-war regional deindustrialization

The deindustrialization of Pennsylvania began well before Second World War. Yet it was only during the 1950s that key sectors began to decompose, beginning with shipbuilding in the Philadelphia region immediately after the end of the war, extending to textiles and apparel in the Philadelphia and Allentown areas, then coal around Scranton and Wilkes-Barre, and

---

1. Even if it once was, the State cannot now be considered an integrated economic region. Regardless, the State government confines its economic development interventions to State boundaries.

finally the collapse of the steel industry in the Pittsburgh region in the early 1980s. Other manufacturing sectors also weakened, but the main plot of the State's deindustrialization is found in these four industries.[2]

From 1950 to 1990, the civilian labour force in the USA more than doubled and the country's manufacturing employment increased by nearly 40 per cent.[3] Pennsylvania lagged behind these national trends. Its civilian labour force grew much more slowly and by 1990 was only 39 per cent larger than it had been in 1950, thus becoming a smaller and smaller share of the nation's labour force. Its national share of manufacturing employment fell by over a half. Across the four decades, Pennsylvania lost nearly one-third of its jobs in manufacturing even though its employment base had increased by over a third.[4]

Throughout these 40 years, Pennsylvania's industrial restructuring, at least in broad outline, paralleled that of the USA. For the country as a whole, and using employment as a measure, manufacturing constituted the dominant industrial sector just after the Second World War. By the 1990s, professional, business, private and entertainment services was the largest sector of the economy, and retail trade was nearly as large as manufacturing in terms of jobs provided. The only major sectors of the national economy to lose employment over these decades were agriculture and mining.

Pennsylvania had absolute employment declines in agriculture, mining, and both durable and non-durable goods manufacturing. Although agriculture was not a critical industry for the State, mining and manufacturing were. Interestingly, Pennsylvania was so dominant in mining that it was responsible for nearly 80 per cent of the nation's net loss in that sector between 1950 and 1990. Overall, in every major industrial sector with the exception of agriculture, Pennsylvania lost national share. Thus, although the State is not declining in absolute terms and in the broad aggregate, it has declined relative to the USA and done so most precipitously in mining and manufacturing. The depth of this deindustrialization becomes more obvious when we look at the four major subregions of the State (Fig. 4.1).

---

2. For a detailed examination of the history of textiles and iron & steel in the USA – two of the industries central to industrialization – see Davis et al. (1972: 418–67).

3. The civilian labour force includes employed individuals and those actively seeking employment, the officially unemployed. Unless otherwise noted, the data used in this section were taken from various documents published by the US Bureau of the Census and collected during decennial censuses.

4. Our discussion of employment change is based on net change; that is, the difference between growth and decline. Any net change is thus a combination of expansions and contractions. A net loss (gain) does not mean that there has been no growth (decline) in employment.

Figure 4.1 The four metropolitan regions of Pennsylvania.

Metropolitan regions

Pennsylvania is quite a diverse region. From colonial times, agriculture was a prime economic activity and, along with food processing, it remains important in the east-central part of the State. The central part of the State is relatively undeveloped, with extensive forest land, although forestry is not the major industry it was in the eighteenth and nineteenth centuries. Commerce and finance drove the early growth of the southeast, where Philadelphia is located. Scranton in the northeast was founded on a major coalfield, and Allentown, also in the northeast, was a centre of textile and steel production. Pittsburgh in the southwest built its early economy on oil, glassworks, coal and iron, and later on steel and machinery.

Because these four metropolitan regions were key centres of industrialization in the nineteenth century and the most highly industrialized areas of the State prior to the 1950s, containing a significant portion of Statewide manufacturing employment in 1950, they will be the focus of our investigation. For centuries, Philadelphia has been the State's largest labour market, now nearly twice as large as the second largest labour market, the Pittsburgh region. Scranton's labour market is about one-third the size of Pittsburgh's, with Allentown's slightly smaller than Scranton's. The Philadelphia region, moreover, extends into the adjacent State of New Jersey, as does part of the Allentown region. Our investigation of these four metropolitan regions will be confined to the four-plus decades after the Second World War.[5]

Over this time, and with the exception of Pittsburgh, the populations of these metropolitan areas have grown, as have those of the State and the nation.[6] However, Pittsburgh lost population (approximately 7%) from 1950 to 1990, and all four metropolitan regions grew more slowly than the country as a whole, as did Pennsylvania itself. Only the Allentown region came close to the national growth rate.

A similar set of conclusions characterizes the growth of the respective civilian labour forces. All grew, but none grew faster than the USA civilian labour force. The Allentown region led the way and Pittsburgh (with an increase of less than 7 per cent over 40 years) was the most anaemic and the only one to fall below the Statewide growth rate.

With the exception of Scranton, manufacturing employment declined in all the metropolitan regions and in the State as a whole. Scranton, though, experienced only a minor increase (3%) in manufacturing jobs. Pittsburgh once more led the way in decline. It lost two thirds of its manufacturing employment, over 200 000 jobs in 40 years.

In all four metropolitan regions at the beginning of the post-war period, manufacturing was the largest employment sector, but by 1990 the service sector had ascended to numerical dominance. In Philadelphia and Scranton, retail employment was close behind manufacturing employment in 1990, and in Pittsburgh the former exceeded the latter. The Pittsburgh and Allentown regions lost employment in their small agricultural sectors, and mining employment declined slightly in Allentown but significantly in Pittsburgh and Scranton.

In sum, when compared to the USA, Pennsylvania and its four major industrial subregions enjoyed modest growth in population and civilian labour force across the post-war period. The State and its subregions also

---

5. Our analysis uses the metropolitan region to characterize these four areas. Metropolitan regions are delineated by the US Bureau of the Census using a combination of commuting patterns and population density to identify integrated economic regions. When we discuss regional labour markets, we use the delineations of the Pennsylvania Department of Labour and Industry. The two delineations are closely aligned but not identical. Data on State labour markets came from various issues of Bureau of Statistics, *Pennsylvania statistical abstract* (Harrisburg, PA: Division of Documents).

6. These metropolitan regions grew, in part, as economic activity decentralized and deconcentrated from the central cities and thus expanded into surrounding areas. As that occurs, the Bureau of the Census extends the official metropolitan boundaries.

experienced a parallel transformation of industrial structure, with a movement away from manufacturing to services and retail trade. Unlike the country as a whole, the State's manufacturing and mining sectors went into precipitous decline – Scranton being the exception as regards manufacturing and Philadelphia and Allentown as regards mining.

Specific industries

Deindustrialization provides the broad theme for the story of the restructuring of Pennsylvania's economy and its four metropolitan areas, but does not capture the distinctiveness of metropolitan economies and the extent to which these early centres of industrialization relied on specific industries for their prosperity. We need to examine the specific industries – coal mining, primary metals, and apparels and textiles – that propelled the State's nineteenth-century industrialization and precipitated the massive loss of jobs a century later. Over the four decades, the State lost over half a million jobs in these industries alone (Fig. 4.2). Let us take each metropolitan region in turn, starting in the northeast portion of the State.

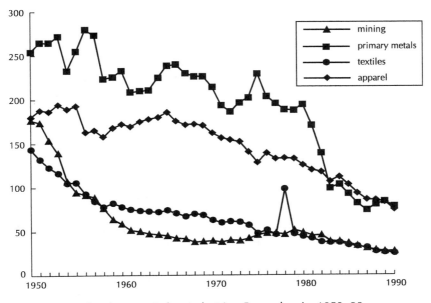

Figure 4.2 Employment in key industries, Pennsylvania, 1950–90.

The Allentown region began as a retail and wholesale trading centre surrounded by a rich agricultural region. At the end of Second World War, the region was producing a diverse array of manufactured goods that included the production of trucks, electronic and gas-generating equipment, textiles and apparel, steel products and cement. Still, it was a relatively specialized economy. In 1950, one out of every two jobs was in manufacturing, trade and agriculture, substantial but not dominant sectors of the economy. The two major industries were apparel and primary iron & steel production. (Bethlehem was the site of the main plant of the Bethlehem Steel Corporation, which employed 31600 workers at its peak in Second World War and by 1994 employed 3600 workers.) Together, one of every five jobs was in these two industries.

Forty years later, the primary metals industry had lost over 60 per cent of its jobs, and apparel had lost over 50 per cent, in total more than 30000 jobs or one-sixth of the 1950 employment base. Whereas in the 1950s these two industries were the largest in the region, by the 1990s they were not even in the top five as measured by employment. Instead, that list was dominated by educational services, construction, hospitals and health services, and insurance and real estate. Textile products was still in the top ten – Number 6 – but was followed closely by various food services, wholesale trade, and business services.

In 1950, the Allentown region was clearly a manufacturing centre, with its major industries all involving goods production, and mainly heavy goods such as steel and stone products but also textiles and apparel. In 1990, only textiles remained as a significant industry, although it was much smaller. Educational services, along with health, business and food services, had experienced major growth and they dominated the regional economy. The education and health sectors employed one out of every six workers in 1990, and fewer than one of ten worked in former dominant industries of primary metals, apparel, and textiles.

Scranton's decline parallels that of Allentown, if one substitutes coal mining for primary metals. Its early industrial base was anchored in anthracite coal, initially used in blast furnaces to produce iron and later steel, but subsequently found more appropriate as a heating fuel. In the 1860s, it provided nearly 80 per cent of the nation's coal (Cochran 1978: 108). Coal mining began its decline in the 1920s, but was still the largest employer in 1950, twice the size of the next largest industries: apparel and textiles. Over the next four decades, the mining industry virtually disappeared. In fact, mining made up 80 per cent of the net job loss in the region. Together, the absolute loss from mining, apparel and textiles was over 60000 jobs, or slightly less than one-half the 1950 employment base.

By 1990, the Scranton regional economy had become more diversified, with the largest industries, as measured by employment, being educational services, construction, hospitals, eating and drinking places, and textile mills. Of the top ten industries, eight came from the services, trade and government sectors.

In both the Allentown and Scranton regions, heavy industry (steel in the first case, coal mining in the second) and apparel and textiles were the moving forces of industrialization and they dominated these regional economies up until the 1950s. Subsequently, these industries virtually collapsed and put thousands of workers into the ranks of the unemployed. Population and employment continued to expand, but reindustrialization did not occur. Instead, these regional economies experienced employment growth in educational and health services and, to a lesser extent, business, real estate and food services.

Philadelphia and Pittsburgh did not fully mimic these smaller metropolitan economies, but did encounter similar forces of deindustrialization. Philadelphia had always had a more diversified economy than the other three and thus was less susceptible to the rapid decline of a single industry (Stull & Madden 1990). Its diversification is apparent in a list of the top ten industries by employment for 1950. Only two were manufacturing industries: apparel and electrical machinery & equipment. The two largest were personal services (mostly in private households) and construction, and were followed by government, apparel, and wholesale trade. In 1990 the economy was slightly more specialized. The top five industries still included construction and government but were joined by education, hospitals, and insurance and real estate. No manufacturing industries appeared in the top ten.

Even though the cluster of industries known as durable manufacturing had the largest 40-year loss of employment – all other major sectors grew – the largest absolute job losses were in specific non-durable manufacturing industries, specifically apparel and textiles, where just over 90000 jobs were lost. Personal services dropped by another 45000 jobs. Compare this to a net gain of nearly 200000 jobs in educational services, over 230000 jobs in health services and hospitals, and over 120000 jobs in insurance and real estate.

At the other end of the State, Pittsburgh's economy has exhibited the poorest performance of the four metropolitan regions. This region began with a highly specialized economy in which nearly one out of every five workers were employed in primary iron & steel production – many in the steel mills lining the Monongahela River, where the famous Carnegie Steel Company (later US Steel) had built in the late nineteenth century. In 1950, the steel industry here was over three times larger than the next largest industry as measured by employment. Construction, personal services, railroads and railway express, and electrical machinery (dominated by Westinghouse) completed the top five. Mining ranked sixth.[7]

Over the subsequent four decades, the Pittsburgh region experienced employment losses in agriculture (a minor sector), mining and both durable and non-durable manufacturing. Over 110000 jobs were lost in primary metals production, devastating the valley towns where steel mills had dominated employment. No other industry had such a precipitous change of fortunes and, when one writes of the deindustrialization of the Pittsburgh region, one is writing about the collapse of the steel industry, an event that culminated in the early 1980s in a rash of plant closings (Giarratani & Houston 1980).

By 1990, schools and colleges, along with hospitals, were the two major sites for employment in the Pittsburgh region. Combining hospitals with health services, the employment in these two industries accounted for over one in every ten jobs and, when combined with educational services, accounted for two in every ten jobs. Pittsburgh was no longer a steel region; primary metals is not even in the top ten employment sectors.

Overall, the deindustrialization of these four metropolitan regions of Pennsylvania centred on the collapse of four key industries: mining, primary metals, apparel, and textiles. Reindustrialization took place primarily through educational and health services, industries that are more regional than national in scope and thus less important as export sectors. At the end of this period of industrial restructuring, and with the exception of Philadelphia, which began the period as a highly diversified economy, these subregional economies were slightly more diversified. In some respects, specialization simply shifted from heavy industry to educational and health services (Table 4.1). The regions continued to expand, moreover, and their employment bases all experienced growth, even if at lower rates than the country as a whole.

Despite aggregate population and employment growth in these metropolitan regions, their central cities, in tandem with other older industrial cities throughout the USA (Beauregard 1989: 1–44), experienced severe

---

7. Whereas bituminous coal was concentrated in the eastern portion of the State, anthracite coal was most prevalent in the southwest, around Pittsburgh. The latter is more appropriate for making coke and producing iron, and the former is more appropriate for heating.

Table 4.1 The top five industries by employment for the four metropolitan regions, 1950 and 1990.

	1950	1990
Allentown	1. Primary iron and steel	1. Education
	2. Fabricated textiles	2. Construction
	3. Professional services	3. Hospitals
	4. Construction	4. Health services
	5. Agriculture	5. Insurance and real estate
Philadelphia	1. Personal services	1. Education
	2. Construction	2. Construction
	3. Public administration	3. Insurance and real estate
	4. Fabricated textiles	4. Hospitals
	5. Wholesale trade	5. Public administration
Pittsburgh	1. Primary iron and steel	1. Education
	2. Construction	2. Hospitals
	3. Personal services	3. Construction
	4. Railroads	4. Eating and drinking
	5. Electrical machinery	5. Wholesale trade
Scranton	1. Mining	1. Education
	2. Fabricated textiles	2. Construction
	3. Yarn, thread, fabrics	3. Hospitals
	4. Education	4. Eating and drinking
	5. Food and dairy stores	5. Textiles

Source: US Bureau of the Census, *Social and economic characteristics* (Washington DC: US Government Printing Office, 1950 and 1990).

population losses and economic shrinkage in the post-war period. The city of Pittsburgh, for example, lost nearly one-half of its 1950 population. Suburbanization combined with industrial decline to weaken urban economies. Regional population and employment growth occurred mainly outside the central cities even though these central cities often maintained dominance in higher-order functions such as banking, corporate legal services and cultural activities.

In economic terms, Pennsylvania is now more like the US economy than it was at the end of Second World War. However, it is no longer a region of national prominence or a leader in national economic growth. Lacking propulsive industries, its prospects for rapid expansion and release from slow growth are problematic, and this is not an unfamiliar story for the northeast and midwest regions of the USA (Perry 1987).

Policy responses after deindustrialization

The revitalization of the State and its metropolitan areas involves a wide variety of governmental and private sector initiatives. Since the 1960s, State and local officials in the USA have been attentive to the condition and trends in the local economy and, with public–private partnerships, have developed many policies and programs to bolster growth. In this section of the chapter, we will consider current State-level responses, but first we need to provide some background.

The USA has never been enamoured with economic planning and only briefly in its history have its citizens tolerated aggressive governmental intervention in the economy (Graham 1976). Although governments tinker with the economy in a variety of ways, from setting interest rates and trade requirements to subsidizing property development and new capital investment, these interventions are not cast as part of a coherent strategy aimed at achieving collective goals or reining in destructive investment decisions and the private property rights of investors (Fainstein & Fainstein 1989).

Additionally, the federal system of government is not designed for dealing with integrated economic regions (Beauregard, forthcoming). Regional or subnational economies often transgress municipal and State jurisdictions and thus are not compatible with the spatial arrangement of political territories. With few metropolitan governments and little inter-State co-operation on economic development initiatives, the problems of subnational economies are usually addressed in a fragmented fashion (Markusen 1987, Rusk 1993). For example, none of the four metropolitan areas discussed above has a region-wide body with a legal mandate to engage in economic development and planning. In most of them, city governments wield the strongest economic development tools, and county governments (made up of multiple municipalities, but not usually metropolitan-wide in scope) are much weaker. Metropolitan planning bodies do exist, such as the Delaware Valley Regional Planning Commission in the Philadelphia region, but they usually function as planning and research organizations having little influence over private investment decisions and few actual programs.

The task of building regional economic development initiatives is left to the State (Eisinger 1988). In the case of the Philadelphia and Allentown regions, which cross State boundaries, this poses major problems.

The city of Pittsburgh represents a good example of how municipalities implement initiatives to reposition a city and a region on a trajectory of growth. Utilizing government and private sector resources, community leaders mobilized in the 1950s to clean up the "Smoky City" and diversify the economy (Beauregard et al. 1992). Early efforts focused on infrastructure (regional highways, an airport), and on air and water pollution caused by the steel mills. Later efforts addressed downtown development and, to a lesser extent, neighbourhood revitalization. By the 1990s, Pittsburgh had put in place a wide variety of regional economic development initiatives. Organizations focused on different sectors, such as reviving heavy manufacturing, software, tourism, foreign trade, re-use of former steelmill sites, retraining, commercial development and housing, to name the major activities.

Many community leaders today refer to Pittsburgh as a "former" steel region, although steel still plays a role in the regional economy. As noted above, the region's growth sectors have shifted to education, health care, financial services and advanced technology, a strategic choice witnessed in deindustrialized regions around the world (Amin & Tomaney 1993). A recent proposal prepared by two non-profit economic development organizations identified five industries as providing growth potential for the region: metalworking, chemicals and plastics, biomedical technologies, environmental technologies, and information and communication products and services (Pittsburgh High Technology Council 1994). Both of these agencies work with firms in these industries through a variety of programs focused on alliances of companies. Their programs range from developing education and training programs, offering specialized services, and disseminating information to providing early-stage venture capital.

Attempts to reindustrialize places such as Pennsylvania, in America's industrial heartland, become increasingly difficult in the context of a continuing westward movement of population and economic activity (Rodwin & Sazanami 1989, Markusen et al. 1991). The growth regions of the USA are now found outside the historical industrial regions. States such as Texas, California, Florida, Arizona and Washington, and their metropolitan areas Dallas, San Diego, Orlando, Phoenix and Seattle, are today's growth centres. In many of the older industrial areas of the Midwest and Northeast, population either declined or remained below the national average during the 1980s, Pennsylvania included. The challenge before these States was to stem the tide of continued stagnation or loss, and find new ways to promote growth.

State governments have led the search for propulsive industries and for a new era of rapid growth. Responding to waves of plant closings and rising unemployment, the Pennsylvania government devised an economic development strategy that is one of the more innovative among States. Thus, whereas local governments attempt to capture capital investment and employment within municipal boundaries, and generally have opted to ignore manufacturing and focus on business services, education, health care, and tourism, the State government has made the commitment to re-industrialize its once-powerful manufacturing base, but not to revive the industries that had collapsed.

PENNSYLVANIA ECONOMIC DEVELOPMENT

During the 1980s, as more and more manufacturing firms laid off workers and shuttered plants, the Commonwealth of Pennsylvania devised new economic development programs to shore up existing businesses, including manufacturing firms, and promote new growth through advanced technology assistance programs. Some programs date as far back as the 1950s, although most are more recent. These programs were put in place to stem the rash of plant closings and to develop new industries and, ultimately, to increase employment.

Two programs represent the centerpiece of these efforts: the Ben Franklin Partnership begun in 1984 and the Industrial Resource Centres (IRC) opened in 1988. Both operate through regional non-profit centres, with the State government co-ordinating programs and allocating funds. Pennsylvania also runs other economic development programs, including the Pennsylvania Industrial Development Authority (PIDA) established in 1956, the Pennsylvania Technical Assistance Program (PENNTAP) begun in 1965, the Pennsylvania Capital Loan Fund, and a State enterprise zone program.

Ben Franklin Partnership At the time of the founding of the Ben Franklin Partnership program in 1984, Pennsylvania had lost 21 per cent of its manufacturing jobs in just six years. Unemployment had reached 14.9 per cent, almost twice the US average. The State's governor, Richard Thornburgh, was forced to act and unlike Ronald Reagan (his Republican counterpart presiding in Washington), Thornburgh and his administration developed an activist economic development policy, called "perhaps the best economic development system in the country" (Osborne 1988: 46).

The Ben Franklin Partnership program represented the heart of the new economic development approach. Building on the State's strong educational institutions, Ben Franklin linked private sector firms to university research in order to increase firm competitiveness and develop new marketable advanced technologies. The Partnership was developed with eight major objectives to:

- maintain and create jobs in new and existing advanced technology firms
- improve productivity, particularly among Pennsylvania's existing industries
- diversify Pennsylvania's economy with special emphasis on increasing the State's share of national advanced technology firms and products
- establish a new consortium to promote economic development, involving the private sector, colleges and universities, and government
- encourage and strengthen research and development between educational establishments and the private sector
- establish and improve scientific education to prepare the State's future workforce
- encourage entrepreneurship through development assistance, and
- assist the creation and expansion of new technology enterprises in the State.

In order to meet these goals, Pennsylvania decentralized the program by setting up the regional centres, each affiliated with a local university. The Ben Franklin Technology Centres provide funds for firms and activities in their regions and specialize in the expertise of local universities and the unique economic strengths of the region. The centres include:

- Northeast Tier Ben Franklin Technology Centre at Lehigh University in Allentown, which specializes in computer-aided design / computer-aided manufacturing, materials, microelectronics, machine or equipment design and biotechnology. This centre also operates offices in the northeast and north-central parts of the State, including West Pittston, near Scranton.
- Ben Franklin Technology Centre of Central/Northern Pennsylvania, located at the Pennsylvania State University in State College, in the largely rural central part of the State, which works in the areas of food, forestry and agricultural sciences, advanced materials, coal and minerals, biotechnology, and manufacturing, management and control systems.
- The Ben Franklin Technology Centre of Western Pennsylvania, affiliated with the University of Pittsburgh and Carnegie–Mellon University in Pittsburgh, which funds projects in computer applications,

biotechnology, advanced materials, processes and devices, robotic and intelligent systems and environmental technologies.

- The Ben Franklin Technology Centre of Southeastern Pennsylvania, in Philadelphia's University City Science Centre, which focuses on sensor technologies, computer science and information processing, biotechnologies, and materials engineering and processing.

Each Ben Franklin Technology Centre operates as a private not-for-profit entity, with its own board of directors comprising members from the private sector, academic community, and trade unions. The centres offer matching grant funds in several areas, including research and development of new technologies, applications for existing technologies and technology transfer, entrepreneurship and small business incubators, education and training programs, and export assistance. Grants range in size from a few thousand dollars to over $100000, with an average of about $50000, and smaller firms are given precedence over larger firms.

Projects are funded by public sector money matched by private sector investments, thereby leveraging limited State economic development resources for greater assistance than outright grants or subsidies would provide. Between 1982 and 1993, the program invested a total of $1.0 billion in the State's economy, with 22 per cent of the funds coming from State investment, 53 per cent from the private sector, and 26 per cent from other sources, including foundations and universities.

Additionally, Ben Franklin proposals are evaluated for their potential economic impact on the firm and ultimately the region in which the firm is located. Over the course of the program, 16294 jobs have been created and 882 new companies started with Ben Franklin assistance. Although these figures cannot begin to account for the jobs lost in each of the regions served – the Northeast Tier Ben Franklin, for instance, has assisted projects that created over 4000 jobs in a region that lost 29000 manufacturing jobs in the 1980s, and the Pittsburgh area Ben Franklin Technology Centre helped to create 3711 jobs, where tens of thousands of manufacturing jobs disappeared – the program's impact on the region and the State is growing, as many of the firms that received Ben Franklin grants expand their markets and increase employment and sales.

The Ben Franklin programs have evolved over their ten-year history, with each centre continuing to refine its special own expertise. In Pittsburgh, for example, the Ben Franklin Technology Centre has created a separate grant program for environmental technology and research that is focused on developing new products from recycled materials and improving the processing of recyclables. The impetus for this program came from recognizing the region's emerging cluster of firms engaged in environmental technologies and related businesses, many of which were established to help the steel industry comply with strict environmental standards promulgated by the national government.

In Allentown, the Ben Franklin program received funding from the US Department of Defence to establish a pilot program called the Agile Web. The program brings together about 20 suppliers in the eastern and northeastern parts of the State (Allentown and Scranton, included), and eight large defence and commercial manufacturing firms to improve interfirm relations and promote manufacturing flexibility within the region's manufacturing base. Firms in the "web" share information across organizations and work together in electronic and mechanical assemblies and products. It is designed to encourage what many analysts call networked production, which seems to be a key to the success of many European and East Asian manufacturers (Harrison 1994).

Industrial resource centers   Although Pennsylvania implemented the Ben Franklin Partnership program to provide grants to firms to engage in advanced technology commercialization, the State also recognized the need to retain its existing manufacturers and increase their competitiveness through modernizing their facilities. The understanding that "manufacturing matters" (Bluestone & Harrison 1982, Cohen & Zysman 1987) is borne out in a region such as Pennsylvania, which, despite the job losses chronicled above, still retained thousands of manufacturing firms. Most of these firms were small to medium-size operations, employing not hundreds or thousands (like the shuttered steel mills) but dozens at the most. The governor after Thornburgh, Robert Casey, made this the centerpiece of his economic development strategy by establishing the Industrial Resource Centers (IRCs).

Like the Ben Franklin program, the IRCs comprise individual centres that operate as private, non-profit entities and receive part of their funding from the State. Eight individual IRCs make up the program:

- Southwestern Pennsylvania Industrial Resource Center (Pittsburgh)
- MANTEC, Inc., the IRC of south-central Pennsylvania (York)
- Delaware Valley Industrial Resource Center (Philadelphia)
- Manufacturers Resource Center, Bethlehem (Allentown)
- Northwestern Pennsylvania Industrial Resource Center (Erie)
- Bioprocessing-Biobusiness Resource Center (University Park)
- Northeastern Pennsylvania Industrial Resource Center (West Pittston, Scranton)

67

- The Industrial Modernization Center (Montoursville)

Unlike the Ben Franklin program, the IRCs work directly with firms to improve their manufacturing processes by offering general business assessments, education and training, and consultancy services such as marketing, plant layout and management reorganization. The IRCs work with manufacturing firms almost exclusively and, like the Ben Franklin Centres, each develops expertise in the specialized manufacturing sectors in the region. Their aim is to remove some of the barriers facing manufacturing firms that are attempting to modernize their operations, by providing technical and business assistance to those firms.

The Southwestern Pennsylvania Industrial Resource Centre (SPIRC) provides an example of how an IRC serves small to medium-size manufacturers in a region. The southwestern part of Pennsylvania is home to 4100 manufacturing firms, employing 170000 workers.[8] Over 40 per cent of the firms SPIRC works with are in the metalworking field, and most of them are small family-run companies.

The heart of SPIRC's assistance is the Operations Review. SPIRC's engineers and consultants evaluate client firms in several areas, depending on the firm's problems, such as product development, process improvements, just-in-time production, quality improvements and labour force participation. Once a review is complete, SPIRC offers matching grants and low-interest loans to help companies operationalize recommendations.

It is difficult to gauge the impact of programs such as SPIRC on a region's economic development. Because SPIRC often works one-on-one with firms, traditional measures of success, such as number of jobs created, may be difficult to ascertain. Furthermore, since SPIRC works with about 100 firms per year, it is able to hit only a fraction of the region's manufacturing firms. Other SPIRC programs, although successful, are also limited in their impact because of their size. Its Apprenticeship/School-to-Work Program operates in local public school districts, and focuses on manufacturing, health care and other service fields. Like other SPIRC activities, small levels of funding mean that it is currently operational in only eight local school districts.

The success of both the Ben Franklin program and the IRCs has prompted greater links between the two, particularly regarding modernization of the region's manufacturing base. Recently, SPIRC created the Manufacturing Extension Partnership, funded in part by the US Departments of Commerce and Defense, and is one of 35 national manufacturing

---

8. SPIRC's region covers 13 counties. This differs from the definition of the Pittsburgh metropolitan region above, which includes six counties.

extension centres. This new partnership brings together 15 regional economic development and educational institutions in a consortium to assist manufacturers. SPIRC and Ben Franklin, along with the other institutions, will continue to work in the areas they have been working, although the increase in funding will allow them to expand their operations.

In light of Pennsylvania's attempts at restoring and modernizing its industrial sector, a major question remains: do these programs help regional economic development? At the individual firm level, successes abound. But the restrictive nature of economic planning at the national level puts these programs under financially strapped State and local governments. In States such as Pennsylvania, the legacy of deindustrialization has diminished revenues from the public sector. Although the State offers innovative economic development programs, and although programs such as the Ben Franklin Centres and the IRCs do not rely entirely on State government funds, the programs remain small in size. The federal government's recent promotion of programs such as Ben Franklin, and the IRCs through their Manufacturing Extension Centres, means that both can expand. Nonetheless, the amount of funds that US Governments spend on assistance to small and medium-size firms is dwarfed by what many other countries spend. The Japanese government, for instance, in a nation whose population is less than half that of the USA, spends 20 times more on financial assistance to small businesses than the US government spends (US Congress 1990: 162). Although Pennsylvania's programs have enjoyed success, they remain modest in size.

Conclusion

This chapter has examined industrial changes and economic restructuring in the Pennsylvania regional economy over the years since 1945. The four major metropolitan regions of the State – Philadelphia, Pittsburgh, Allentown and Scranton – all witnessed the erosion of their economic base in manufacturing and mining between 1950 and 1990. In Scranton and Allentown, the decline of heavy industry – coalmining in Scranton and steel in Allentown – along with a shrinking apparel and textile industry, left the metropolitan economies more diversified and less dependent on specialized manufacturing. Both economies have experienced job gains in local- and regional-orientated activities, such as construction, health, education and other services. Specialization in Pittsburgh was even more pronounced. The collapse of the steel industry in this regional economy put tens of thousands out of work by the mid-1980s. Today's growth sectors, as in Scranton and Allentown, are found largely in the service industries, with health and education leading the way. Philadelphia, the largest metropolitan region, also lost thousands of manufacturing jobs over the period, and again, as in the other cases, regionally based services employed growing numbers of workers.

These metropolitan area economies, once specialized in propulsive manufacturing and mining activities of an earlier era, have come to look more like the USA as a whole in terms of their composition. More important, though, is that all four metropolitan regions, along with the State as a whole, registered growth levels below US rates, whether measured in terms of population or employment. (In Pittsburgh, population change between 1950 and 1990 was negative.) The State's relative position in the nation has contracted, as has its share of the nation's manufacturing. No new high-growth sectors have emerged that appear likely to change this trend.

The State government responded to these changes by devising new economic development programs designed to assist private business. It first centred its efforts on advanced technology activities through the Ben Franklin Partnership program. Later, it developed new programs focusing on manufacturing modernization. Education and training, matching grants, and business assessments are the main components of these programs. The programs are decentralized throughout the State, with each location specializing in the key industries and activities of firms and universities in their location.

Did the State consider other policies to retain existing industries? The State's response to manufacturing grew stronger after the dominant industries collapsed, and today the State does place emphasis on retaining existing industries.[9] Generally, though, State and local governments have had little interest in promoting the former dominant industries in their regions. Their sentiments are based on these industries' problems in the marketplace, which led to their collapse, as well as what happens to a regional economy dependent only a few sectors. Diversified economies came to be valued over specialized ones (Beauregard 1993). Coupled with this is the ideological reluctance to engage in industrial policies that involve "targeting" select sectors, except in defence areas at the national level.

---

9. The State administers a program called the Governor's Response Team, a program to identify and assist small manufacturing companies that are in danger of failing, but would be viable with business assistance or a new owner.

Economic restructuring – deindustrialization – changed some of those views. Local and State manufacturing-based policies increased in number across the USA as more and more local and State economies felt the hardships incurred with closing factories and rising unemployment. Although service jobs were on the increase, their generally lower wages and regional orientation meant fewer growth sectors for the industrial States. Manufacturing gained as a focus of public policy formulation, because policymakers recognized the importance of industries that export beyond State borders. Generating higher multiplier effects through greater regional linkages, manufacturing came into focus in the public policy arena.

Finally, where is the State likely to focus its future economic development efforts? It appears that the State will concentrate its activities as it has, with an emphasis on advanced technology sectors and specific manufacturing ones. Current economic development initiatives place little emphasis on today's growth sectors: education, health services and hospitals, construction, real estate, and eating & drinking places. The reasons for this inattention are many. Most of them (especially the latter three) are local sectors with few out-of-State exports. Local activities generate lower multiplier effects than export-based activities (because of scale effects), so most public policies focus on the latter, hoping to realize the most "bang for the buck."

Additionally, when economic development in the USA has focused on non-manufacturing activities, it has been in sectors such as tourism and real estate. Some local economic development organizations in the State are recognizing the importance of other sectors, especially health services, and offer programs related to them, including education and training. These are just beginning, however, and have no record to evaluate.

Are these programs enough? Given the story of Pennsylvania and its four major metropolitan economies, no. Can the State turn around its stagnant growth and regain some of its industrial past? That is the more difficult question. Regional economies in the USA grow unevenly. The miracle growth economy in Massachusetts in the 1980s fell quickly into recession by the end of the decade. California, likewise, has seen its growth halted by recession and cuts in defence spending. Whether Pennsylvania can find new propulsive industries, promote growth in its major metropolitan areas, and attract younger workers to the State, depends on many factors, but most of these are outside local and State control. Its economic development programs represent a start. Only in the coming years though will their impacts become known.

CHAPTER FIVE

The restructuring of the steel industries in Germany and Great Britain

Jonathan Morris & Rolf Plake

Structural change in the steel industry

In 1992/1993 the iron & steel industry all over Europe entered into one of the most serious crises in post-war history. The surplus capacity caused by this crisis is estimated at 30 million tonnes in the crude steel sector and approximately 20 million tonnes in the rolled steel sector. The cut in employment needed to cope with this overcapacity is likely to reach a scale of 50000 to 60000 jobs in the next few years (ILO 1992). In Germany in 1992:

- the production of pig-iron fell by 8 per cent to 28.5 million tonnes
- the production of crude/natural steel fell by 5.7 per cent to 39.9 million tonnes
- the production of rolled steel finished products fell by 4 per cent to 31.4 million tonnes.

A further reduction of 5–6 per cent in the consumption of crude steel was expected for 1993. Again it is the workers who bear the brunt of this development. In 1992 15000 lost their jobs, in the next two years a further 35000–40000 were expected to follow. If you add to these job losses those in the steel supply sector and the endangered jobs in the coal sector and its suppliers, then the coal and steel industry is threatened with a reduction of 100000–200000 jobs in the next three years.

If this process is not reversed, then in the medium term, employment in the German iron & steel industry will fall from its current 175000 to under 100000. However, in contrast to earlier crisis periods, this cut in employment is caused not by part-closures in individual areas but by the closing down of whole sites.

It may seem strange, when pondering the revitalization of two old industrial regions, to be discussing an industry (steel) that was a bastion of the old order in both Wales and North-Rhine–Westphalia. Indeed, the other elder statesman of the Welsh economy, the coal industry, is notable in its absence. What justification, therefore, is there for the inclusion of steel; why not concentrate upon electronics and the Japanese presence or financial services, or some other "Sunrise" sector? The justification is two-fold. For all the talk of the "decline" of the industry (and employment levels have certainly declined markedly), it remains a key player in Welsh economy, and British Steel (the dominant force) remains one of the largest private sector employers in the region. Secondly, and more important, the so-often ascribed sobriquet, a "declining industry", is somewhat if not largely misplaced; news of its death is premature.

The prominence of the industry in Wales, and arguably its continued vitality, are a base for the argument, but are not enough in themselves. What justification can be offered for its place in any discussion on revitalization and, given the nature of the industry, in what ways can we reasonably expect the industry to participate in the revitalization process? In many ways the industry has a limited impact beyond its immediate size; it provides a building block for other industries and, therefore, unlike other industries, has limited "trickle-down" potential. However, in this chapter we will argue that in many ways, despite its laggard image, the industry is at the leading edge of new manufacturing practices and therefore it is in certain respects an exemplar of best (and sometimes worst) practice. The industry is, for example, stocked with new computerized technology, is introducing novel forms of work organization more readily associated with Japanese car producers and, as a result of both developments, along with a much stronger emphasis on cognitive skills, has invested heavily in training initiatives, both on the job and off the job, the latter in conjunction with local vocational education and training providers (Blyton et al. 1993). In many ways the industry is also locked into a single product, which in the short to medium term is extremely dependent upon the business cycles of other industries, notably construction and automotive, which are in the longer term reducing their unit steel use. The obvious way in which to escape from this ensnarement is to diversify into other related downstream (and possibly higher value-added) areas, or to diversify out of the industry completely. These concerns will provide the basis of the paper, which will describe, among other things, changes in working practices, training initiatives and diversification measures.

Welsh and German steel industries in the 1990s

The steel industry generally is becoming increasingly segmented into two types of producers. First are those found in the developed countries, which have turned to new types of steel and more value-added activities in processing. In turn, they have increasingly left production of standard steels to producers from the developing countries, which have certain competitive advantages, most notably in labour cost factors (ILO 1992). Technological change in the industry has fundamentally altered the way in which both iron & steel are produced. The major changes have been in the main functional areas of (blast) furnaces, the casting process, the rolling phase, all allied to computerization of production and energy conservation. The result for the workforce has been that an industry that once hired on the basis of biceps-size now has to recruit and retrain workers into using a more cognitive process. That is, brain power is replacing brawn.

In conjunction with new process technologies, and in part as a direct result of them, steel producers in the developed countries have striven to introduce new "products" and improve the quality (e.g. tensile strength) of steels. This has been achieved, for example, through the extended use of automatic process controls and through greater use of continuous casting (Blyton 1993). More specifically, the steel industry has sought such improvements as higher strength, improved toughness, greater welding suitability and increased corrosion resistance. Improved quality has also been the result of new product development. The industry has developed steels with higher strength, lighter weight and improved coatings with greater resistance and durability. These new high-strength low alloy plates and strip steels have helped the steel industry to meet competition from other materials in certain industries, notably automotive and white goods. The new coated strip products have also rejuvenated steel use in buildings, cars and consumer durables, whereas higher quality tinplate has to a certain extent fended off competition from aluminium in the canning market.

Many of these improvements have been user-driven or developed in close collaboration with purchasers in the metal processing industry. That is, end-user companies and industries are increasingly demanding higher-quality steel output in order to maintain their own competitive position. Automotive firms are a good example of such a development. The car industry started making lighter cars after the initial oil price shock of the mid-1970s. This led to a situation in which, wherever possible, steel was

74

replaced by lighter materials. Where steel could not be adequately replaced, it had to be thinner and lighter, yet still meet increasingly rigorous stability and safety requirements. Moreover, the car industry has demanded better standards on rust resistance, with the result that the refining and coating of plates has become an increasingly important production stage.

Investment in the iron & steel producing industry between 1980 and 1990 was above average; as a result the German steel industry today is a modern production sector of a high technical standard and is by no means a "washed-out old industry". Despite the structural changes in the steel markets described it cannot be assumed that steel as a material will lose its key economic role in the near future. Steel is rather an "old" and a "new" material at the same time. For many applications, steel will remain one of the most efficient materials in the future, also in the car industry (Franz & Lichte 1991). In the long term, steel has a high potential for innovation, for both new alloys and new procedures. Steel also benefits from technical advances (e.g. just-in-time delivery) so that, in competition with other materials, it won't be left behind. As well as areas in production that are likely to continue losing in importance (mass steel manufacture, pipes), there are also areas with a positive future development (e.g. steels of high versatility, new alloys and laminated materials). In the long term, however, these will not be able to compensate for the sales losses in standard products. In this respect the structural change in iron & steel production will continue. As a result of a continuing worldwide overcapacity, the transition to a second phase of restructuring in the steel industry is taking place through the companies. This restructuring lies above all in co-operation and mergers between companies.

The diversification policy of the large companies dominant in the Ruhr are attributable to purely business management criteria and strategies, whereby questions of regional development are not considered. This policy was realized in the main through the buying up of companies considered innovative in other areas of Germany or abroad. For example, the Mannesmann group acquired the hydraulics company Rexroth in Lohr, the mechanical engineering and installations company Demag in Duisburg, the engineering manufacturer Harmann & Braun in Frankfurt, the Swabian Kienzle-Apparate GmbH, the Stuttgart ANT telecommunications GmbH and the American data-processing printer firm Tally Corporation. Since 1988, the Thyssen group, which includes complete systems for transport technology, environmental technology, energy technology and processing technology, including flexible production systems and CNC processing centres in its range of products in its sector" capital goods and processing", has had a share in the leading Stuttgart software house Ikoss. Thyssen spent over DM1700 million alone on the buying up of the American Budd Company (car manufacture supplier with over 10000 employees) a few years before. Such diversification strategies may be advantageous for the balance sheets of these companies, but for the region they are critical. The withdrawal of the coal and steel concerns from traditional production sectors is the same as if they left the area completely.

This problematic dividing up of company and regional development has been intensified in the past by the fact that in the heyday of the steel economy some companies actively prevented the appearance of new economic activities in the region. All over the Ruhr, large industrial areas are owned by the coal and steel companies. (In Duisburg, for example, a mere five companies own about 70 per cent of the industrial area.) For a long time these companies refused to allow new enterprises to settle here, so that the local authorities' hands were tied and regional diversification was blocked.

New work-practices and training

British Steel has embarked on a series of new working practices in an industry characterized by what might be termed very old practices, many of which have their origins in the nineteenth century. These have been approached as a response to the rapid development of new technology, to the new imperative for quality production, and a continuous drive for labour cost reductions (Morris et al. 1992). Thus, although the industry in Wales may be said to be at the leading edge of implementing new manufacturing methods, it is no different from the steel industry elsewhere in the UK and western Europe, including Germany.

Essentially, these new working practices can be grouped into three major categories: first, generalized moves to increase functional flexibility and reduced demarcation barriers, secondly, more specific measures to introduce multi-skilling; and, finally, the introduction of team-working. Although there were attempts to implement greater flexibility in the 1970s, these largely foundered (Blyton 1992, Bacon et al. 1994). However, this changed in the watershed period following the defeat of the major 1980 UK strike when management started to reassert its prerogative. Subsequently, management used two vehicles to push through these major changes in work organization. The first was the so-called local "Slimline Agreements", which local unions were effectively forced to sign in order to ensure their plants' survival. Secondly, a localized lump-sum bonus (LSB) was introduced, amounting to up to 20 per cent of pay in certain cases. Moreover, unless the terms for the LSB were agreed, then the ordinary annual increase was not paid either. Thus, the bonus became a potent management tool for forcing through what were, to the workers, unwelcome changes (Kelly 1984, Avis 1990, Morris et al. 1992).

The main training initiatives developed in BS plants in Wales have been associated with the craft restructuring programme. The craft restructuring programme has involved two main elements: first, it has involved reorganizing training of all new apprentices into the two major disciplines (mechanical and electrical); and, secondly, the retraining of current craftsmen, or at least a proportion of them. A competency-tested three-tier grading and promotion system has also been introduced within the skill groups at certain of the BS plants to include craftsmen, supervisors and technicians. The importance of the craft restructuring programme is reflected in the training budgets and in the time allocated to the programme. At the BS Llanwern works, for example, in 1990–91 apprentice training and craft training took over half of the total training time (34% and 21% respectively). The only other group to be allocated anything like this amount of time were process workers (14%). These figures are even more stark when compared to those for 1986–7, when only 3 per cent of time was allocated to craft workers training and retraining.

However, the agreement and introduction of craft restructuring has not proved unproblematic. Indeed, in some situations it has given rise to long-running disputes between management and craft unions. This is despite craft unions welcoming the idea of changes that improve the promotional and career prospects of craftsmen. These disputes have centred particularly around selection criteria for retraining, and the wage implications of the retraining. On selection issues, the disagreement has been strongest where management have selected workers for retraining on criteria challenged by the union (for example, subjective judgements such as the worker's "attitude to change"). At many British Steel plants, selection has led to a situation of a proportion of the existing staff being selected for retraining, whereas others are excluded from the retraining programme.

Innovation and worker involvement in the Ruhr

One really decisive weakness of the Ruhr economy lies in the fact that the companies lack innovative dynamism. It is clear that the jobs being lost cannot be compensated for by the production of services or through the location of new industries and companies. In view of this need to renew jobs, the dynamic development of the resources of existing companies acquires a central significance in the Ruhr area. However, the ability of the companies to innovate is the decisive criterion for the safeguarding of their resources and the permanent restructuring of them along the lines of the new requirements of the market.

It is now important to say something about the new role of employees in this complicated business, as well as something about the processes, scopes and limits of a bottom-up corporate innovation policy. A bottom-up innovation policy is not suited to a conflict-orientated trade union policy. Innovation projects in companies can succeed only if they are common endeavours. As one can easily understand, they cannot be realized against the wishes of top executives and middle management, and in the same way it is not possible to order innovation and diversification from the top down without creating considerable friction. In the end, arriving at an understanding on corporate improvements and innovation measures is gaining more and more significance in this age of **lean production**.

The potential of the formal technical and informal know-how of the staff is a decisive pawn in the successful organization of an innovation and diversification process. The knowledge needed for the operative implementation of innovation and the detailed work on problems is often patchy at management level. Here the perspective is all too often determined by the three- to five-year contract, and detailed insight into the informal workings of the complicated structure of a company is lacking.

Many works councils want to organize their work in representing the interests of their colleagues professionally. They would like to examine problems and take steps to overcome them as early as possible, before the stable door is locked after the proverbial horse has bolted, because with high losses carried forward and drastic management measures for reorganization presented to the works councils for rapid approval, the negotiating process is as arduous as one can imagine. Nevertheless, section 80.3 of the Employee's Representation Act plays an important instrumental role here: the law entitles works councils to call in outside experts in questions of substantial company changes. The process of examination by these experts often results in alternative proposals for the reorganization of the company. Usually these proposals are linked with measures to shape the future of the company and for technical and organizational innovation. These changes in the work of works councils and trade unions are only hesitatingly acknowledged by the political and business sectors. The words of a works councillor might serve as a way of looking at things: "We can still occupy the factory gates if necessary – we intend to use every small possibility to save jobs and implement future-orientated measures".

As an example of worker-involvement in steel company innovation, the following case is relevant. E+H GmbH is a services company belonging to Thyssen Stahl AG (TST) and Ruhrkohle AG (RAG) in the western Ruhr area. As a private railway company, it carries the materials of the steelworks in in-company transit and trans-ships goods at two harbours it owns on the Rhine. On the whole the approximately 70 million tonnes of cargo transported by E+H each year is made up of ore, sinter, coal, coke, hot iron and hot crude steel, as well as semi-finished steel products and finished rolled steel products. Here, with 8 tonnes having to be transported to produce 1 tonne of steel, a high tonnage arises that demands a cheap means of mass transportation. The structural changes in the steel industry and cost structures in the transport sector place narrow constraints on the future transport and employment volume at E+H. For E+H this means at best stagnating handling figures.

Together with the employees and company management, IKS (Innovations und Stukturpolitische Beratungsagentur für die Metallindustrie) has worked out proposals for the modification of the rail-bound traffic in the steelworks. One possibility of returning the transport of slabs back to rail is offered by the *isolated, radio-controlled self-propelled car (IFSV car)*. Above all, this type of vehicle, using trucks, saves the cost of locomotive-based shunting. Moreover, in view of the threat of staff cuts in in-company transit, new fields of business have to be found in which E+H can apply its strengths profitably. Here are several conceivable options:

- *Container handling* There would be sufficient space and good transport connections by land and by water available in the harbours.
- *Participation in suburban public transport* The E+H rail net offers excellent opportunities for the development of suburban public transport if E+H can succeed in establishing co-operation agreements with the German federal railways and the Rhine–Ruhr public transport company VRR.
- *Metropolitan goods transportation by rail* This would above all be used for carrying goods in metropolitan transit, for instance the mass transportation of goods or the transport of the semi-finished products

of the steel sector. This metropolitan goods transportation by rail can also be developed into a complete system for transport and logistics services.

This example also shows that diversification and innovation in the "old" companies of the coal-and-steel association can succeed. However, it also shows how important the know-how of the employees is in this process and how much energy is required to transform good proposals into reality. All too often good ideas fail because of narrow-minded attitudes in companies. The fate of the "modernizer" (and almost every company has one) provides an excellent statement in this regard. In view of the inertia of old structures hostile to innovation (also in many traditional medium-size companies), often all that remains of an innovation policy is the "slow boring of thick boards".

Non-diversification: the "ragged frontier"

Given the low multiplier effect in this industry, one potential way in which the Welsh steel industry could have benefited the Welsh economy is through diversification outside core competencies or areas. There was extensive diversification by world steel producers during the 1980s; this is in part a response to continued recessionary problems within the industry and steel's particular position in the market place. The steel industry is particularly prone to business cycles, as there is such a high level of capital intensity, and plant cannot be closed or opened quickly or cheaply as in other industries. Moreover, the steel industry is extremely dependent on the fortunes of two major users, construction and the automotive industry, which are themselves extremely cyclical. Thus, firms have sought to diversify out of core steel competencies. At the same time the industry has undergone a degree of liberalization. From 1945 to 1965, the European steel industry was largely characterized by public sector monopolies operating in monopolistic markets protected by international cartels, in turn operating in a fast-growing general market. To a certain degree this has changed with far greater liberalization of markets, privatized entities (most obviously British Steel) and far less willingness on the part of the EC to allow open-ended national subsidization.

Steel firms, therefore, have sought diversification in two major forms. First, they have diversified horizontally, that is by acquisition, merger, joint-venture activity. Given the limited opportunities to do so nationally (as the industry is characterized by national champions), this has often taken an international form. Although there have been several pan-European deals, the best examples of these have been between US and Japanese steel producers.

The second form of diversification of steel producers has been "vertical" into related or non-related business areas. In this case the best examples are the German and Japanese producers. In the latter case, there has been a wholesale (but not wholly successful) move into microchip production, in an attempt to jump an innovation generation into the new "industrial race". In Germany, meanwhile, the diversification has been somewhat more complex, with takeovers of related downstream companies (in industrial plant and the automotive components sector) and unrelated companies in areas such as electronics. The most obvious case in point would be Mannesman, which has diversified virtually completely out of steel into automotive components, plant and machinery and electronics. This shift has not been so stark at Hoesch (still Europe's eighth largest steel producer), but less than half the company's turnover now comes from steel.

This vertical diversification of the German steel producers has crossed international boundaries; In the UK, for example, German companies have bought several successful engineering and steel-using companies in the automotive components industry. Thyssen, for example, have bought Tallent Engineering, a major supplier to Nissan, and Albion Pressed Metal (a Toyota supplier), while Hoesch have acquired Camford Engineering, a large pressings concern.

This diversification strategy is in direct contrast to British Steel, where acquisition activity has been limited to the purchase of several steel stockholders. Indeed, British Steel remains one of the least vertically integrated major producers. The reasons for this emanate from the peculiar ownership history of the industry in the UK, and in particular its nationalization in 1949, its shift to the private sector in 1951, renationalization in 1967 and privatization in 1988. The key date in the context of this argument is 1967. This nationalization was the first "true" nationalization, as the 1949–1951 phase had been too short to effect major change. However, the 1967 nationalization nationalized not the whole of the industry but only plants with an annual output of 0.475 million tonnes per annum. Although this nationalized the bulk of the industry (90% plus) a small but important part was in private hands. Moreover, the small steel plants and producers were not bulk producers but specialist steel producers. This created the so-called "ragged frontier", comprising originally some 200 small specialized producers and processors, many of which relied on British Steel for crude and semi-finished steel. Thus, specialized areas, such as re-rolling, high-alloy steel, high-speed steel, tools and stainless steel, were produced only in the private sector. This was complicated in the "Phoenix" schemes of the 1980s (an attempt to "bail-out" large parts of the private sector), when British Steel took a share in the private sector. The end result is perhaps best illustrated by steel production at Cardiff in the 1970s, when British Steel supplied to a private producer (GKN) that produced finished products such as rod and bar on virtually the same site. Thus, what was in effect an integrated steel production site was owned by two companies, one public and one private (Vaizey 1974, Abromeit 1986, Cockerill & Cole 1986). The net results of this complex industry ownership structure was that, as a nationalized company, for 20 years British Steel was effectively locked out of the *immediate* downstream activities at a time when German firms were diversifying apace. By the time the company was privatized in the late 1980s, it faced the imperative of survival and, arguably, had lost many of the skills necessary to diversify. The end result is that, far from British Steel boosting the Welsh economy by diversification into downstream activities, the major diversification into this area in Wales is Hoesch's ownership of Camford Engineering and Gwent Steels.

Conclusions

To return to the point of departure, what justification is there for including the steel industry in a study of rejuvenation? The evidence provided in this chapter would suggest that there is. The industry is a major employer and is likely to remain so. Moreover, although British Steel headquarters are to be found outside Wales, there are still major divisional headquarters to be found inside (with associated professional and managerial positions) and a substantial research and development capacity, functions rarely found in the new Sunrise branch-plant economy.

The industry has also been innovative in other respects. There has been major investment in state of the art technology and there have been innovations in work practices. For example, although multi-skilling has become a subject of management rhetoric elsewhere, in the steel industry it exists. That the management tactics owe much to the "rottweiler" school of management, though, is part of a wider discussion, although certainly the degree of union–management consensus that exists in the corporatist system of Germany is sadly absent. Perhaps the weakest area of "contribution" has been the relative lack of diversification in (or outside of) the Welsh economy. As has been illustrated, this is an historical legacy, although it would seem to be a continuing blind-spot among managers.

The origin of a job-orientated policy in North-Rhine–Westphalia lay, on the one hand, in the efforts of the trade unions and, on the other, in the reorientation of the State of North-Rhine–Westphalia in favour of a regionalization of its structural policy. An example that should be named here are the efforts of the ZIM meetings (Zukunftsinitiative Montanregionen, or initiative for the future of the coal & steel regions), which were later carried on in the ZIN meetings (Zukunftsinitiative Nordrhein–Westfalen or initiative for the future of North-Rhine–Westphalia). Here the State tried to pick up on main structural and regional aspects in the structural change and develop, above all, labour-market and technology initiatives aimed at "help for self-help".

A concept for organized industrial change, an involvement-orientated structural policy, must begin with the modernization of the existing industrial core and resources, and furnish concrete help and support measures. The jobs in existing companies are far easier and cheaper to retain and modernize than through the classical path of "creative destruction". The dynamic development of resources is thus a core point of a job-orientated structural policy. Conversely, it is also true that the subsidized preservation of industrial structures has a disastrous impact on jobs in the medium and long term.

The innovative ability of companies must be retained and developed if the existing jobs in industrial production are to be saved and expanded. The problems with the lack of willingness in companies to innovate, which penetrates right through to the psychological aspects of the company's orientation, show that a structural policy that sets store on the promotion of technology, high tech developments and their financial backing alone is inadequate. A company innovation and diversification strategy must accompany the selection and development of technology. Questions on the reorientation of complete branches, on company innovation projects, the promotion of product innovation in addition to process innovation, the development of individual associations and the development of co-operative measures between individual companies – thus stand at the centre of a job-orientated structural policy.

The ability to innovate and assist industrial structural change stand and fall by the different viewpoints and instruments of regional and sectoral structural policy becoming compatible with each other. Many initiatives in regional structural policy fail because they are unable to come close to and grasp corporate problems. In addition, important players (chambers of commerce and industry, branch associations) are often blocked in achieving the aim of interlinking regional and company level by their views on organizational policy. However, in the interlocking of both aims lies the key for the development of branch-orientated early warning systems, which identify problems in good time and develop the necessary instruments to respond to them. Only through the development of individual, regionally embedded innovation associations and the development of intercompany co-operation agreements can the tasks in structural policy be mastered in the future. In this context the role of employees in corporate innovation policy as described here is of importance and central significance.

CHAPTER SIX

Disintegration and reintegration of production clusters in the Ruhr area

Dieter Rehfeld

Introduction

About ten years ago, when Piore & Sabel (1985) published their "Second Industrial Divide", they initiated a discussion about the new meaning of flexible specialization for the future of industrial development. Referring to the industrial districts in the Third Italy or in Baden–Württemberg, they also highlighted the new meaning of a flexible and innovative regional base of global competitiveness. Industrial districts and synergies, agglomeration advantages and regional networks: these are the most prominent topics of the new discussion about regional developments, which promises the possibility of a sustainable development for all regions, for both high tech regions and traditional.

But we should be careful dealing with simple concepts and high expectations. On the one hand the most promising models of flexible specialization, the Third Italy and Baden–Württemberg, are today experiencing a fundamental structural shift. On the other hand we should not forget the fate of older industrial regions. These older industrial regions had been organized as agglomerations or networks for a long time, but only very few older industrial regions have been able to handle the challenges of structural change in successfully.

Talking about the meaning of regional networks therefore also includes talking about the risks of failure, about the problems of organizing a durable regional restructuring and, not least, about the limits of regional strategies in the context of global economies and national and European politics.

Looking at the Ruhr Area, we can discuss the problems of traditional regional networks – production clusters – as well as the possible development of new regional networks. Doing this, we will focus on three aspects:

- First, I want to outline the concept of the production cluster and to illustrate that there are different types of regional production clusters in relation to the specific preconditions of the different regions.
- Secondly, I will contrast the old steel and mining production cluster in the Ruhr Area and a new one in the same region, the production cluster grouped around environmental technology and waste management.
- Thirdly, I will discuss some problems in context with the rise and future development of the new production cluster in the Ruhr Area.

Production chains and production clusters

In discussing the problems of regional restructuring in the Ruhr Area regional development is conceived to be a process subject to both internal and external opportunities and constraints. The economic interlinkages inside the region and their integration into supra-regional economic networks are of central importance. To analyze this relation between internal and external interlinkages, we start from the concept of production chains.

A production chain is the sum of all production and service functions necessary for developing, producing and marketing a certain product or a group of products. Besides the production itself, elements of this production chain are those functions preceding and following production, and those necessary to carry out the manufacturing process and the integrative function of standardization (Fig. 6.1).

In analyzing production chains, three aspects are important. First, they differ with regard to their significance for the overall economy – just as over the past hundred years the production chains grouped around the railway, power-generating facilities, automobiles or microcomputers have taken on core functions in the economy as a whole at certain times.

Secondly, the internal organization and cohesion of a production chain have to be looked at – some elements of this are the size of a company, the mode of co-operation and the technical, material or organizational connections between the different segments of the production chain. Thirdly, in the course of time the importance of groups of products changes in the structural context of industrial systems.

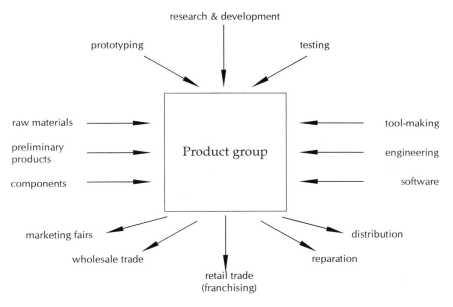

Figure 6.1 Elements of a production chain.

Further on, we see a production cluster as the spatially concentrated parts of a production chain. If all functions necessary for the development, production and marketing of a product are concentrated within one region, we call it an integrated production cluster. Our own studies about economically successful regions show that all exhibit a wide range of occupational categories focused on a relatively limited range of industries (Kilper/Rehfeld 1991, Rehfeld 1993).

Functional differentiation and specialization are two key prior conditions for regional networking: there are very few opportunities for strong regional ties if the regional industrial system is very broadly diversified and/or if there is a lack of important functions (e.g. decision-making) of a production cluster or a concentration on only one or two functions.

In order to illustrate this argument, we can group different regions along two axes: specialization and functional differentiation (Fig. 6.2).

We can identify four types of regions:

First, there are regions with a high level of functional differentiation and specialization, that is, integrated production clusters. In this type we can find nearly all successful regions of the 1980s: high tech regions such as Silicon Valley or Boston's Route 128, industrial districts such as the Third Italy (north-central Italy), or Baden–Württemberg, or world cities with a

87

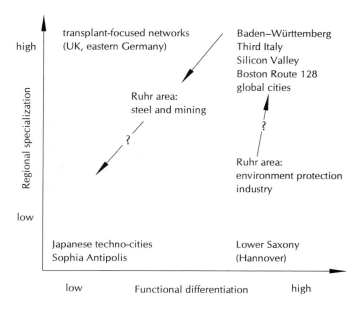

Figure 6.2 Functional differentiation and specialization: types of regions.

high degree of specialization in production- and headquarter-related functions such as financing, research and advertising.

Secondly, at the opposite end of the figure we find regions with a low level of specialization as well as a low level of functional differentiation. Examples are the French high tech centre Sophia Antopolis or most of the Japanese Techo-Cities; here predominately high-value functions such as research and development are concentrated, but without further links with productive functions.

Thirdly, there are regions with a high degree of specialization but dominated by one function, especially component assembly. Traditionally there are former rural or peripheral regions with a high level of public investment subsidies. These regions grew until the early 1970s. And since the 1980s we find regions with a production system grouped around one new plant of a global company. The most prominent are the Japanese car-assembling transplants in Great Britain or some new plants in eastern Germany.

Fourthly, there are only few examples concerning regions with a high degree of functional differentiation but without any further specialization. One German example we have studied is Hannover in Lower Saxony, where different functions are related to various products or production groups, for instance cars, rubber, electronics, and so on.

Only in the first type of region can we find an important degree of inter-linkage between the different companies. Nevertheless, within the second and the third types of region we find examples of high rates of occupational growth. But this growth depends on external impulses and/or subsidies, not on an innovative regional base. In the long run, it will be crucial for these regions to change direction to become an integrated production cluster.

The Ruhr Area is an example to study both the disintegration of former integrated production clusters and the problems of building new production clusters. Looking again at Figure 6.2, two important production clusters within the Ruhr Area are actually changing: the steel and mining cluster is disintegrating and the cluster grouped around environmental technology and waste management is (possibly) in a process of integration.

Trends in disintegration

The Ruhr Area is located within North-Rhine–Westphalia, one of the largest federal States of Germany. Nowadays, it is a polycentric urban agglomeration with more than five million inhabitants. After growth began during the 1850s it became the leading region in the process of industrialization in Germany. During the past 30 years, the Ruhr Area has suffered a high degree of industrial decline.

The nineteenth century's evolution of the production cluster around coal and steel in the Ruhr Area and this region's rise to be Germany's main industrial area have been described often before (for the following see Schlieper 1986; Hamm/Wienert 1990: 144ff.; Kiesewetter 1989: 187ff.; Radkau 1989 p. 115ff.; Weber 1990).

Looking back to the roots of industrialization in the middle of the nineteenth century, it was not a local technological competence that explains the rise of the Ruhr Area: the most important innovations in steel production came from England, and the most important technical universities for the mining sector had been founded outside the Ruhr Area in Aachen and Clausthal–Zellerfeld. It was the utilization of technologies developed in foreign regions that brought out the materially related connection of coal and steel. Over time, the integrated elements of the two industries developed first by expansion into product processing segments, via either a direct material relation (such as the one between foundries and blast-furnaces) or the ensuing progress in thermal economics. Two more industries were integrated into the production cluster based on coal, iron and steel:

- In 1902, power generation and steel production became connected by steel producers, Stinnes and Thyssen taking over 86 per cent of RWE's shares (the regional power generating and distribution companies); power stations and steel plants exchanged raw materials and energy over the following years. This initiated the boom in large lignite power stations, which rendered possible low energy prices, which, in turn, attracted high energy consuming heavy industries.
- Around this time, by-products of both the mining and the steel industries, such as alum or sulphur, were increasingly used as raw materials for the chemical industry (which was to become rather important during 1939–45 policy of autarky through its autonomous company, the Kohlechemie).

The organization of the production cluster in the Ruhr Area should be viewed in the context of the industrial linkage opportunities. Whereas steel production and steel-working industry had been spatially separated up to the middle of the nineteenth century, the corporate policy of the Ruhrgebiet's steel companies aimed at concentrating many production and distributive functions of this production chain – mining as well as processing and even scrap collecting for recycling purposes – into integrated groups.

So, the evolution of groups and consortia became, once again, a structural element of the Ruhr Area as it had in its early expansion phase. The product groups of small and medium-size enterprises, especially of those in mechanical engineering, remained closely related to the large-scale enterprises of the coal, iron and steel industry. Contrary to other regions' production clusters, the Ruhrgebiet's large companies succeeded in keeping the most important engineers, so that outsourcing and the emergence of new competitors were correspondingly few (cf. Weber 1990: 222, 228).

The growth of this production cluster constituted the success story of the Ruhr Area, as well as being the main reason for the problems within the region, as coal mining in the Ruhr Area came under pressure from global competition from the late 1950s and steel production since the early 1970s. The process of deindustrialization in the Ruhr Area is widely accepted as the origin of the downturn of the industrial core in this region (cf. Petzina 1987, Loewe/Wand 1987, Montankommission 1989). Therefore, we will focus on another aspect of this development: the disintegration of the production cluster.

There are two main reasons for this trend towards disintegration.

90

First, there is a trend of dissolving the materially related production interlinkages. In this context, for instance, we can consider:

- new technologies in steel-generating or downstream production such as the foundries, these new technologies facilitated the organizational and spatial separation of production steps that had been strongly interconnected;
- the change from coal-based chemistry in the Ruhr Area to petrochemicals, as well as the decline of coal for steel generating;
- the rising use of microelectronic and sensor-technical components in mining; these components cannot be delivered by the local mining suppliers and have to be imported from outside; that is one reason why traditional supplier–user relations are becoming weak;
- very low transportation costs; therefore, very heavy and bulky components can also be transported on a global level.

Secondly, there is the reaction of the dominant groups to changed global conditions. Their strategies led to a change in organizational integration, which became possible by dismantling materially related production linkages mentioned above. The dominant groups in the coal, iron and steel production cluster restructured in three ways:

- The dominating Ruhr area enterprises (especially those of the steel industry) have grown to multinational groups. In the 1950s they established steel works in Third World countries and then founded branch enterprises, mainly in the area of further processing.
- Because of growing problems in export markets, the steel groups started a diversification of group activities in the 1960s. They bought both plant and companies in the mechanical engineering industry, as well as those engaged in the construction of plant, in supplying the motor industry and in ship building. Since these activities are mainly located outside the Ruhr area, there was a large outflow of capital (cf. Petzina/Plumpe/Unger 1990).
- Some steel groups, such as Mannesmann and Gutehoffnungshütte, have closed down most of their steel-making core production and are now mainly engaged in further processing and mechanical engineering. Although the coal, iron and steel sector remains the basis of these groups, their activities are more export orientated.

Despite the deindustrialization and disintegration, there is still a cluster of coal, iron and steel and related industries (cf. Fig. 6.3) that, albeit considerably smaller, still dominate the region with their economic and organizational power and their importance concerning the employment situation: even today, more than two thirds of the west German coal

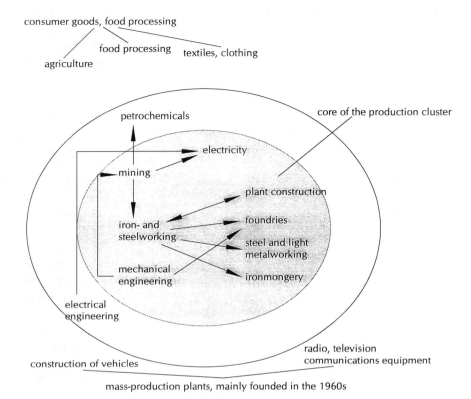

consumer goods, food processing

food processing   textiles, clothing

agriculture

Figure 6.3   The industrial cluster in the Ruhr Area.

output and iron & steel production is concentrated in the Ruhr Area.

In the early 1990s, nearly the half of the overall industrial employment in the Ruhr Area still depended on this cluster. Another 12 per cent of industrial employment depends on further energy-consuming heavy industries. Only a quarter of industrial workers are occupied in the formerly dominating industries such as mechanical and electrical engineering, the motor and plastic industries and those parts of the chemical industry that do not belong to primary industry. Finally, about one tenth of industrial employment depends on consumer-related industries.

Currently, the Ruhr Area is experiencing another far-reaching decline of not only steel, mining and related industries, but also in others such as mechanical engineering and automobile components. Obviously, such a decline cannot be compensated for by the settlement of single new plants. If the Ruhr Area is to survive as an industrial core region in the long run, the regional productive system needs to be reintegrated, that is, to enable new and self-sustaining production clusters to grow.

Trends in (re)integration

There are several trends in the development of new clusters in the Ruhr area (cf. Fig. 6.4). The reorganization of car component production, the emergence of environmental technologies and waste management, and the modernization of transportation services provide scope for new production clusters. There is little hope that the Ruhr Area will become a leading region in microelectronics. But there is a great opportunity, if the new production clusters mentioned above develop, of bringing out further growth in cross-cluster activities such as measurement, controlling and processing, new materials or biotechnologies.

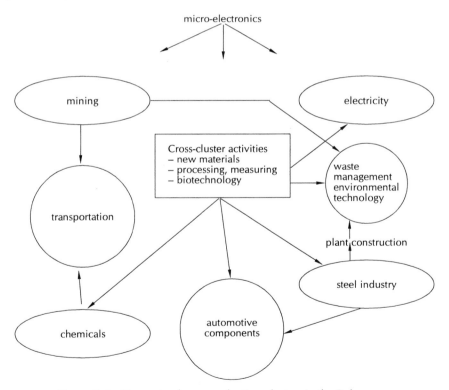

Figure 6.4 Elements of new production clusters in the Ruhr area.

In general, there are three very important preconditions to establish new production clusters in a region such as the Ruhr area:
- they have to be related to global markets: only if there is a global demand for new products and services can we expect sustained growth of new production clusters;
- they have to build on indigenous regional potential, because there is little hope of reorganizing the industrial system of a region such as the Ruhr area mainly by investment from outside;
- indigenous growth potential includes the need for co-ordination of the diversification strategies of the dominating regional companies and selected public support (e.g. an advanced infrastructure such as advertising, or research and development, or in initiating supply and demand).

The most promising of these new production clusters is the environmental protection industry, which includes environmental technology and waste management. In discussing this example, I will outline the challenges in creating new production clusters.

Because of the many problems with soil contamination at old industrial sites – air and water pollution, consumers and industries waste on the one hand; public environmental regulations such as water and soil protecting regulations or recycling duties on the other – a wide range of different new production activities grew up in the Ruhr area in the 1980s.

Grabher (1990: 17) points out that the environmental technology industry in North-Rhine–Westphalia at the end of the 1980s accounts for more than 600 firms, with about 100000 jobs. The North-Rhine–Westphalian State government even talks about a thousand enterprises active in North-Rhine–Westphalia in ecological technology and as suppliers of every imaginable environmental protection apparatus (NRW 1990). And a study of the ecological industry's related small enterprises in the Ruhr area talks about 551 enterprises with fewer than 50 employees in the Ruhr area (KVR 1992).

Various evaluations (cf. the overview in Wackerbauer 1992) about the spatial distribution of the environmental protection industry in Germany show that about a third of companies engaged in activities related to environmental protection are located in North-Rhine–Westphalia. This degree of spatial concentration indicates a strong relationship between environmental problems and the growth of the environmental protection industry. Nearly half of industrial investment in environmental protection takes place in North-Rhine–Westphalia, because of the high share of environment-contaminating industry (such as the petroleum products industry, iron & steel works, non-ferrous industry, chemical industry, mining, power production, and water supply), especially in the Ruhr area.

Despite the fact that the environmental protection industry started to develop in the Ruhr area only in the 1960s, a wide range of new enterprises are now active in this market. The most important groups of enterprises are:

- builders of machinery and facilities (mainly engineering companies from the regional steel producers, constructors of power plants and power plant components),
- engaged in environmental technology and the construction of systems and facilities such as purification plants and detoxification systems
- regionally based mining and energy companies, which have diversified in recent years and in many cases have externalized their activities in waste management by founding new companies
- regionally based plants and companies, especially automobile assembling plants and the chemical industry, which announced new policies for recycling
- specialized regionally based enterprises with a long tradition in waste management and soil recycling, especially construction and service firms
- diversifying suppliers of the mining industry, especially mechanical engineers (these started to construct systems for dust removal or air pollution prevention in the 1960s)
- a wide range of new small and medium-size firms, engaged for instance in planning and advertising, software development, producing systems and apparatus for measuring and controlling, special components and basic chemical materials
- enterprises, engaged in related activities such as transport, biotechnology, processing,

and so on.

Despite the fact that environmental technologies is a young and growing industry that will change in the future, we have to point out that a new production chain has become established in recent years. Figure 6.5 summarizes the most important production and service tasks included in this production chain. Starting with the production process, we have waste resulting from that itself (recent and historical waste, and waste resulting from cleaning technologies) as well as from the product and its packaging. This waste has to be collected, separated, sorted and classified, and processed. The resulting materials have to be recycled, or, if that is not possible, burned or deposited. The recycled materials are intended to be used again

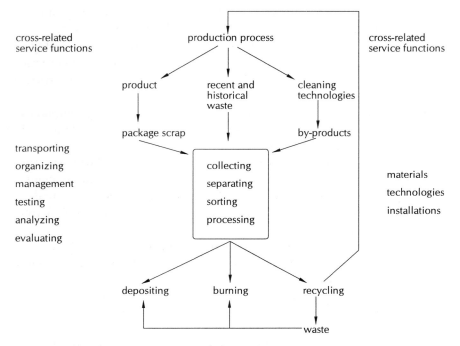

Figure 6.5 Environmental technologies and waste management – elements of the production chain

in the production process. In each part of this chain, links are needed to transport, logistics, management, analysis, testing and evaluating, and – one of the main productive functions – the development and construction of the technological equipment, and the associated physical, chemical and biological materials. The industries profiting from this task are mainly the chemical industry and electrical and mechanical engineering, but also transport, the construction industry and energy supply.

In contrast to others, this production chain can be summed up as follows:

- a wide range of business profiles, for instance the prevention of air pollution, the treatment of drinking water, the purification of waste water, the protection of water, the sanitation of the soil, the eradication of waste, and so on
- a certain independence from cyclical movements, but a high degree of dependence on political issues and regulations
- a high degree of research and development intensity, including the capability to develop customized solutions

- an impetus towards cross-firm co-operation because a wide range of expertise is required
- the dominance of small and medium-size enterprises in recent years (now multinational concerns are engaging in this new market, too)
- an interchange of ideas, know-how, qualified workers, and a demand for specific supplier components such as equipment for processing and measuring; these innovative interlinkages create a regional milieu that initiates the development of new products and the formation of new enterprises.

This new production cluster is fundamentally different from the traditional steel and mining cluster in the Ruhr area (Table 6.1). At first sight, it is surprising that the change not only takes place in the same region but is increasingly organized by the enterprises engaged in both the old and the new fields. Thus, the rise of the new cluster can be regarded as an example of a regionally based diversification strategy.

The following two questions focus on the preconditions and the problems of such regionally based diversification:

- what are the origins of this new production cluster in an older industrial region?
- what are the problems that arise out of close links between old and new enterprises' strategies and organizations?

Table 6.1 Contrasting production clusters in the Ruhr area.

	Steel and mining cluster	Environmental protection industry cluster
Scope	Homogeneous	Heterogeneous
Demand	Highly dependent on cyclical movements	Highly dependent on political regulations
Research and development intensity	Low to medium	High
Enterprise structure	Integrated companies	Small and medium enterprises
Organization of the production cluster	Hierarchical	Co-operative
Mode of integration of the production cluster	Materially based interlinkages	Innovative interlinkages: lead user–supplier, know-how transfer, outsourcing

A new production cluster in the Ruhr area

The environmental condition of the Ruhr area is not a problem caused but rather perceived during the past 20 years. Waste water and air pollution, contaminated soil and hazardous waste have long been closely connected to the process of economic growth in this region. In the early 1970s there was for the first time a broad discussion about environmental problems and the start of different political measures aimed at the reduction of pollution and contamination. This was the crucial point concerning the rise of the environmental protection industry in the Ruhr area, because these new measures were organized in a way that facilitated the transformation of problems into market opportunities.

No doubt, in the early 1970s, the new political focus on environmental protection generated much discussion about the costs of implementing environmental technologies. But soon it was perceived that environmental protection could also create new markets and jobs.

The rise of the environmental protection industry in the Ruhrgebiet cannot be understood without considering the State's involvement in initiating, supporting and organizing the formation of this new production chain. More than half of environmental protection investment is made directly by the public sector, mainly by local authorities. The private sector investment in environmental technology is generated indirectly by State activities, responding to laws to reduce emissions, waste, noise and so on. These are mostly federal laws, but there are additional NRW government activities, such as funds to decontaminate soil, financial assistance in environmental investment, laws to organize waste management, and so on.

Furthermore, State activities focus on implementing the complementary infrastructural preconditions. These activities are mainly initiated by the NRW administration and include:

- the organization and support of specific training programmes (e.g. the training of environmental protection advisors for small and medium-size enterprises);
- the foundation of research and development institutes (e.g. universities);
- the foundation of technology centres or industrial areas for environmental technology production (for instance in Essen or in context with the IBA).

The creation of new markets and the infrastructural support of new industries are two of three important aspects of the rise of environmental technology in the Ruhr area. The other decisive aspect concerns the proximity of problem-causing and problem-solving industrial activities. Nearly half of German industrial investment in environmental technologies occurred in North-Rhine–Westphalia, most of it in the Ruhr.

Therefore, the great steel, energy, mining and chemical companies can be regarded as lead-users who force their suppliers (in mechanical engineering) first to develop new technologies for the reduction of pollution, contamination and waste.

Furthermore, another precondition has been that the regional suppliers were able to master these new tasks. This question is of great interest to the discussion of regionally based diversification strategies. In NRW it focuses attention less upon dominating technical competence and more upon the ways in which firms identify and penetrate new markets:

- a long tradition in waste management, especially in scrap collecting for recycling purposes
- experience in the construction of ventilation systems for the mining companies
- traditions in co-operation with local authorities, especially in energy supply or water purification
- experiences in the transportation of hazardous waste
- the availability of deposits and sites for incineration facilities.

But the strong connections between lead-users and specialized suppliers could become a bottleneck in further development for the following two reasons.

First, as mentioned above, there is a need for flexibility and co-operation between the different enterprises engaged in the environmental protection industry. Indeed, there are many different forms of co-operation in the Ruhr. Figure 6.6 provides an overview of selected forms of co-operation in the different tasks of waste management, including different types of enterprises and local authorities:

1. between regional-based mining, steel and energy companies (Ruhrkohle, RWE, Thyssen, Hoesch), specialized enterprises engaged in waste management (Heitkamp, Edelhoff) and affected producers (Opel, Bayer) aiming at developing new concepts in car recycling
2. Thyssen, RWE, and the local authorities in Duisburg, organizing the "Entsorgungszentrum Duisburg" in order to develop new concepts in hazardous waste removal and others
3. between three regionally based enterprises (Veba Kraftwerke Ruhr, Teerbau, Ruhrkohle Umwelt) in cleaning contaminated soil
4. between Veba Kraftwerke Ruhr, VEW, Edelhoff and Rethmann in a waste utilization company

5. between chemical industry companies (BASF, Hoechst, VEBA), a steel producer (Klöckner) and a public research institute in implementing a facility to transfer used plastics to oil products

6. regionally based enterprises in the context of the Institute for Environmental Technology in Duisburg

7. the above institute, another regionally based enterprise (Babcock) and local authorities in Essen and others in electronic waste removing

8. the local authorities in Gladbeck, Bottrop and Gelsenkirchen and the RWE-Entsorgung planning a facility to sort packaging waste

9. local authorities from the above cities and Essen and a regionally based construction company to manage rubble.

Since the end of the 1980s there has been a strong trend of concentration, especially in waste-management related activities. The great mining, energy and steel companies in the Ruhr area have become increasingly engaged in waste management, not only by an outsourcing of related activities but also by taking over former small and medium enterprises. The consequences are different: on the one hand the integration of large companies offers new possibilities for investment, financing or foreign

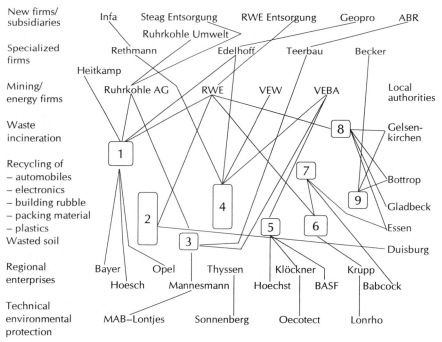

Figure 6.6 Selected co-operations in waste management in the Ruhr area.

investment; on the other hand the companies that have acquired may risk losing previously loyal customers to other companies.

Secondly, because of its origins, the environmental protection industry in the Ruhr area has a strong position in water and wastewater cleaning activities, in waste management, prevention of air pollution and in noise abatement. But companies are weak on research and strategic management in the fields of energy and environment. Measurement, analysis, systems control, planning and advertising are below the average for German environmental protection activities. This pattern is a product of the specialization of the Ruhr area's industry in general, especially the below-average shares in electrical engineering and precision engineering and optics.

This specialization refers to the dominant way in which the problem has been handled in the past 20 years. The main response to increased regulation has been ad hoc solutions, most of them can be called "end-of-pipe-solutions". That means that the solutions take place after the problems have arisen. However, there is a new trend to focus more on waste avoidance than on waste management. The main reason for this trend is the growing understanding that the traditional methods of waste management will produce more problems or will be very expensive in future. For instance, new waste management regulations in Germany have raised the issue of transport and logistics costs, as well as those concerning the recycling process and the emissions from waste incineration.

The obligation to reduce waste, traffic and energy is thus increasing. In this respect, environmental protection does not refer primarily to paying to reduce waste but to avoiding the production of waste in the first place. Therefore, the crucial task for the Ruhr area's environmental protection enterprises in the years to come will be not only the organization of waste management but also bringing on new activities to reduce waste, traffic and energy use in the interests of increasing the quality of life. Serious and committed action and the development of an integrated waste-management industry will be necessary to create public confidence and support for this new industry and to avoid the risk of developing an industrial specialization in the Ruhr area that enjoys short-term success but suffers long-term problems. Moreover, it is vital that this is achieved early if the Ruhr area is to maintain its recent leading position in the environmental protection industry – especially when we remember that support for this industry and engagement in new activities are a the subject of regionally based industrial policy in almost all regions experiencing industrial decline, with the consequence that competition between these regions will grow.

Note

This chapter is based on two studies of the Ruhr area (Rehfeld 1992a, 1993a). Further empirical information about the two production clusters in the Ruhr area is provided by these studies.

CHAPTER SEVEN

Groping towards reflexivity: responding to industrial change in Ontario

Meric S. Gertler

Introduction

Industrialized societies are currently undergoing a period of difficult restructuring, and Canada is no exception. The process of industrial change has been particularly painful for Ontario, Canada's largest and most industrialized province, which since 1990 has experienced economic dislocation, instability and social hardship on a scale not witnessed since the Great Depression. With this kind of economic backdrop, it should come as no surprise that policy-makers in the province have become increasingly furtive in their pursuit of new approaches to industrial strategy.

In searching for new directions, economic policy-makers have pursued a series of initiatives intended to fix Ontario onto a high-wage, high-value-added growth path. The rationale underlying this shift has been to facilitate the economy's transition to "new" competitive realities, in line with Best's (1990) conception of the "new competition", by encouraging the adoption of "network" principles throughout the province's manufacturing economy. The object of these reforms has been to bring about changes to firms' *internal* work practices, organization, and products, as well as to help transform the *relations between individual firms* and their suppliers, customers, competitors, and related institutional entities. In so doing, policy-makers in the province have aspired increasingly to the role of *animateurs* of change in the private sector, and have sought in recent years to develop the kind of *institutional reflexivity* said to characterize Europe's most innovative regions (see Cooke & Morgan 1993, Cooke 1994).

This chapter analyzes this recent and continuing experience in Ontario, and offers a mid-term assessment of the effectiveness of the efforts mentioned above. It begins by presenting the basic contours of economic structure and change in the province, focusing on the noteworthy impacts of the most recent recession. Later I discuss some of the forces that have been operating upon the Canadian and Ontario economies, originating both nationally and internationally, to produce the changes described in the first part of the chapter.

One such force is the Canadian government's adoption of a macroeconomic policy based on the ideology of continental free trade, signified by the signing of the Canada–USA Free Trade Agreement (FTA) in 1987, precursor to the larger NAFTA agreement that took effect 1 January 1994. As will become evident, this policy stance has not only intensified the process of structural change in the Ontario economy, producing serious adjustment problems along the way, but has also created a regulatory environment in which activism at the subnational (provincial) scale has become increasingly constrained. Furthermore, it has served to move the national macroregulatory framework for economic relations in a direction that is anything but conducive to the encouragement of network (or what Sayer & Walker 1992, might refer to as "social economy") relations between firms, making it even more difficult to establish true partnerships between the dominant economic stakeholders in Ontario.

Consequently, I provide an overview of industrial policy in Ontario in recent years. I then examine the broader macroregulatory structure more systematically, noting how it continues to present obstacles to policy-makers whose intention has been to develop "network" or "social economy" relations within the province's economy. This leads to a more general discussion of the relationship between these two different scales of economic regulation: the region-State and the nation-State. Ultimately, I conclude with a sobering appraisal of the challenges facing Ontario (and many other subnational political jurisdictions) as it strives to attain true institutional reflexivity in the face of external constraints.

Restructuring of the Ontario economy

Ontario is Canada's most populous province and has long dominated the country's national economy. In 1994, its population was close to 11 million (roughly 38% of Canada's total population), indicating that nearly two in five Canadians currently reside in the province.

AGGREGATE PATTERNS OF PERFORMANCE

Coming out of the 1981–2 national recession, Ontario experienced strong and consistent economic growth, exceeding 4 per cent (in real terms) every year from 1983 through 1988 (see Table 7.1). Its unemployment rate declined from 10.3 per cent in 1983 to only 5 per cent by 1988. By the end of the 1980s, virtually two in five Canadians found employment in the province, which accounted for more than 40 per cent of the nation's gross domestic product. Moreover, Ontario's manufacturing sector was responsible for producing more than *one-half* of the nation's manufacturing output, and the province also accounted for a similar proportion of Canada's international trade in merchandise. Clearly, in both demographic and economic terms, Ontario had reaffirmed its position as Canada's heartland.

However, the end of the 1980s brought a set of changes that would begin to undermine Ontario's national economic supremacy and challenge its long-term stability. The Canadian economy entered another recession in 1990 and, for Ontario, it was soon clear that this downturn would be most unlike other recessions before it. Between 1990 and 1992 the region's unemployment rate climbed steadily, approaching the national average rate of unemployment. Furthermore, Ontario's unemployment rate remained stubbornly high: in 1994, the rate stood at 9.7 per cent, the fourth year in a row that it had exceeded 9.5 per cent. In a labour force of 5.4 million workers, over half a million remained unemployed. Furthermore, the share of jobless workers made up by the long-term unemployed (i.e. those without work for six months or more) increased dramatically over this period, from just over 13 per cent in 1989 to some 33 per cent in 1994 (Ministry of Finance 1995). In the recession of the early 1980s, this share had reached a peak of only 26 per cent in 1983, and had declined steadily thereafter. In the early 1990s downturn, this share has equalled or exceeded 30 per cent for the three years of 1992–4, and still shows little sign of subsiding quickly.

Hence, although the 1981–2 recession was relatively short-lived, with a consistent and rapid improvement in the region's employment and output picture, the more recent downturn has proved far more difficult to shake off. And in further distinction to the earlier episode, Ontario's performance relative to the rest of the country has been substantially worse than in previous years. By the end of 1992, *more than one-half* of all the jobs lost in Canada since 1990 were lost in the Toronto metropolitan area alone. Since reaching an employment peak of just over 1.9 million workers in 1989, the Toronto region lost approximately 180,000 jobs up to the end of 1993.

105

Table 7.1 Economic indicators for the Province of Ontario and Canada, 1981–93.

	1981	1982	1983	1984	1985	1986	1987	1988	1989	1990	1991	1992	1993
Real GDP ($B 1986)													
Ontario	165.5	158.9	166.1	181.3	191.0	202.7	211.9	226.1	231.0	224.1	217.7	218.9	223.5
Canada	440.1	426.0	439.4	467.2	489.4	505.7	526.7	553.0	566.5	565.2	554.7	558.2	570.5
Ontario–Canada (%)	37.6	37.3	37.8	38.8	39.0	40.1	40.2	40.9	40.8	39.6	39.2	39.2	39.2
Employment (000s)													
Ontario	4171	4063	4089	4235	4377	4524	4689	4862	4949	4937	4770	4714	4793
Canada	11001	10618	10675	10932	11221	11531	11861	12245	12486	12572	12340	12240	12383
Ontario–Canada (%)	37.9	38.3	38.3	38.7	39.0	39.2	39.5	39.7	39.6	39.3	38.7	38.5	38.7
Unemployment rate (%)													
Ontario	6.6	9.7	10.3	9.0	8.0	7.0	6.1	5.0	5.1	6.3	9.6	10.8	10.6
Canada	7.5	11.0	11.8	11.2	10.5	9.5	8.8	7.8	7.5	8.1	10.3	11.3	11.2
Ontario–Canada	-0.9	-1.3	-1.5	-2.2	-2.5	-2.5	-2.7	-2.8	-2.4	-1.8	-0.7	-0.5	-0.6

Source: Ontario Ministry of Finance, *Ontario economic outlook 1994–1998.*

While Ontario (and the Toronto region in particular) have struggled to escape the grasp of recession, the rest of Canada's economy had largely recovered to its pre-recession levels of employment by early 1994. And relative to Canada's two other metropolitan areas with populations over one million, Toronto's position has seriously suffered (Fig. 7.1). Vancouver now has the lowest unemployment rate of the three (in January 1995, its rate stood at 7.9%). While Montreal remains in the worst economic shape of the three (12.3%), Toronto's performance (9.0%, January 1995) has moved sharply in the direction of Montreal's. With the lowest unemployment of any metropolitan region in the country during the boom years of the 1980s, it relinquished this position to Vancouver some time during 1990. These figures suggest what other data have confirmed: that the recession of the early 1990s has begun to realign Canada's economic geography in a significant way. The most salient aspect of this realignment has been Ontario's fall from grace.

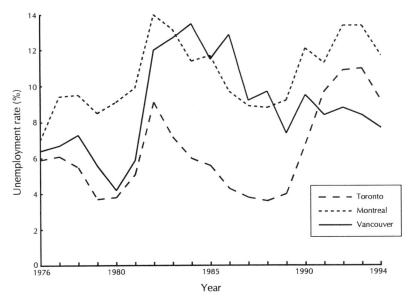

Figure 7.1 Unemployment trends: Toronto, Montreal and Vancouver, 1976–93.

SECTORAL AND OCCUPATIONAL DISAGGREGATION

When the general patterns described above are disaggregated, further important dimensions of economic change become evident. One of the most apparent trends is the consistent decline of manufacturing employment in both absolute and relative terms (Table 7.2). While manufacturing employed roughly one in four Ontario workers in 1981, this figure had declined to something much closer to one in six by 1993. Over the same

Table 7.2 Ontario's changing industrial structure, by employment.

	1981	1983	1989	1993
Total employment (000s)	4171	4089	4949	4793
Manufacturing (000s)	1034	932	1029	837
(%)	24.8	22.8	20.8	17.5
Services* (000s)	2715	2772	3420	3546
(%)	65.1	67.8	69.1	74.0
Other** (000s)	422	385	500	410
(%)	10.1	9.4	10.1	8.5

Source: Ontario Ministry of Finance, *Ontario economic outlook 1994–1998.*
* Services includes private and public sector services.
** Other includes agriculture, other primary, and construction.

period, service activities (both private and government) have grown from about two-thirds to just shy of three-quarters of the employed labour force. Table 7.3, which provides a more detailed view of the province's changing industrial structure, suggests that the same trends are evident (although somewhat less muted) when one measures these changes

Table 7.3 Changing industrial structure, by share of GDP (measured at factor cost).

	1984	1989	1993
Real GDP ($1986) ($millions)	163101	205311	200060
Goods producing (%)			
Agriculture	38.3	35.8	32.2
Other primary	1.7	1.3	1.1
Manufacturing	1.7	1.5	1.3
Construction/utilities	26.6	24.8	23.4
Service producing (%)	8.1	8.2	6.3
Transportation/	61.7	64.2	67.8
Communication	6.4	6.8	7.1
Wholesale/retail trade	11.3	12.8	13.9
Finance, insurance, real estate	14.3	15.0	16.4
Government services	6.7	5.7	6.2
Community, business, personal and other services	23.1	23.9	24.2

Source: Ontario Ministry of Finance, *Ontario economic outlook 1994–1998.*

according to output rather than employment. By this yardstick, manufacturing is still a very significant component of the Ontario economy, generating close to one-quarter of the province's net output, despite the more marked decline in employment.

A more detailed profile of the manufacturing economy is conveyed in Table 7.4, which provides trade data for Ontario's leading export sectors. These data make clear that the province's manufacturing economy is heavily orientated toward the production of automobiles and automotive parts, for which it enjoys a large trade surplus. They also demonstrate Ontario's continuing dependence on foreign sources for technology-intensive inputs to production, such as electrical and non-electrical machinery and equipment. At the same time, the province's more traditional resource-related products, including pulp and paper, iron, steel and various other metals, and wood products, also figure prominently in the list of leading export sectors.

Table 7.4 Top ten exporting product sectors, 1993 (CAN$ millions).

	Exports	Share of total Ont. exports (%)	Imports
1. Motor vehicles, parts	41215	43.4	24338
2. Machinery, mechanical appliances	11208	11.8	21550
3. Electrical machinery & equipment	4269	4.5	12854
4. Non-ferrous metals	3702	3.9	3406
5. Pulp, paper & allied products	3254	3.4	1865
6. Precious metals	2969	3.1	1667
7. Iron and steel	2181	2.3	1678
8. Plastics, plastic articles	2089	2.2	3490
9. Prepared foods, beverages, tobacco	2062	2.2	2604
10. Wood & wood products	1723	1.8	650
TOTAL (all sectors, Ontario)*	95037		106725
TOTAL (all sectors, Canada)*	187348		169951
Ontario as a share of Canada (%)	50.7		62.8

Source: Ontario Ministry of Finance, *Ontario economic outlook* 1994–1998.
* For merchandise trade only

Table 7.5 provides another perspective on economic structure by focusing on occupational change in the province. By 1993 the Ontario workforce was dominated by managerial, professional and administrative workers, at over one-third of the employed labour force – a proportion that has risen fairly steadily at least since the early 1980s. The next nearest category (clerical) approaches 16 per cent, which is actually down from its 1981 and 1989 shares. Meanwhile, those in the traditional manufacturing occupations of processing, machining, product fabrication, assembly and repair constitute a shrinking but still significant 13 per cent of regional employment.

In summary, then, it would appear that the Ontario economy has recently experienced a recession of historic significance. Furthermore, there is evidence to suggest that this recession has not been just another "business cycle event", but that the changes sweeping over the province are qualitatively different from earlier rounds. This is *not* business as usual.

Table 7.5   Occupational composition of employment in Ontario.

	1981	1989*	1993
Total employment (000s)	4171	4949	4793
Occupational shares (%)			
Managerial/Professional	23.8	29.9	33.8
Clerical	18.4	17.2	15.8
Sales	10.1	9.3	9.9
Services	13.3	12.2	13.3
Primary	4.5	3.1	3.2
Manufacturing**	17.1	15.1	12.7
Other†	12.8	13.3	11.4
TOTAL	100.0	100.0	100.0

Source: Ontario Ministry of Finance, *Ontario economic outlook 1994–1998.*
* 1989 represents the peak year for total employment.
** Includes processing, machinery, product fabrication, assembly and repair.
† Includes construction, transportation equipment, operation, materials handling.

Forces of change

Given the various indications that "things are not the same as they used to be" for the Ontario economy, then what forces have been producing major change in the province? I would suggest that the economic transformation under way has been produced through the combination of three different sources of change, some of which represent fundamental shifts in the structure and geography of production systems.

MACROECONOMIC POLICY

One must acknowledge a set of macroeconomic policies pursued in Ottawa by Conservative federal administrations since at least 1984, when former Prime Minister Brian Mulroney was first elected. The dominant objective of such policies was to reduce inflation and secure price stability, and this was achieved through a rather draconian regime of high interest rates implemented by the Bank of Canada. The Bank's prime rate increased sharply between 1987 and 1990, even while inflationary pressures remained modest. While the annual inflation rate was somewhat higher in the Toronto region than the rest of the country in the second half of the 1980s (and indeed, the "overheated Southern Ontario economy" was frequently singled out as the target of Ottawa's anti-inflation rhetoric), by 1992 inflation had been virtually "wrung out" of both the national and regional economies (Gertler 1991, Metropolitan Toronto 1994).

Accompanying rising interest rates in the late 1980s was a rapidly appreciating Canadian dollar, which led to declining short-term competitiveness and shrinking sales for Ontario's exports. The combined impact of sustained high interest rates and a rising dollar was sufficient to send the Canadian economy into recession, notably before the other G7 countries. While interest rates have been allowed to decline to single-digit levels since 1992, with a parallel decline in the value of the Canadian dollar, the national (and especially, the Ontario) economy has been slow to recover. The reasons for this probably have much to do with the next two forces of change.

NORTH AMERICAN FREE TRADE

A second source of economic change is the Canada–USA Free Trade Agreement that came into effect in 1988. The full effects of this major event are difficult to discern, for two reasons. First, it is difficult to disentangle the influence of trade-related adjustment from the other forces acting upon the Canadian and Ontario economies during the same period (including the macroeconomic events just discussed). Secondly, by their very nature, major changes to trade regimes set in motion a set of responses and restructurings that may take several years to complete. Consequently, any assessment of the impacts of the FTA (or the subsequent NAFTA agreement) on the Ontario economy must be couched in cautious and tentative terms at this stage. Nevertheless, several trends seem apparent. For the most part, I would argue that these have worked against rather than in favour of the economic vitality of the region.

The FTA triggered or accelerated a process of major spatial and functional restructuring of corporate organization on a continental scale, to which even companies headquartered outside Canada and the USA have been induced to respond. This restructuring has several apparent manifestations. Many USA-based multinationals that had formerly operated branch plants inside Canada to serve the relatively small Canadian market

111

(roughly the equivalent of California) chose one of two likely options. Some chose to close such plants and to serve the Canadian market from larger US plants with spare capacity and greater scale economies. The most vulnerable plants appear to have been those operations that were at least 10–15 years old, in formerly protected sectors (such as textiles, apparel, footwear, food and beverage, and furniture), employing labour-intensive technology to produce mature, standardized products in relatively small runs (Mahood 1991).

Other owners of branch plants chose to reconfigure their Canadian operations to become part of a continentally rationalized production system. In such cases, the product lines in Canadian plants were narrowed, and instead these plants specialized in the production of fewer products for the entire North American market. Generally speaking, corporations implementing *either* form of reorganization have reduced both the number of plants operating in Canada and the number of employees on their payroll. There is also at least anecdotal evidence to suggest that, even in cases where Canadian plants have secured a mandate to produce particular products for the entire North American market, the Canadian corporate subsidiaries have undergone substantial "hollowing out", as many of the functions related to strategic management, product development and marketing have been taken over by head office.

A vivid case in point is Campbell Soup (a producer of soups and other prepared foods), whose US parent is based in Camden, New Jersey. As a result of the FTA, the parent firm took its Canadian operations out of its international division, making them instead a division within North American operations. This set the stage for a geographical and product-mix restructuring aimed at making use of excess capacity in the company's more efficient US plants, while closing down the most inefficient Canadian operations. The net result has been a reduction in the number of Canadian plants from 11 in 1985 to 4 by 1991. In making these changes, Campbell divested itself of certain non-core product lines, and designated plants in Toronto and the Ontario towns of Chatham and Listowel as specialized operations with mandates to serve the company's entire North American market (Bertin 1990, 1991).

For Japanese "transplants" in Ontario (operating primarily in the automotive and consumer electronics sectors), and even for Canadian-owned firms, a similar southward pull has been evident. Many of these companies have responded to two imperatives that make the diversion of new productive investments to US sites a strategically rational action. First, despite the existence of an agreement that was supposed to guarantee access to the US market for Canadian-based plants, a constant series of hostile trade actions launched by US-based producers, coupled with the absence of explicit definitions of dumping and subsidies, has created tremendous uncertainty, delays, and costs for Canadian-based exporters. In the face of such uncertainty, continued expansion of production capacity in Canada to serve the US market appears to be less and less sensible. In the case of Japanese automotive transplants (Honda, Toyota and Suzuki all have operations at greenfield sites in Southern Ontario), disputes between Canada and the USA concerning definitions of "North American content" placed a chill on further investments in Ontario until very recently.

Secondly, in light of such geopolitical realities, and given the relative importance of the US market compared to a Canadian market (which is one-tenth its size), the shift to a US base of operations need not imply surrendering the Canadian market, because access to it by American-based producers in the post-FTA (and NAFTA) era has been relatively unimpeded. For Canadian firms in relatively labour-intensive sectors (including even the "lower-tech" end of the automotive parts sector), the move to a southern US location also offers the further advantages of a low-wage, non-union, "permissive" regulatory environment. Such producers can thus enjoy the best of both worlds: secure access to the US and Canadian markets, and a low-cost, flexible production environment.

In the automotive assembly sector, Canada still enjoys a significant labour cost advantage over US sites (estimated in 1995 at between US$7 and US$9 per hour), attributable largely to the efficiencies of socially provided medical insurance that reduce employers' costs. The Canadian dollar's decline since the end of 1991 has also widened this gap. Successful product mixes, relatively new capital stock and high quality ratings (reflecting a better educated workforce) further strengthen the strategic position of the Canadian automotive assembly sector. Nevertheless, lest the industry become complacent, it is worth noting that at least two German up-market automotive manufacturers – BMW, Mercedes–Benz – have announced major new investments in the southern USA within the past couple of years. Furthermore, the passing of the NAFTA agreement has made Mexico a viable, low-cost site for production destined for the North American market. Ford and Volkswagen already operate assembly operations there, and more producers are following their lead.

The net result of these trends will not be known for some time. However, available data suggest that the impact until now has been distinctly negative. Figure 7.2 reveals that, in contrast to the last recession in 1981–2, a very high proportion of the job loss in Ontario in the downturn of the

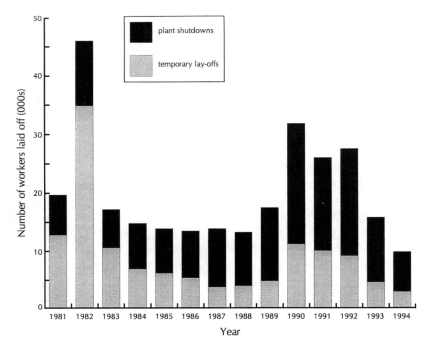

Figure 7.2 Temporary and permanent lay-offs in Ontario, 1981–94 (*Source:* Ontario Ministry of Finance, *Ontario economic outlook, 1994–1998*; includes lay-offs affecting 50 or more employees; 1994 data are for the first ten months.)

early 1990s came in the form of permanent lay-offs from the shutdown of operations, instead of temporary lay-offs from reductions in output. This stark difference would appear to indicate the profound effect that trade-related restructuring has had on the Ontario economy since the late 1980s.

LONG-TERM TRANSFORMATION: THE "SOCIAL ECONOMY" OR THE "FLEXIBLE ECONOMY"?

In addition to the two sources of change just discussed, there is a third set of changes influencing production systems within Ontario. As with trade liberalization under the FTA, this form of change is still very much under way, and the resulting outcomes are also difficult to forecast.

I refer here to a fundamental shift in the nature of national economies, away from the characteristics of the so-called "Fordist" age: mass production and consumption; well paid, full-time, unionized workers; large, rigid

114

and vertically integrated corporations; and so on. It is easier to describe what we are moving away from than what we are moving towards. However, the emerging economy seems to be based on some combination of the following characteristics (Cooke & Morgan 1993):

- New forms of work *within* the firm: terms of competition shifting from cost alone to include quality, responsiveness and time-to-market with new products; greater flexibility of output (both quantitative and qualitative); an accompanying flexibility of labour, and the increasing versatility of machinery; departure from traditional union-based work rules and wage determination practices, toward more individualistic, performance-based systems; flattening and "de-layering" of organizations, reintegration of design, production, and marketing processes.

- New forms of *inter-firm* relations: a shift from competition to a greater role for collaboration; vertical disintegration of large organizations, leading to a greater externalization of functions; subcontracting, external purchasing, strategic alliances, longer-term and closer relations between suppliers and buyers; new forms of governance (both private and public institutions)

The precise form that the Ontario variant of this transformation will take is the subject of much present discussion, debate and conjecture. Some commentators have chosen to emphasize the fundamentally *social* nature of emerging production systems, claiming that collaboration has come to play a larger role both within the individual firm (in relations between newly empowered workers and their managers) and in the closer relations between firms (demonstrated by, for example, the sharing of information and the establishment of trust-based relations). Others emphasize the objective of *flexibility*, particularly those aspects less favourable to workers (greater uncertainty of job tenure, increasing use of part-time and temporary labour, wage erosion). Clearly, these two visions are somewhat at odds with one another, and both figure in the current debate concerning the future shape of the economy in Ontario. One path is relatively high-wage and "worker-friendly", while the other seems to be based more on wage competition and less satisfactory work experiences (Bakker 1992).

Thus far, the signals coming from changes in the Ontario economy are mixed. On the one hand, one hears almost daily stories of firms that are restructuring their business and their workplaces to tap more effectively the full potential of their workers. One also hears frequent comments about the adoption of new, flexible, quality-enhancing machinery and pro-

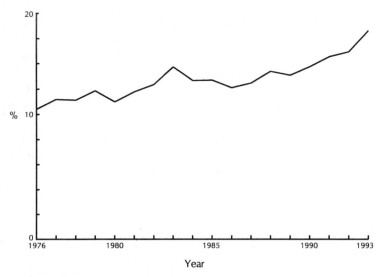

Figure 7.3 Part-time employment as a percentage of total employment, Toronto CMA, 1976–93.

duction systems. On the other hand, the use of "contingent" labour such as part-time workers is clearly on the rise (Fig. 7.3). This practice, combined with the increasingly common use of overtime and temporary workers to handle upswings in demand, has contributed to a weak recovery described by many as being "jobless": despite some rise in output, full-time employment levels remain slow to move upwards. With real incomes having been eroded by these forces, house prices have declined dramatically, especially within major urban centres such as Toronto. Similar declines are evident in Toronto's slumping office market (Metropolitan Toronto 1994).

Some Ontario-based firms have succeeded in becoming global players. However, under the current competitive regime, they have been compelled to follow a strategy of *global localization*, which entails the creation of new operations at sites outside Ontario (and Canada) for production and research. One such case in point is Northern Telecom (NorTel), the well known producer of telecommunications switching and telephone equipment, which is based in Mississauga (just west of Toronto). Being a major player in the telecommunications market (in which most customers are publicly owned or regulated utilities), NorTel has pursued a strategy of relocating both production and R&D activities inside foreign markets in Europe, Asia, and the USA. In 1994, NorTel closed or reduced the scale of operations at two of its four Ontario production plants, in London and

116

Bramalea (*The Globe and Mail* 1994a). Meanwhile, it has expanded its investments in the USA, France, Ireland, China, Malaysia, Thailand and Australia. Its research arm, Bell Northern Research, has laboratories in the UK and the USA, and as the research being conducted at it flagship labs in Ottawa comes to be tied increasingly to product developers now located in the firm's network of far-flung plants, there is growing pressure to decentralize more of the research effort to sites outside Ontario (Bagnall 1991, Surtees 1991, *The Globe and Mail* 1994b). The consequence for Ontario has been a loss of high-quality, knowledge-intensive jobs, ironically despite (or because of) the continued success of the firm.

Another example of the same phenomenon is the auto parts producer Magna International, based in Markham, Ontario. This highly successful firm has expanded aggressively into the USA, Mexico, and Europe, motivated by the need to design and produce its products close to its customers in the automotive assembly business. Most recently, it has acquired an ownership stake in seven plants in Europe (in Germany, Austria and the Ukraine) and has announced plans to set up a management training centre in Europe as well (Pritchard 1993a,b).

The policy sphere: challenges and responses

It should be clear by now that the changes taking place within the Ontario economy since the late 1980s constitute something much more than a simple "business cycle event". In that sense, this recent economic change, resulting from the interaction between national economic policy choices and international economic forces, seems remarkably reminiscent of the kinds of changes that took place in the US Midwest region some ten to 12 years earlier (see Markusen & Carlson 1989). As in the case of the Midwest, where a brisk recovery has recently become apparent (Prowse 1995), there are some stirrings of recovery in the Ontario economy. However, to date, this fragile recovery has been highly uneven geographically. While the areas west of the Greater Toronto Area have rebounded notably in the past year, taking root most firmly in communities such as Kitchener–Waterloo, Cambridge, Hamilton and London (recently dubbed as Ontario's "boom belt"), the Toronto region has continued to struggle (Little 1994).

Instead, the economic changes discussed in the previous section signal the beginnings of a more fundamental transformation of production systems and organization whose ultimate form is still very much "up for

117

grabs". The lure of low-wage regulatory havens in the southern USA and Mexico, made all the more seductive by the FTA and NAFTA, has posed a fundamental challenge to Ontario's economic policy-makers. As low-wage, labour-intensive, lower value-added manufacturing activity has shifted to sites south of the border, it has fallen to the provincial government to devise a strategy to ensure that the lost jobs are replaced. Similarly, confronted with the kind of choices posed by the two paths to a "flexible future", policy-makers in Ontario have, not surprisingly, sought to devise ways to ensure that the economy moves along the "high road" rather than the "low". Finally, given the kinds of international pressures confronting even the "model" flagship firms in the region such as Northern Telecom and Magna, the economic ministries of the Ontario government have come under pressure to protect and enhance the province's status as a centre of innovation and knowledge-intensive production.

The Rae (New Democratic Party) government assumed power in September 1990, just as the Ontario economy was heading into its steep downturn. Hence, economic and industrial policy matters very quickly acquired a strong sense of urgency. Moreover, the NDP's social democratic orientation, their strong historic links to the labour movement and their legacy of concern for less powerful segments of Ontario society raised expectations that the new government's approach to economic policy would depart significantly from previous practice. However, the history of industrial policy-making in the province over the previous decade, under first Conservative and then Liberal administrations, had been marked by a growing emphasis on shaping the economy's developmental path in a proactive way, and the transition to an industrial policy strategy under the NDP was marked by a surprising degree of continuity (Wolfe 1994).

In particular, the previous Liberal administration (1985–90) had initiated a multi-stakeholder strategic planning process, erected around the Premier's Council (established in 1986), a high-level body made up of representatives of Ontario's leading businesses, a handful of Cabinet ministers, several senior academics, and leaders in the Ontario union movement. This body produced a landmark document (Premier's Council 1988) that, while never fully implemented, has nevertheless remained highly influential. As Wolfe (1994: 16) notes:

> The study, and the policy solutions it advocated, were noteworthy
> for the dramatic break they constituted with the prevailing neo-
> conservative orthodoxy in North America. Rather than viewing
> international competition as a threat to workers' wages, the Pre-

mier's Council depicted effective international competition as the key to a high wage economic strategy and higher standards of living.

The Council advocated the raising of worker productivity (and wages) as the central objective for industrial policy. This was to be achieved both by raising productivity as much as possible in all sectors of the economy and by stimulating a shift in the composition of Ontario's economy towards higher-value-added activities. In particular, they advocated focusing upon Ontario's export (or "traded" sectors), since it was in these sectors that the harsh winds of international competition were most strongly felt.

Well before the Premier's Council report was completed, the Liberal government created a Technology Fund, endowed with CAN$1 billion. This money, which was partly administered by the Premier's Council, went to fund both short- and long-term university research in areas of competitive significance (in co-operation with industry partners), private sector applied industrial research in strategic new technologies, assistance to small and medium-size enterprise (SMEs) to help them hire scientific, engineering and other technical workers, and labour-sponsored research on the workplace impacts of new technologies. A set of other proposals emanating from the 1988 report, including plans to enrich tax incentives to encourage industrial R&D, a strategic government procurement program (to upgrade the technological sophistication of the province's suppliers), a CAN$100 million venture capital loan fund, a scheme to encourage worker ownership, and programs to facilitate labour market adjustment never saw the light of day while the Liberals were in office.

With the NDP regime's ascension to power in 1990, the new government found itself in agreement with many of the principles espoused by the Liberal Premier's Council – particularly the goal of the high-wage economy. Although it reconstituted the body as the Premier's Council on Economic Renewal, the objectives were broadened to achieve a better balance between enhancing competitiveness, protecting the rights and welfare of Ontario's workers, and achieving environmental sustainability. Indeed, the general direction charted by the NDP government was one that sought to emulate European approaches based on *sectoral* initiatives, as developed in Germany, Italy, and the UK.

The 1992 document *An industrial policy framework for Ontario* (MITT 1992) articulated a more comprehensive vision of a strategy founded on upgrading the productivity, innovativeness and value-adding capacity of Ontario firms, to be achieved primarily by pursuing a corporatist model of strate-

119

gic sectoral partnerships in which labour unions would come to the table as equal partners with producer associations and other representatives of the business community. The aim of this strategy was not only to encourage the widespread adoption of continuous improvement principles and other forms of quality-enhancing workplace reorganization, but also to set in motion a dynamic to *build and reinforce institutions* throughout the provincial economy. These institutions would, after the European fashion, stimulate interfirm co-operation, collaboration and learning, as well as facilitating more fundamental, consensus-based collaboration between labour and management – in essence, to achieve network relations between (and within) individual workplaces.

By engaging in the promotion of this institution-building, the provincial government (and particularly the Ministry of Industry, Trade and Technology – soon to be renamed Economic Development and Trade) sought to *animate* and "encourage co-operative actions to enhance competitiveness" (MITT 1992: 23). This co-operation was foreseen as taking place between workers and employers (through which greater employment flexibility would be achieved in exchange for enhanced job security), between suppliers and buyers (to raise quality jointly), between innovators and performers of R&D (as a way of managing risk and cost), between members of a common industry (who may save by collaborating on sector-specific marketing and training initiatives), and between partners in strategic alliances (to enhance access to technology or markets). The Ministry also sought to engage in international co-operation with similar agencies at the subnational level (largely in Europe) in order to facilitate co-operation between firms in each region.

The mechanism for achieving most of this, and the centrepiece of the *Industrial policy framework*, was the Sectoral Partnership Fund (or SPF), funded initially at $150 million for three years. This Fund was designed to provide seed money to catalyze multi-firm and multi-stakeholder co-operation around important sectors in the Ontario economy. The target areas included projects or organizations to strengthen the sector's technological capability – for example, through the creation of a centre for applied R&D and technology diffusion in the tool, die and mould industry – initiatives to assist the sectoral development of joint promotion or marketing, and to facilitate access to market intelligence, and the support of sector-specific education and training initiatives (developed jointly between stronger producer associations and the relevant labour unions).

Thus far, sectoral co-operation – at least to the point of producing a joint plan of action – has been stimulated in a wide range of industries, including telecommunications, plastics, automotive, tourism, "green industries", biotechnology, furniture and electrical/electronic products (Wolfe 1994). While the degree of consultation and co-operation at the stage of formulating general plans has been impressive, Wolfe notes that "concrete initiatives have been somewhat slow to develop out of the broader strategies developed to date" (p. 26), with sector-based centres for the diffusion of technologies being the most common form of tangible achievement.

Hence, the recent experience in Ontario suggests that successive governments have pursued increasingly comprehensive industrial strategies. This has culminated with the NDP approach, where policy-makers have demonstrated at least the desire to address industrial and economic change across a broad front. Furthermore, they have shown an eagerness to emulate (and to learn from) the experiments of other subnational, high-wage jurisdictions. In doing so, they have themselves arguably begun to exhibit the kind of continuous learning, innovation, and self-reflection said to characterize best practice in the firms whose behaviour they seek to modify. In this sense, they have actively aspired to make Ontario an intelligent, institutionally reflexive region-State.

Nevertheless, progress has been slower than hoped for, in the face of several unanticipated obstacles. According to Wolfe (1994), a major weakness of the current policy set is the lack of sufficiently strong co-ordination to ensure coherence across the many individual initiatives (sectoral and otherwise) that have emerged. There is a need to ensure that potential cross-sectoral synergies are identified and exploited. Furthermore, the connections between the crop of new institutions being created and preexisting institutions (particularly in research, education and training sectors) have often been weak or non-existent. As a result, the present constellation of industrial policy initiatives falls well short of constituting a fully developed and integrated regional system of innovation.

The problems, however, may run somewhat deeper than is implied by the above discussion. The obstacles to achieving institutional reflexivity and network relations (both within and between firms) are likely to arise from other causes. First, the problem of insufficient coherence and the need for greater co-ordination arises in very large measure because of the absence of an *explicitly geographical* framework in which the initiatives just described have been conceived of and delivered. Although Ontario may be nominally referred to as a "region-State" (given its subnational political status), it is itself a vast province exceeding 1 million km^2 in area. Even if analysis is confined to the heavily urbanized and industrial southern half of the province, one can still discern quite a number of distinct economic

121

subregions. By European standards, Southern Ontario would be considered to be made up of several individual industrial regions. If it is indeed necessary to ensure the presence nearby of all the major ingredients of a regional industrial system (Saxenian 1994), then it should come as no surprise that the current endowment of institutions in Ontario (devised without due regard to economic geography) should appear to lack coherence and co-ordination. Although it made some sense for industrial policy-makers to adopt a sectoral approach as the quickest way to instigate joint dialogue between firms, unions, and other stakeholders, the fact that this was done apparently without "one eye on the map" may now be responsible for some significant logistical and co-ordination difficulties.

Secondly, many of the recent industrial policy initiatives have been devised to change the behaviour of individual firms and the workers and managers within them. For instance, objectives include encouraging the upgrading of workers' skills and democratizing the workplace, the successful adoption of more advanced technologies and work methods, co-operation with suppliers or customers in order to produce jointly supported innovations and quality improvements, and collaboration with former or current competitors in order to realize complementarities, synergies, or simple cost savings from pooling the acquisition of production inputs. However, the record thus far for effecting such change is actually somewhat disappointing.

True collaborative action has proved to be especially elusive in Ontario, and more difficult to instigate than was originally hoped. There are several important reasons for this. To begin with, the simple absence of a well established legacy or tradition of interfirm co-operation, the strongly entrenched ethic of "rugged individualism", and a history of adversarial relations between unions and employers all create an enduring and powerful inertia that has stymied the government's attempts to move the sectoral partnerships from dialogue to action (and sometimes even limited the effectiveness of dialogue).

However, this problem does not arise out of some set of organic traits endemic to North American "business culture". Rather it can be linked to the characteristics of the broader regulatory framework, defined jointly by federal and provincial legislation governing labour markets, industrial relations and finance (Drache 1992). Hence, because labour market and industrial relations institutions foster employer practices that create relatively high rates of labour force turnover, the incentive for employers to invest voluntarily in training remains low. In the absence of a comprehensive public training policy (in which employer participation is mandatory), the uptake of new technologies and work practices has been slower and less effective than it might otherwise be, and quality improvements have been more difficult to achieve. But more to the point, employers are induced to poach skilled workers from other firms in their industry – and most likely within the same community – thereby undermining the development of trust, openness and information-sharing between firms, which is said to be essential to the achievement of collaboration. Add to this the consideration that managers' well known tendency to favour short-term returns over longer-term benefits, which itself arises from the characteristics of the larger (nationally defined) system through which most firms obtain their capital, further undermines efforts to develop the kind of stable, long-term relations with suppliers or customers (or workers, for that matter) that are so important to the achievement of network interaction.

As a result, institutions such as producer associations remain, on the whole, quite underdeveloped and, where they do exist, unambitious. In the face of strong disincentives to collaborate, there is little motivation to breathe new life into these organizations. Furthermore, they have tended not to develop the structure of active local affiliates that is so typical in Germany and Italy. Because of this, it remains an even more difficult task to mesh sectorally defined priorities and initiatives with locally coherent development strategies.

Furthermore, the institutional ambiguity of the industrial relations system in Ontario hamstrings the strengthening of interfirm co-operation. Although large employers in sectors such as automotive assembly and steel production remain largely unionized, a much smaller proportion of SME firms (which are the actual and potential suppliers to the large-firm segment) are union shops. Not surprisingly, this has created a dynamic of conflict within the larger plants, in which unions have been reluctant to agree to outsourcing arrangements (including external network links of a collaborative nature), as these are generally perceived as undermining the power of established unions. This is problematic, since without the willing participation of workers many network initiatives are doomed to fail.

Conclusions

The Ontario experience is interesting and unique for several reasons. It represents a case of growing activism on the part of the region-State to reshape the sectoral composition of the province's economy, to encourage a shift in firms' competitive strategies, and to bring about a qualitative change in the nature of social relations between economic actors. Furthermore, Ontario's policy-makers have consciously sought to emulate the more laudable attributes of economic systems in Europe and elsewhere. All of these tasks have taken on considerably greater urgency with the profound economic restructuring that began to take hold in the province starting in the late 1980s. The experience has been further enriched by the 1990 ascent to power of a social democratic government intent on forging a high-wage, knowledge-intensive, but equitable path for the province's economy.

The experience since 1990 suggests that the ability of this particular region-State to effect such an ambitious program of industrial change has been limited. It has been seriously curtailed by being embedded within a somewhat unsympathetic national (and international) regulatory regime whose characteristics encourage counterproductive practices on the part of economic stakeholders in the province. In some areas, such as labour relations, the province does have significant jurisdiction over legislation, and at least the theoretical ability to enact changes that might make the system more conducive to the establishment and maintenance of network relations. However, in practical terms, its power to make major change in this field is limited by the political power of the business community, backed up by the possibility that Ontario firms will disinvest and shift their operations to more permissive sites south of the border. In this sense the dynamic for policy harmonization between the Canada and the USA, which was strengthened by the FTA and NAFTA, operates as a major impediment to progressive industrial change in the province.

Thus, the Ontario experience says as much about the limits to comprehensive industrial change led by the region-State as it does about the possibilities. It therefore makes clear at least some of the reasons why the transposition of European approaches to the Anglo-American (and particularly North American) sphere will be difficult.

CHAPTER EIGHT

Industrial restructuring and further training in North-Rhine–Westphalia

Gerhard Bosch

Training and regional economic development

It is generally agreed in Germany today that vocational training is an important factor in regional development. It is universally accepted that training may even play a decisive role in triggering innovation and attracting investment into the region. Thus, a report compiled by the North-Rhine–Westphalian State government's Committee for the Coal and Steel Producing Region States that, "... As an active presence in the region, training centres function as catalysts in the modernization of the regional economy" (Kommission Montanregionen 1989: 345). Thus, the widespread introduction of CNC technology and other innovations has been furthered to a very considerable extent, particularly in small and medium-size firms, by the training provided for key personnel in joint training centres. Thus, for example, a State government report on the training of master craftsmen (Meister) in CNC technology states: "The intention behind the training is to foster future economic development, i.e. to encourage the future transfer of skills to firms by providing training, technical knowledge and information" (MWMT 1985: 31).

Scepticism towards the unco-ordinated promotion of investment and technology has on the whole been growing. Many companies and public-sector economic and technological development agencies have, at great expense, had to alter their view that all applications programmes could be solved just by providing hardware. A great deal of investment in expensive plant and equipment has been wasted because of a lack of adequate skills on the part of users. Attempts are increasingly being made in

125

regional structural policy to remove the boundaries between formerly strictly separated policy spheres in order that different areas of policy can be linked and co-ordinated at an early stage. Regional development can no longer be promoted through a single sphere of policy, such as technology or investment policy.

However, the need for such co-ordination is also increasing within the field of further training itself. As a result of the enormous expansion in this area, there is a great deal of overlapping of courses and duplication of provision; from the consumers' point of view, the provision of training has become less and less transparent, whereas for providers its profitability is increasingly being called into question. Furthermore, the need for new investment is continuing to rise." For individual training centres, this means that they are having to invest ever larger sums of money when they are no longer in a position to carry the burden alone. This is where regional forms of co-operation between the providers of vocational training may provide a solution." (Berufsförderungszentrum Essen, PTQ-Projektgruppe, Projektinformation 1.89).

The "regionalization of regional policy" and the exploitation of a region's endogenous development potential are now seen as offering opportunities for improving the co-ordination of regional employment policy. The aim of "regionalized regional policy" is to move away from subsidizing the total cost of individual investment projects and instead to provide assistance for projects that have been developed in the region itself. Such a policy would seek to exploit the development potential that already exists within a region, thereby triggering a process of innovation based on training, new technologies and new products (Derenbach 1984: 84). The starting points for such structural policy strategies lie in the activation or conversion of regional development potential, particularly in the spheres of training, infrastructure and the environment (cleaning up land contaminated by industrial waste) and in the development of otherwise inhibiting potential (e.g. ecological damage; cf. Table 8.1; Hahne 1984).

Problems of regional further training policy

Statements on the linking of further training with regional economic policy are often full of slogans and devoid of content. As a result, it is all too easy to fall into the trap of legitimizing an unchanged policy by attaching new labels to it. It has in fact proved particularly difficult to integrate

Table 8.1 A typology of endogenous regional potential

Potential	Available/ awaiting activation	Available but requiring conversion to be cut back	Pressures and burdens
Human resources	– Unemployed – Hidden reserve – Training reserves – Reserves of technical know-how – Reserves of planning and innovation	– Retraining reserves – Opportunities for restructuring in the training system	– Excessive use of work capacity (overtime, high work intensity, etc. – Noise pollution – Environmental pollution
Equipment and physical infrastructure	– Reserve capacity in secondary and tertiary sectors – Opportunities for extending and intensifying the use of railways, waterways and public transport – Empty housing stock	– Opportunities for product and process innovation; opportunities for product switching – Opportunities for restructuring in the R&D system (universities)	– Environmentally dubious processes and products – Road schemes – Area of country under concrete
Materials and energy	– Extraction of materials from waste – Degree of energy utilization – Utilization of polymineral materials	– Refuse conversion – Heat–power connection – Inefficient energy use (public vs private transport)	– Waste products – Waste incineration – Energy consumption – Short life of consumer goods
Natural sources	– Renewable energy sources – Natural resources (e.g. compost, wood, etc.)	– Rehabilitation of contaminated land and polluted water	– Use of countryside – Pollution and wasteful use of land, and air

Source: Scholz et al. (1991).

further training into regional structural policy. On the one hand, further vocational training cannot be easily co-ordinated at the regional level, because of its institutional diversity and the differing interests of the various providers. On the other hand, long-term training objectives (extension of individual competences, greater mobility on the labour market as a whole, and not just at the regional level) are not readily compatible with what are frequently short-term economic demands.

INSTITUTIONAL DIVERSITY

Unlike the initial education and vocational training system, the further education and training sector in Germany is characterized by institutional diversity (Fig. 8.1):

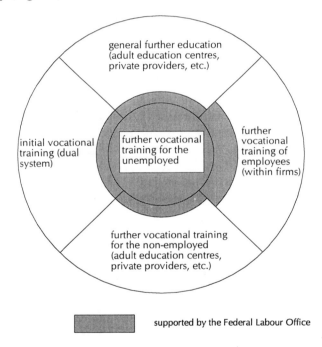

supported by the Federal Labour Office

Figure 8.1 The role of the Federal Labour Office in the further training system (*Source:* Bosch 92: 40).

1. Basic subjects (e.g. German and arithmetic) that are a precondition for successful further vocational training. 2. Additional training for employees seeking promotion or needing refresher courses, training of unskilled and semi-skilled workers, as well as those threatened with unemployment. 3. Training for people formerly in insurable employment who have interrupted their working lives (e.g. in order to raise a family). 4. Young people who have not found a training place in the dual system (Programme for the Disadvantaged).

128

- General further education is financed to a large extent by participants themselves. Courses are offered by public (mainly adult education centres and private providers).
- Further vocational training for employees is largely financed by firms. However, subsidies from the Federal Labour Office are available, particularly for the training of unskilled and semi-skilled workers and for new recruits
- Further training for the unemployed or those threatened by unemployment is financed by the Federal Labour Office. Training is delivered by private providers (chambers of commerce and industry, trade union training centres, firms, etc.).
- Vocational training for those not in employment and who have not paid contributions to the Federal Labour Office is again financed privately by the individuals concerned.

The major players in the further training sphere are the Federal Labour Office in Nuremberg and firms, who have until now shouldered by far the greatest share of the burden. In 1992, firms spent about DM30 billion on further vocational training, with the Federal Labour Office contributing DM10 billion.

Further vocational training programmes are offered by many competing providers. During a comprehensive survey of providers in North-Rhine–Westphalia, our institute identified about 2400 establishments. It is very difficult to discern any sort of regional interest in this sphere. In such a competitive market, any attempt to establish an inadmissible centrally planned economy is domed to failure.

"The planning of further vocational training is an empirical process" said an official of the Ruhr Chamber of Industry and Commerce in a recent interview. It could also be described more negatively as an unsystematic or even random process. In a somewhat caricatured form, the organization of further vocational training at regional level can be characterized as follows. Individual training providers try to stay in touch with the market by maintaining informal contacts with firms, through participants surveys and by researching the destinations of successful participants (Sauter & Fink 1980). They modify their provision if they receive strong signals from the market. "The provision of further vocational training is based ... largely on obvious demand and experience with the courses already being provided. As a result, programme planning and the establishing of priorities often fail to go beyond a continuation of existing provision, supplemented here and there with new courses introduced a reaction to current requirements" (Braun et al. 1984: 144).

The tendency to continue with existing provision arises to a large extent out of the providers' own interest in utilizing to the full plant and equipment they have purchased. "There are obvious deficiencies in the systematization and institutionalization of co-operation (Kommission Montanregionen 1989: 298). As a result, courses overlap, the same new curricula are developed by more than one provider and costly investment is duplicated. For the potential trainees, the provision of further training is confusing and lacking in transparency." The consequences are full-blown "retraining-careers" that are very costly and lead to regular employment only after a very long time, if all at all" (ibid. p. 297). Individual training providers consider themselves responsible only for certain segments of the market. The chambers of industry and commerce, for example, still concentrate largely on further training programmes for employees and are happy to leave more difficult groups, such as the long-term unemployed, to training centres run by trade unions or churches. Large firms with their own training facilities are to a certain extent independent of the regional further training market; only smaller firms require regional provision.

Nevertheless, a system of regional training programmes does exist; it concentrates primarily on courses leading to recognized qualifications and has its roots not in local attempts to manage training provision but in the nationwide funding system for initial vocational training (Sauter 1993) and the nationwide structuring of occupational labour markets. Almost 60 per cent of all young people in Germany now complete a training course in a recognized occupation. These occupations have in recent years been reformed and adapted to meet new technological and organizational requirements. These new occupational profiles also offer several points of reference for further training policy. Thus, curricula and quality standards development at supra-regional level relieve the strain at regional level. The development of occupational labour markets guarantees the acceptance of standardized training programmes, both by firms, that tailor their job profiles to such standard programmes, and by individual workers, who know that their qualifications will be recognized by firms throughout the country (Sengenberger 1987).

THE DIFFICULTY OF IDENTIFYING REGIONAL FURTHER TRAINING NEEDS

Demands are constantly being made for the provision of further training to be more closely tailored to "regional requirements". However, these requirements are not easily established or "called up". Many fruitless attempts have been made to ascertain firms' requirements. In many places, for example, the local employment offices have organized conferences with local employers and further training experts in order to gain from them some precise information on local training needs. The results are sobering. No concrete advice has been given on additional training programmes. Even surveys of employers and training providers have usually proved fruitless. Evaluation of an expensive survey of almost 2000 industrial and craft firms leads only to the crude, almost trivial conclusion that further training needs will rise in future in connection with the introduction of new technologies (Braun-Henze et al. 1986). Despite the disappointing results obtained from surveys of further training needs, the mistake of using them to assess need is made repeatedly. Thus, the Siegen Chamber of Industry and Commerce obviously fell flat on its face with a recent survey of approximately 1600 firms, which states: "Thus, many firms, predominantly small and medium-size ones, had difficulty in ascertaining their training needs ... In future surveys, it will be necessary to obtain more detailed information from firms on expected technological developments, for example, in order to be able to make a meaningful assessment of future training needs" (IHK Siegen, Info-1990). Many firms have still not analyzed their training requirements and are thus not in a position to articulate their possible training needs in any way other than through ad hoc decision-making (Semlinger 1989: 336 ff.) If we are to proceed from analysis of needs to the development of concrete training programmes, this strategy of the "blind leading the blind" will have to be abandoned (Staudt 1985).

Market and further processes have different and conflicting time horizons: markets are orientated towards the present, whereas further training has to look to the future because the qualifications acquired are supposed to last beyond the current situation. Moreover, demanding, capital-intensive further training programmes in particular cannot usually be made available in a short period of time. Curricula have first to be developed and providers have to put the necessary infrastructure in place. Thus, even relatively short programmes (such as CNC courses, for example) require fairly long lead times. Other further training programmes, particularly retraining courses, last up to 2–4 years. The planning time required and the length of the courses themselves mean there is a risk that the market will develop in a different direction in the interim. Consequently, further training policy has to be future-orientated, particularly when it comes to infrastructure decisions and long-term programme planning.

The response to the problems outlined above is that further training policy cannot simply react passively to economic developments but has to have a strongly supply-orientated active component. Infrastructure decisions have to be taken and the content of programmes developed level relieve the regions of the uncertainties and cost of planning and enable providers at regional level to respond more rapidly at change (Table 8.2 provides an overview of the scope for action in the sphere of further training at regional and supra-regional level).

Table 8.2 Responsibilities and activities at the various levels of the further training system.

Level	Responsibilities/activities
Local–regional	– Planning and development of training offered by training providers (firms, external providers) on the basis of an analysis of regional needs – Co-ordination of provision with a view to establishing a coherent regional programme (e.g. Through co-operation between the various providers) – Introducing transparency, e.g. By setting up data banks, publishing further training reports and compiling lists of courses – Provision of information and advice for potential trainees and providers, e.g. through data banks, chambers of industry and commerce, employment offices, local authorities – Implementation of programmes (incl. Methodology and materials, examinations and evaluation) – Infrastructure development, with institutional support – Linking economic development to training programmes – Measures to ensure quality of provision, e.g. Through self-regulation or through employment offices under the provisions of the Employment Promotion Law
Supra-regional	– Laying down framework for the planning of training provision, e.g. Through – Regulations on further training and certification – Establishing quality standards for programmes and providers (incl. Training for teaching personnel) – Regulation of targets for promoting access to and participation in further training, by: – Drawing up regulations and/or agreements on finance and release from work – Providing support for information and advice centres – Establishing conditions for introducing transparency into the further training system, by – Compiling national statistics on further training – Conducting regular representative surveys and quality assessments

Source: Sauter (1993).

Further training policy in NRW

In view of the institutional diversity and many actors in the further training sphere, greater control of structural policy cannot be achieved with rigid organizational models and ready-made answers. What can be observed at present in this sphere is rather some exploratory processes through which appropriate practical solutions are being tested, as well as what is financially and politically feasible. In what follows, we shall seek to outline some of the elements of regional further education policy. Since little systematic research has been carried out in this field to date, our data are somewhat fragmentary. However, it should be recognized that initiatives for the development of a more systematic further training policy are coming from very different quarters. I shall start with those initiatives coming from below, for it is only if such attempts are made that the State of North-Rhine–Westphalia will be able to incorporate further training into structural policy.

THE SYSTEMATIZATION OF PLANNING WITHIN INDIVIDUAL ORGANIZATIONS

Until a few years ago, those responsible for planning further training programmes in the region did not co-ordinate provision, even within their own organizations. This was particularly true of adult education centres, employment offices and the chambers of industry and commerce. For example, the following was reported in an interview from a chamber of industry and commerce in the Ruhr; until 1987, the individual departments of the Chamber (initial training, commercial and industrial training) planned and advertised their programmes independently of each other. Thus, very similar data-processing courses were offered in both the commercial and industrial departments, without the one knowing what the other was doing. All the training programmes offered by the Chamber are drawn together and advertised jointly. Department heads now meet once a week and there are many joint activities, such as training for examiners in initial and further training.

ON-SITE CO-OPERATION BETWEEN TRAINING PROVIDERS

Networks of training providers have now been established in several places in North-Rhine–Westphalia. The following objectives are to be achieved with the help of these networkers:

133

- improvement of the region's position by means of a systematic training policy
- increased transparency in the supply of training
- exchange of experiences between training providers
- co-operation in the implementation of programmes.

One example of this is the Siegen Training Association, which has now been imitated several times in North-Rhine–Westphalia. In 1988 in Siegen a centre was set up to provide information on the further training programmes offered by the chambers of commerce and industry; a regional databank offering an overview of training provision in the region was established. In 1989 a training association was established with a membership of 30 further training providers in the region. The members of the association, together with the district authorities, contribute to the financing of the information centre. The association reached agreement at an early state on voluntary self-control on the maintenance of quality standards and it provides the corresponding courses in the databank with a quality seal. The seal is awarded on the basis of the following criteria: lecturers qualified in both their subject and in teaching methods, technical equipment appropriate to "a standard modern work place", detailed breakdown of course objectives, content and scope. The association lays down standards for hardware and software, but does not monitor their implementation with on-site checks. There is now a great variety of bilateral and trilateral co-operation between the members of the association. In the initial training sphere, for example, Krupp apprentices receive instruction in typing and book-keeping at the trade union advanced training centre. In turn, the trade union training centre sends trainees for individual training modules to the chamber of industry and commerce. As a result, the local training system has become so flexible that it was possible within a short space of time to offer further training to 1000 Krupp employees who where to be made redundant. The development of these associations undoubtedly smacks of cartel building, but they are the only way of guaranteeing the quality of a competitive provider structure, since the rapid expansion of the further training sector has led to the emergence of several shady training providers who simply "want to make a fast buck". The important thing is that the regional training associations should not exclude any important or innovative providers, and not represent any special interests.

EMPLOYMENT PLANS IN FIRMS

Until the mid-1980s, firms in the Federal Republic took no responsibility for the training of employees made redundant. They paid redundancy money or transition allowances to those taking early retirement. In particular, unskilled and semi-skilled workers and skilled workers with out-of-date training were left behind by the pace of structural change and remained out of work after their dismissal. In consequence, the trade unions demanded that agreement be reached on so-called "employment plans". Those employees made redundant were not merely to receive passive assistance in the form of redundancy pay but were also to be offered training. Firms were to be involved in the planning and implementation of the training programmes. Legislation was introduced to create greater scope for action in this area. Thus, in industries facing crisis, workers on short time, whose short-time allowance is paid by the Federal Labour office, can also be offered training.

In the Ruhr, employees threatened by employment in some firms have been given training: The new regulations affecting workers on short time were used at Mannesmann and workers "surplus to requirements" received training. At Klöckner–Becorit, a supplier to the mining industry, about 120 of 350 employees made redundant were given a guarantee of re-employment after 18 months at the earliest, provided that they had by then successfully completed a further training course. The maintenance allowance was topped up with redundancy money. Around 70 employees have begun a course of training and around 30 have returned to their former employer. The State of North-Rhine–Westphalia has now taken up this first attempt at developing a preventive labour market policy. Between 1989 and 1993, and with assistance from the Objective 2 programme of the EC structural fund, it provided support for the further training of around 23500 workers in the coal and steel producing regions threatened by unemployment. The current job losses in the mining and steel industries are being cushioned by special training programmes. A total of 1600 people in the mining industry and 1100 in the steel industry are receiving training. The State (*Land*) is paying the costs of the training courses, the Federal Labour office is providing maintenance money and the firms are paying any remaining costs. Workers are being trained for external mobility. Most of the courses are provided by external training agencies.

VOCATIONAL TRAINING IN THE COAL AND STEEL INDUSTRY AND THE TRAINING CENTRES' MOVE TOWARDS INDEPENDENCE

The coal and steel companies in the Ruhr are noted for the quality of their vocational training. Through the system of co-determination that exists in the coal and steel industry, the trade unions have a great deal of influence in these companies and pushed early on for increased vocational training. As a result, the training rate in the industry was very high. Many of those who received training went to work in other companies. As a result, the coal and steel industry contributed a great deal to the development of the regional stock of skilled workers. At Ruhrkohle AG, for example, the trade unions made their agreement to the job losses of the 1980s conditional upon the training quota remaining at 9 per cent of the workforce. The closure of many pits and steelworks brought with it the question of what was to be done with the training centres at the closed mines and factories. In recent years, many of these training centres have become independent in order to retain their capacity for the regional training market. With starting or bridging capital provided by the government, they are now turning to the market.

REGIONAL AND TRAINING CONFERENCES

In 1990, the State government of NRW asked the regions to put forward regional development plans. The objective was to establish a systematic framework to be used for guidance in the drawing up and selecting of regional structural projects. Views on further training policy for the future were an important part of these development plans. In many places, special training working parties were set up, some of which put forward proposals for training policy in the future. In order to enhance the status of these activities, which in the region are often regarded as of only secondary importance compared with economic and technological development, the State government offered to organize special regional training conferences if the regional authorities considered this necessary. Between 1991 and mid-1994 (Vanselow 1995), ten training conferences were held in North-Rhine–Westphalia and two more are planned. The State government organized and funded these conferences. The regions nominated the participants and speakers. There were between 80 and 160 participants, mainly representatives of local authorities, further training establishments, firms, the public employment service and the trade unions. The purpose of these conferences was to discuss concrete further training

136

projects. This succeeded in those places where working parties had drawn up plans prior to the conferences. Thus, in some regions there was a debate on how to develop special programmes for small and medium-size firms. In other regions there were demands for the various sources of information on further training, e.g. in the chambers of industry and commerce and the public employment service, to be drawn together into a single system. The coal mining regions, for which a special assistance programme has been drawn up, have now requested the State government to set up local further training information centres, further training advice centres, co-ordination offices and further training fairs. The State government regards such activities as the responsibility of local authorities, but will probably provide some start-up funds. In sum, it can be said that the regional and training conferences brought the various actors at local level around the same table. This has undoubtedly supported or accelerated the establishment of local networks.

Conclusion

Regional policy cannot be confined solely to promoting the two production factors "capital" and "land", but must also be concerned with the development of human resources in the regions. A properly functioning further training system is becoming increasingly important for successful regional development. This applies particularly to old industrial regions in which workers often have to be prepared for completely new jobs. Because of increased demand from both the public and private sectors, the number of further training providers in the German regions has increased significantly in recent years. However, this new industry, which has emerged spontaneously in response to a new market, has considerable shortcomings. There has been duplication of provision and double investment, while at the same time important courses that are essential to regional development are either not provided at all or are of insufficiently high quality. It is quite clear that regional policy cannot simply leave events to the markets but must actively intervene.

One proposal frequently put forward as an instant recipe for success is that regional training policy should be orientated towards the needs of firms. However, practical experience shows that firms – and this applies particularly to small and medium-size firms – are themselves unable to formulate their long-term training needs, but first have to work them out

137

in close collaboration with regional further training providers. Firms do not generally have access to the sort of forward-looking human resource planning that would provide reliable estimates of future needs for the purposes of regional further training policy. As a result, the regions have to manage the demand side without any fixed guidelines and help to determine the course of future development by adopting a supply-orientated further training policy.

The question of how best to proceed remains largely unresolved. A great deal of experimentation can be observed in the regions. Among other things, co-operation between training providers is being encouraged, networks linking training providers and firms are being established, regional training conferences are being held, and user protection is being improved through quality control measures or self-regulation. The greatest difficulty lies in persuading private training providers to co-operate voluntarily with each other. Moreover, the regions are dependent on supra-regional assistance. In particular, the development of new curricula and of certificates for standard courses that are accepted in the labour market has to take place at supra-regional level, so that the wheel does not have to be constantly reinvented and resources are not unnecessarily tied down in work duplicated in several regions. Thus, a successful regional training policy depends both on a climate of co-operation within the region and on an active supra-regional environment.

CHAPTER 9

Training policy and practice in Wales and North-Rhine–Westphalia

Sara Davies

Introduction

Training strategies are central to the process of regenerating old industrialized regions. Although the need to invest increased resources in further and retraining in order to assist industry improve levels of quality and productivity is felt throughout Europe, regions that were once dependent on traditional heavy industries face even greater difficulties. As well as initial training programmes for young people and further training for people in employment, particular measures are needed to upgrade retraining opportunities for workers who are made redundant in traditional industries. North-Rhine–Westphalia (NRW) in Germany and Wales in the UK are two regions that have experienced acute structural decline and which have developed very different training policies and programmes.

Regenerating old industrialized regions

Structural decline not only impacts upon firms that are directly involved in, for example, coal and steel, but reverberates throughout the entire regional economies. Regeneration is particularly difficult in regions that have fallen into the trap of "rigid specialization" (Grabher 1993), that is, which have become so concentrated on one or more interrelated industries that all support structures and networks (including R&D centres, training bodies, employers' associations and trade unions) have become geared to the needs of those industries. When the core sectors decline, not only are the main firms and their suppliers forced to diversify or disappear, but all aspects of the region's economic and social framework are brought into question and come under pressure to restructure in order to adapt to a changing environment. In such a situation, new economic development strategies, whether they are based on attracting inward investment or on creating indigenous firms in new growth sectors, must aim to upgrade training structures and provision. In particular, training policies must address the need to improve skills levels within existing firms, as well as providing workers with the appropriate skills to gain employment in new sectors. As long as the training infrastructure remains focused on the needs of declining industries, the types of training provided are unlikely to answer industry's needs. Information exchange and co-operative endeavour between a wide range of public and private actors are vital if such difficulties are to be resolved. Local networks of training providers can facilitate the process of adapting training supply to the changing needs of a region's economy. Moreover, collaborative action is often necessary if adequate conversion training opportunities are to be made available to workers who are made redundant from traditional heavy industries.

Regenerating North-Rhine–Westphalia and Wales

The economies of the South Wales Valleys and NRW's *Ruhrgebiet* were formed by the dominating industries of coal and steel. With cuts to these industries continuing to the present day (and set to continue into the foreseeable future in the *Ruhrgebiet)*, the question is raised of how new sectors are to be developed, and how redundant workers from these industries are to be reintegrated into the labour market. Restructuring processes in the two regions have taken very different forms, particularly in the past fifteen years. Although coal and steel had been in decline in South Wales for many years, cuts in the early 1980s were particularly harsh. Between June 1980 and June 1982, the official working population of Wales fell by 106 000 (from a peak of 1 022 000 in 1979), which included 38 000 steel employees, or half the Welsh steel workforce (Williams 1985). Mining employment fell from 270 000 to 23 000 between 1921 and 1982 and, by 1994, one deep mine was left in South Wales and one in North Wales. The rationale of such a strategy must be that, although such cuts are harsh and painful when they occur, they should send renewing forces through the economy. Drastic action demands a response, and increases pressure upon remaining firms to innovate and become more competitive in order to survive. In fact, Thatcherism's "free hand of the market" strategy was tempered in Wales by interventionism, such as Secretary of State Peter Walker's Valleys Initiative. Moreover, both regional aid and an enterprising attitude on the part of the Welsh Office, Welsh Development Agency (WDA) and other bodies has meant that Wales attracted large amounts of inward investment in the 1980s and 1990s. Between 1981 and 1989, 14 per cent of all capital investment projects into the UK came to Wales (Hill & Munday 1991), resulting in 14.5 per cent of all new jobs created in the UK by overseas companies (even though, in 1989, Wales accounted for only 4.4% of the UK workforce). Levels of investment peaked in the late 1980s yet, despite increasing competition in the early 1990s, Wales continues to receive significant amounts of inward investment; between 1983 and 1993, more than 1, 100 projects invested over \$8.25 billion in the Welsh economy, creating or safeguarding over 110000 jobs (*The European*, April 1994). The arrival of prestige Japanese and German firms is believed to have sent regenerative impulses into the Welsh economy, as such firms have demanded high quality goods and services from local supplier-firms and local support structures. Training provision is improving rapidly, not only to meet the needs of the new world class manufacturing firms, but also to assist indigenous firms to upgrade in terms of both quality and productivity in order to become suppliers to these global firms.

Nevertheless, although the Welsh economy now appears to be recovering from the aftermath of rapid and violent restructuring, many of the coalminers and steelworkers who lost their jobs have been less fortunate. The UK government's reliance on market adjustment to provide a solution to structural change seems at best naive and at worst brutal. This approach contrasts dramatically with that of the *Land* government in North-Rhine–Westphalia, which is committed to "managing" structural decline and to minimizing social disjuncture (Rehfeld 1993). Its strategy has been supported by key actors in the region, including NRW's powerful coal and steel corporations. Major cuts in employment have been – and are still being – implemented, with 240000 coal jobs and 100000 steel jobs disappearing in the past 30 years; the RWI economic research institute in Essen estimates that a further 50000 steel jobs will be lost as a result of structural change (*Financial Times*, September 1993). Nevertheless, cuts have been planned to take place over an extended period of time, so that the knock-on effect on firms in other sectors is minimized, firms have time to adjust and social consequences are minimized. The *Land* does not simply aim to lessen the impact of restructuring on individuals, but also believes that the gradual adjustment of economic structures creates an environment more favourable to the generation of new entrepreneurial and employment opportunities. NRW has, therefore, adopted a policy of attempting to construct new industries (for example, the environmental protection industry) parallel to the decline of traditional industries so that, as employment has decreased in the latter, it has increased in new sectors. NRW has thus based its economic development strategy on endogenous potential rather than on attracting inward investment, partly because it recognizes that high wage costs make the *Land* less attractive than other regions in the EU or in central and eastern Europe. In 1991, manufacturing labour costs per hour were US$22.2 in Germany, compared with an EU average of US$18, a UK rate of US$13 (*Financial Times*, June 1993) and a Welsh rate of around US$12.

Vocational training in NRW and Wales

One key component in any regeneration strategy must be training and retraining programmes, yet the content and structure of such programmes are determined by the environment in which they are formed and implemented. This is clearly illustrated by the contrast between German and British training policies (Mackay 1993). One of the main differences is that German manufacturing industry generally produces higher value-added products than do UK firms. German industry bases its competitive advantage on quality, whereas, in the UK, particularly in the 1980s, growth was based on unskilled low-wage sectors. In Germany, new technologies are used to complement employees' skills and to produce higher quality goods, rather than, as in the UK, to de-skill work and to replace labour (Cassels 1990). Lower skills levels in Britain are perceived as a major cause of the difference in labour productivity in similar establishments across several sectors in Britain, France and Germany (for example, Prais 1993). Whereas Britain has tended to emphasize academic excellence for an elite at the expense of technical and vocational skills, Germany has recognized the importance of having a critical mass of well qualified people. Whereas less than a quarter of the German labour force lacks a recognized qualification at craft level or above, two thirds of the Welsh labour force falls into this category. The presence of many workers with a foundation of broad-based skills on which to build is increasingly perceived as crucial in today's changing economic environment. Industry not only requires

142

higher skills levels but also adaptability and a capacity for continuous learning and retraining – both of which are extremely difficult if workers lack initial qualifications and are unaccustomed to education (Freeman & Soete 1987).

Germany has a particular advantage over Britain in initial vocational training for young people (Her Majesty's Inspectorate 1991; Sako 1990). The *Duale System* provides training for two thirds of 15–18 year olds in Germany and combines in-house training in industry or commerce with day-release training in *Berufschulen* (vocational training schools), normally for a three year period. The system is financed jointly by industry and government; the *Länder* fund the *Berufschulen*, whereas employers finance their part of the training. The system is managed by the chambers of industry and commerce *(Industrie und Handelskammer – IHK)*, which also run the examinations and award certificates, and it is regulated by federal government *(Bund)* legislation. Workers must have a recognized vocational qualification in order to gain employment in most fields, and companies are obliged to employ only those individuals that have the necessary qualification. Industry supports the system, partly because of financial incentives (with trainees receiving between one third and one quarter of adult wages) and partly because of the German consensus that effective vocational training is necessary. The *Duale System* was reorganized in the late 1980s because it was perceived as inadequate to changing training requirements.

In Britain, however, there is no legal obligation on either firms or workers to undertake training. Particularly since the fall in the number of apprenticeships since 1979, vocational training is now overwhelmingly provided by public bodies, such as further education (FE) colleges and Youth Training (YT) programmes, which are administered by the county-based Training and Enterprise Councils (TECs). As the jobs market for 16 year olds has collapsed, the number of 16–19 year olds in education and training is increasing. According to the Careers Service in Wales (1994), the proportion of over 16 year olds remaining in education rose from 45 per cent in 1989 to 65 per cent in 1993. Moreover, enrolments in FE colleges increased by 23 per cent in Wales between 1987/88 and 1991/92 (FEFCW 1993a); worryingly, however, the level of increase in enrolments on engineering and technology FE courses was lower than the total increase (FEFCW 1993a), and there is a relatively high drop-out rate from engineering courses (OFSTED / Audit Commission 1993). In general, training opportunities and skills levels in Wales are below the British average (Huggins 1992, Morgan & Rees 1994); for example, Wales lags behind the rest of the

UK in National Vocational Qualifications (NVQs) and National Education and Training Targets (NETTs), the government's most recent attempts to upgrade and regulate the type of training provided by YT (NACETT 1994; Department of Education and Science 1991). Fundamental problems remain in the provision of initial training for young people, with YT trainees experiencing difficulties in finding employment after they have completed the courses. There is, moreover, a high drop-out rate; the proportion of YT leavers in Wales who gained a full qualification was 30 per cent compared with the British average of 33 per cent, and the proportion of those who completed courses in Wales was 47 per cent compared with 53 per cent in Britain (Employment Department 1993b). Some TECs offer a limited number of more innovative training programmes for young people; South Glamorgan TEC, for example, manages a training programme, "Blueprint", in manufacturing engineering for 16- 19 year olds. The course lasts three years in two local FE colleges, and involves one year of full-time college-based training, and two years of work and training in co-operation with local firms. However, such schemes are limited in scope and, alone, cannot meet increased demands for workers with higher skills levels. The Employment Department (1993a) predicts a fall of 19 per cent in the number of plant and machine operatives in Wales by the year 2001; as yet, the training structures that would improve skills levels to compensate for this decrease are inadequate.

The major difference between the two systems may be explained by the fact that vocational training in Germany is well respected, whereas in Britain it has traditionally been perceived as a second-rate alternative to a university education (Finegold & Soskice 1988, Keep & Mayhew 1988). Moreover, higher wage levels in Germany reinforce companies' emphasis on quality, thereby underlining the need for an efficient training strategy. The German system is also perceived as effective because it is managed by the chambers of trade and commerce, in other words it is employer-led; this enables a mismatch of training supply and demand to be minimized. TECs are also industry led yet do not have either the strategic or financial muscle of the German chambers, mainly because companies' involvement in TECs – and in training as whole – is on a purely voluntary basis. Although Welsh and British firms report high levels of recruitment difficulties – 37 per cent in Wales and 46 per cent in Britain, rising to 45 per cent and 60 per cent in engineering sectors (TEED 1992), many do not have effective training strategies. Four fifths of Welsh employers claim to have training strategies for their staff, yet it is estimated that less than a third of employees annually receive training. Wales comes last in a table of British regions illustrating the incidence of job-related training, with 8.6 per cent of the population of working age receiving job-related training, compared with a British average of 9.9 per cent (Employment Department 1993b). A survey by Mid Glamorgan TEC suggests that, in 1990–91, only one quarter of firms in the county had formal training plans, only one tenth had a formal training budget, and 44 per cent of firms spent nothing on training (Mid Glamorgan TEC 1991). Moreover, the type of training undertaken by UK employers is low quality because it is mainly "on-the-job", the cheapest and least effective form of training; the Training Agency (1989) reported that, in the sample of 4, 200 employers interviewed, 58 per cent of their gross expenditure on training was "on the-job".

Government action on training in NRW

As well as private sector training initiatives, various layers of government in both NRW and Wales have policies that impact upon the level of training available. In Germany, central government labour market measures are generally aimed at employment creation (for example, by subsidizing employment for the long-term unemployed) and are implemented by local authorities (*Kreise*, at county council level). For example:

- *Arbeitsbeschaffungsmaßnahme* (employment creation measures) under the*Arbeitsförderungsgesetz* (law to promote employment – AFG), which was passed in 1969, and for which funding was increased in 1986. To date, 48 job creation programmes in NRW have been funded by ABM, with around DM52 million (*Land* NRW 1992)
- *Bundessozialhilfegesetz* (federal law on social welfare) – which in NRW is reinforced by the *Arbeit statt Sozialhilfe* programme (work instead of social welfare). In 1991, this programme created 2400 jobs in NRW, with wages being paid by the *Land* (*Land* NRW 1992)
- the federal government's *Aktion Beschäftigungshilfen für Langzeitsar- beitslose* (action on employment aid for the long-term unemployed) started in July 1989
- the federal government's *Maßnahmen für besonders beeinträchtigte Langzeitsarbeitslose* (measures aimed at disadvantaged long-term unemployed people) German job centres (*Arbeitsämte*) offer retrain- ing courses, for example:
- *Arbeiten und Lernen* (working and learning) for young people and women returners

145

- two year retraining courses leading to a recognized vocational quali-fication (although requirements for these courses are so high that places are often not filled)
- shorter training courses and workshops which offer no recognized qualifications.

NRW *Land* has prioritized investment in higher education and further training since the 1960s; the *Land* now has 51 HEIs (universities, technical universities and polytechnics) and 139 adult education colleges (*Volkshoch-schulen*). Additional labour market measures have been introduced by the *Land* government, with the aim of addressing problems caused by struc-tural change and of upgrading training opportunities in the face of a changing economic climate. In the late 1980s and early 1990s, NRW *Land* allocated DM250 million *per annum* to further education and training, the largest amount of any German *Land* (*Land* NRW 1992). In 1987, NRW's total budget for further and retraining amounted to DM1.6 billion, or around one third of that spent by all the German *Länder.* This compared with a the total budget of DM700 million in 1980; funding more than doubled within the next 7 years.

NRW *Land* measures include:

- *Arbeitsmarktpolitische Sonderprogramme "90* (special labour market programme 1990) which receives funding from the EU's Structural Funds under Objectives 3 and 4, that is, for young unemployed peo-ple and for the long-term unemployed, as well as from the *Land.* In 1990–92, around DM150 million was allocated to this programme (*Land* NRW 1992)
- *Förderung von sozialen Maßnahmen zum Strukturwandel in den Ziel-2Gebieten* (promotion of social measures aimed at structural change in NRW's Objective 2 regions), which applies to parts of NRW particularly affected by cuts to the coal and steel industries, for example the *Ruhrgebiet.* The programme aims to mitigate the effects of structural change and long-term unemployment, and includes retraining opportunities for people threatened by unemployment or who have never had a job, as well as for the unemployed. By the end of 1991, around DM200 million had been allocated to this programme. A fur-ther initiative under this programme, *Qualifizierung im Mittelstand* (training in SMEs) is aimed specifically at firms with fewer than 500 employees; 50 per cent of training costs are met by this programme. (*Land* NRW 1992, Stöbe 1992).
- *Zukunftsinitiative Montanregionen; Zukunftsinitiative für die Regionen* NRW (initiatives for the future of the coal and steel regions and for all

NRW's regions – ZIM / ZIN) both include an emphasis on upgrading training opportunities. For example, ZIM provided finance to improve equipment and facilities in vocational schools *(Berufschulen)* and in industrial training centres (Stöbe 1992).

Government action on training in Wales

The Welsh Office has responsibility for higher and further education and for training policy in Wales. It distributes funding, implements central government policy and conducts research into skill shortages and training needs. In 1994, the Welsh Office's Industry Department took over training policy from TEED, the Training, Education and Enterprise Department (previously the Training Agency), in an attempt to integrate labour market and industrial policy within a broader economic development framework. Two new Non-Departmental Public Bodies (NDPBs), answerable to the Welsh Office, were established in 1992 to take responsibility for funding further and higher education, the Further and Higher Education Funding Councils for Wales (FEFCW and HEFCW). The Welsh Office has a certain amount of discretion in the way it prioritizes policies for Wales and has targeted three main areas in the sphere of vocational training:

- to reinforce the gains made to the Welsh economy from inward investment in recent years, particularly by upgrading training levels in supplier firms and providing support services to large inward investors
- to improve training levels in SMEs
- to focus on the problems of specific areas, particularly the South Wales Valleys and rural Wales. (TEED 1992).

The Welsh Office co-ordinates the work of Wales's 7 Training and Enterprise Councils (TECs), and allocates finance to them (although TECs may also charge for some services in order to gain extra finance). The TECs were set up in 1990, roughly at county level, and in Wales have budgets of between £4.27 million and £29.83 million, depending on the size of the populations they cover. TECs originally had the ambitious dual aim of upgrading training and boosting local economic development:

> . . . the fundamental aim of every TEC will be to foster economic growth and contribute to the regeneration of the community it serves. Its special focus will be on strengthening the skill base and

147

assisting local enterprise to expand and compete more effectively.
(TECs Prospectus 1989)

The structure of TECs was intended to draw private sector dynamism
into an area previously managed by the public sector. TECs are public-
private partnerships with company status and a board of directors who
are key local actors. In theory, two thirds of the directors should be from
industry and the remainder from education, local government, trade
unions and the voluntary sector; many TECs, however, have had difficulty
in recruiting high calibre participants from local companies and the public
sector is often overrepresented on boards. TECs do not themselves organize
or manage training courses, but rather act as co-ordinators and information providers for courses run by FE colleges and private trainers. Nevertheless, although TECs originally aimed to integrate training and enterprise and to empower local business leaders to address skills needs, their
main activity is providing training for young and unemployed people. In
1993/94, 74 per cent of the TECs' £2.3 billion budget in Wales and England
was spent on unemployment training programmes (Bennett et al. 1994).
TECs are contractually obliged to provide training for young and unemployed people, who are guaranteed training places on Youth Training or
Training for Work (which has replaced Employment Training). In Wales,
over 16000 people were on YT courses at any one time in 1990–91, and the
total expenditure for that year was nearly £43 million; figures for Employment Training in the same period were 23000 trainees and £29.6 million
(TEED 1992). TECs aim to raise the participation level of young people in
education and training; the UK participation rate of 18 year olds is one
third of that of major competitors such as the USA, Japan, Germany and
France (Bennett et al. 1994), with the consequence that British workers
have relatively low skills levels and are unused to education and training.
There is, however, real conflict between TECs' contractual obligations to
provide training places for unemployed people and the strategic need to
promote retraining and further training in local industry. Some schemes
aimed at boosting enterprise and tackling skills shortages have been instituted, such as the Investors in People programme, under which companies
commit themselves to developing and implementing continuous training
strategies, and which aims to induce a pro-training attitude among
employers. Nevertheless, the TECs' difficulties are compounded by the
government's policy of reducing finance for training, on the assumption
that the TECs will induce the private sector to invest more heavily. Between
1987 and 1992, Employment Department funding (in constant prices) to

the TECs and LECs (Local Enterprise Companies, in Scotland) decreased by over £2 billion (Peck & Emmerich 1993) and, although it levelled out thereafter, funding is projected to fall again in 1995/96. A further reason for the decrease in funding, particularly for Employment Training / Training for Work, is that the scheme is perceived as ineffective. Trainees tend to leave ET courses early; in 1989–90 there was a "drop-out" rate of 70 per cent (Cooke 1990). The main reason for this is that the courses do not assist unemployed people to find work; according to an unpublished survey in March 1992 (Unemployment Unit 1992), only 19 per cent of Employment Training leavers found work. The hope that TECs would be able to "customize" ET courses to meet the needs of their localities and thus stem the "drop-out" rate, has yet to be translated into reality.

Conflicting pressures on TECs have meant the abandoning – in reality if not in principle – of some of their original aims, not only upgrading skills levels in local industry but also, for example, providing strategic support for the long-term unemployed, for disadvantaged groups and for people who are made redundant as a result of structural change. It is difficult to avoid the conclusion that "TECs have become a QUANGO: a business-led body mainly doing government's job for the unemployed" (Bennett et al. 1994: 314).

Larger amounts of finance are needed for training, both from government and from industry. Yet this is hindered by the UK government's ideologically based reliance on the market, which leads it to underfund training for the unemployed and to refuse to induce industry to invest in the skills of the existing workforce, for example, via a training levy, or via tax incentives for firms with effective training policies. The current situation deters companies from implementing training strategies, as they may be penalized for doing so if their employees are "poached" by other firms, with the consequence that their investment in human capital is lost. A further obstacle placed in the path of TECs by government is the lack of a strategic context for action. Wales is, perhaps, more fortunate than England because the Welsh Office acts as a regional co-ordinator and because formal and informal co-operation between the Welsh TECs already exists, for example in the Council of TECs in Wales and in day-to-day communication, particularly between the four TECs in industrial South Wales. Nevertheless, the lack of strategic planning and a disjuncture between overlapping local initiatives also affects Wales. This is, in part, attributable to the large number and variety of organizations that are involved in training provision and in economic development. The lack of a coherent strategy means that training provision is formed solely by customer demand.

149

Publicly funded training provision in the South Wales Valleys, for example, is focused on administrative and clerical jobs, receiving around a third of all available finance. Only 5 per cent of funding is allocated to electrical and electronic manufacturing, even though this is the region's most important manufacturing sector, with one sixth of all manufacturing employment (Employment Department 1993a). Moreover, there is frequently a lack of coherence between local authority economic development plans and TECs' labour market assessments. The TECs' lack of local accountability (Peck & Emmerich 1993) can further exacerbate policy fragmentation and lead to the creation of conflicting power blocs. Nevertheless, if integrated within a regional strategy, TECs can assist in upgrading the quality of local training provision and in co-ordinating local training strategy (for example, by relating NETTs to the needs of the local economy and ensuring progress towards the targets). Some TECs, such as South Glamorgan, undertook quality audits of labour market requirements and training provision when they were set up and proceeded to develop a strategy aimed at reorganizing and upgrading their local training networks. This function of local co-ordination is increasingly important, now that FE colleges are no longer under the wing of Local Education Authorities (LEAs) but are self-governing. As FEFCW has decided that funding for FE colleges is to be based on levels of recruitment, learning and completion (FEFCW 1993b), there is a danger that the resulting increase in competition between colleges will further fragment training provision and possibly lead to the closure of weaker colleges.

Training requirements in NRW and Wales

Although economic restructuring strategies in NRW and Wales take very different forms, the two regions share several key difficulties with regard to training provision. In particular, as two regions whose economies and support infrastructures were moulded by the coal and steel industries, both have experienced difficulties in adjusting to a changed and changing situation. Existing training structures do not meet the needs of economies in a state of flux, either in terms of the skills or sectors that are addressed, or in the structures themselves, which appear both inappropriate and inadequate for today's training needs. In NRW in particular, the traditional training providers were the *Montan* (coal and steel) corporations, which ran vocational schools and educated more apprentices than they required.

However, as the coal and steel industries in NRW and particularly the *Ruhrgebiet* have declined, the *Montan* corporations have cut back their training schools (for example, Thyssen in Duisburg has closed two out of its three training centres); this means that a key source of local vocational training expertise is disappearing. Smaller firms are now having to take responsibility for training their own workers, rather than recruiting those trained by *Montan* corporations, yet SMEs frequently lack the resources to undertake strategic action on training. The situation is exacerbated by NRW's changing economic structure, which means that the type of skills and sectors that used to be targeted by training providers are no longer important, and that there is a need for employees with new skills and in new fields.

There is a danger that workers who are made redundant from the coal and steel industries will never work again. Although NRW *Land* would consider the social misery and dislocation caused by such a prospect sufficient reason to take action to create new employment opportunities, there are also convincing economic reasons for attempting to reintegrate redundant workers. Demographic changes mean that the populations of Western European countries are ageing, and that the number of young people in the labour market is set to decrease steadily. Firms will therefore have to retain and retrain their staff in the future if they are to have a skilled and committed workforce. In this context, it would be foolish to neglect the skills of workers from the coal and steel industries. This problem has come to be recognized by the European Union, which, in the Maastricht Treaty (Title VIII Article 123) amended the role of the European Social Fund so that it now also aims "to facilitate (workers') adaptation to industrial changes and to changes in production systems, in particular through vocational training and retraining."

In the past, in both NRW and Wales, many workers have been induced to take early retirement; yet the average age of coalminers in the *Ruhrgebiet* is 33 years old *(Ruhr Nachrichten*, March 1993). Early retirement can, therefore, no longer be used as a less painful means of implementing job cuts. Women still make up a distinct minority of the Ruhrgebiet workforce; in June 1991 *(IHK NRW* 1992), 37.4 per cent of the total workforce was female (compared with a *Land* average of 39.2% and a *Bund* average of 41.3%). Wales, however, has experienced a higher rate of growth in female employment than the British average, increasing from 39.3 per cent in 1981 to 43.7 per cent in 1991 (Morris, June 1993). This trend may be attributed both to cuts to traditional male employment opportunities and to growth in part-time, low-paid and low-skilled manufacturing and service sector jobs. Although opportunities exist for firms to continue to draw on "green" female employees, retraining programmes should be implemented that will allow redundant coal and steel workers (who are predominantly male) to re-enter the labour market, rather than being consigned to long-term unemployment, with all its consequent problems.

Retraining strategies

The private coal corporation, *Ruhrkohle AG*, and the (formerly) nationalized body, British Coal, both assumed some form of responsibility towards miners who have been made redundant, by offering aid in retraining and gaining new employment. British Coal Enterprise (a subsidiary of BC) provides support (training, advice, business loans and low-rent enterprise units) to redundant miners who wish to become self-employed. British Coal Enterprise (BCE) also has a Job and Career Change Scheme (JACCS), which offers career guidance, counselling and practical help with job hunting. Within six months of being made redundant, workers can apply for retraining grants; each case is judged on merit and no limit is set on finance available to individual workers. Although BCE has three training centres in Britain (one in the Midlands, and two in the North of England), most training in South Wales is provided by FE colleges or private trainers. BCE determines the type of training that is appropriate in each case and then liaises with training organizations to obtain the necessary training provision; one-to-one training is often negotiated, as workers seeking retraining tend to be scattered both spatially and temporally. BCE is currently attempting to move from simple training provision to assisting ex-miners to obtain jobs in which they can be retrained. Employers who are willing to guarantee employment receive finance from BCE towards on and off the job training.

Although Wales has attracted a large amount of inward investment in the past decade, most firms have either recruited skilled and intermediate workers from existing firms (particularly in the electronics sector) or "green" labour, particularly women, for low-skilled employment. However, some firms have specifically targeted ex-miners and steelworkers in a desire to draw on South Wales' existing skills base. One such firm is the British Airways Maintenance Centre (BAMC), which has been constructed near Rhoose (South Glamorgan) and which became fully operational in 1994. BAMC recruits three types of workers; highly skilled licensed aircraft engineers, technicians with aircraft maintenance experience, and mechanics with some technical skills, including miners and steelworkers as well as, for example, motor vehicle fitters. BAMC recruits mechanics, who will make up 48 per cent of the workforce, from within a 50 mile radius of the plant, and sends them on a two month intensive training course at Barry College. One difficulty facing examiners who are considering retraining with BAMC is that it means taking a severe wage cut; whereas miners earn £20000–30000 annually, a new mechanic recruit to BAMC can expect to earn around £10000–12000. However, opportunities exist for mechanics to upgrade to technician level via continuous and further training programmes – facilitated by BAMC's special relationship with Barry College, which would enable younger workers in particular to upgrade to a higher skill and wage level within a growing industry. BAMC has a training agreement with Barry FE College, which also trains young apprentice technicians, offering craft studies and BTEC National and Higher Certificates in aeronautical engineering. However, such tailor-made initiatives (particularly ones aimed at redundant miners and steelworkers) must be seen as the exception rather than the rule, although Barry College also has training agreements with firms such as ICI, Bosch and British Airways Avionics. Although several South Wales FE colleges have similar contracts with prestige inward-investing firms, in general they lack the resources to provide customized services to large numbers of firms.

Ruhrkohle AG (RAG) still produces 80 per cent of Germany's hard coal output despite the fact that its coal production has decreased from 115.4 million tonnes in 1960 to barely 50 million tonnes in 1993 (*Financial Times*, September 1993). Today only 89000 people are employed as coalminers in the *Ruhrgebiet* and a further 20000 jobs are scheduled to disappear by the end of 1995, as a result of declining industrial orders from steel mills (particularly with the closure of the Klöckner coke works) and a slowdown in electricity consumption. State subsidies to the coal industry are set to decline to 50 million tonnes by the year 2005, as they can no longer be justified now that the sector's importance has decreased. RAG is maintaining its viability as a company by diversifying into other fields, such as environmental technology, trading, power engineering and construction, which today account for 39 per cent of RAG's turnover; 20 years ago, 98 per cent of the company's turnover derived from coal.

Like many coal and steel corporations based in the *Ruhrgebiet*, RAG has a paternalistic tradition, which not only means that it attempts to "manage" decline, but also that it actively pursues policies of aiding workers who are faced with redundancy to retrain and to find alternative employ-

153

ment. RAG has long been encouraging its workers to retrain in other fields, and in 1990 set up a subsidiary company that provides vocational training for 6000 employees annually. Of these, 3500 are involved in projects in the new *Bundesländer,* such as waste management and land reclamation with another RAG subsidiary, *Ruhrkohle Umwelt,* which undertakes environmental protection projects. The most recent rounds of cuts in the coal industry have prompted further action. Of the 20000 employees scheduled to be made redundant in 1993–95, RAG has estimated that 11000 will take early retirement, and a further 5000 will find alternative employment without great difficulty. It has therefore targeted its efforts at providing practical support for the remaining 4000 workers, some of whom will be offered jobs by other firms within the *Ruhrkohle* group. In March 1993, a new subsidiary, *Industrie Service GmbH* was set up to undertake plant maintenance and demolition, as well as land reclamation (400ha in the *Ruhrgebiet,* at a cost of DM350 million) for RAG; its 400–600 jobs will be reserved for redundant miners. In September 1992, RAG instituted a retraining programme to address the needs of workers faced with redundancy. By the end of 1993, 700–900 employees were participating in retraining programmes, in such diverse fields as manufacturing engineering, specialist construction work, land reclamation and waste disposal, nursing and sales. Retraining courses last between three months and three years, during which time workers generally continue to be employed by RAG, although some also receive benefit from the *Arbeitsämte.* The courses are managed by a variety of training providers, and the entire project is co-ordinated by the subsidiary company, *Ruhrkohle Bildungsgesellschaft* (Ruhrkohle training association), which co-operates with other actors involved in retraining, for example the *Arbeitsämte, Industrie und Handelskammer* (chambers of industry and commerce – IHK) and *Handwerkskammer* (craft chambers). It is anticipated that there will be a need for such programmes to be extended after 1995. Reductions in wages when moving from mining to another sector can also impact on the success of retraining schemes in Germany; however, some careers offered to RAG miners also provide high wages (for example, in parts of the construction industry). RAG workers are offered the additional incentive of being allowed to remain in cheap miners' accommodation if they take up retraining opportunities.

Whereas BCE's attempts to assist redundant miners are fragmented and reactive, RAG's strategy is based upon preventive long-term measures. RAG's retraining programmes are organized more efficiently and give the corporation and individual workers the time to adapt, plan ahead and take informed decisions. BCE's individual approach would not appear to be cost-effective, either for BCE or for training providers. Moreover, a strategy of regulating decline benefits SME suppliers (such as mining engineering firms), which are allowed time adapt to a changed environment. SME suppliers in NRW can participate in the *Land*'s retraining programmes for workers whose companies are threatened by redundancy. Such inputs into increasing skill levels may help a firm survive and, even if it does not, its workers will be better equipped to re-enter the job market and to gain alternative employment.

SME *networks and training consortia*

In recent years, a spotlight has increasingly come to be focused on SMEs, partly because they constitute the majority of firms (in 1989, 89.5% of firms in Wales employed fewer than 25 employees, Employment Department 1993a) and partly because SMEs are viewed as having considerable innovative potential attributable to their organizational flexibility. However, SMEs are less likely to formulate strategic business plans (which should include further training) than larger firms, and also find it difficult to release staff for training because of a lack of resources. Support programmes that offer access to technological advice, training and R&D can therefore enable SMEs to implement modernization strategies. Because collaborative action is perceived as a means of reducing costs and increasing information exchange, there have been attempts to bring small firms together in training projects in both NRW and Wales. SMEs often need to be encouraged to use available training facilities, which they do not perceive as being relevant to their needs; a survey by Mid Glamorgan TEC (1992) demonstrated that one quarter of firms with fewer than 25 employees saw training as being of little value to them (compared with 8% of firms with 25–199 employees, and zero per cent of firms employing over 200 workers). TECs attempt to promote training in SMEs by subsidizing programmes, so that 66 per cent of the costs are met by the TECs. There have been moves in recent years to encourage SMEs to form training networks, with organizations such as the Welsh Development Agency, the TECs and Cardiff Business School involved in setting up such initiatives. This trend was sparked off by the arrival of inward investing firms in Wales, some of which encourage their (potential) suppliers to co-operate in training in order to upgrade quality and productivity levels. The prospect of gaining such valuable customers can counteract local industry's fear of losing employees

155

to the customer-firm or to other suppliers, which frequently deters companies from investing in training and from collaborating with other firms. Training consortia have been developed in automotive engineering, electronics and information technology. For example, the Welsh Automotive Training Consortium was set up in 1993 with the assistance of the WDA and the four TECs in industrial South Wales, which each invested £20000. The consortium currently has 22 member-firms and aims to identify and deliver quality related skills training on a collaborative basis.

NRW has had considerable success in creating SME network projects in initial vocational training, although less in further training. As further training tends to be more firm-specific, companies fear that they will lose sensitive information to their competitors and that their employees may be "poached" by partner-firms. Moreover, unlike initial training, German firms are not legally obliged to undertake further training. Existing collaborative arrangements between SMEs in initial training are, however, regarded as a useful basis for developing programmes in further and retraining.

Networks of training providers

In both regions, large numbers of organizations are involved in training, so that spheres of interest can overlap and conflict, and non-productive competition can develop between training providers. NRW is attempting to solve this problem by creating local training networks. Further training courses in NRW are run by chambers of industry and commerce, craft chambers, job centres, individual firms, vocational schools, adult education colleges, trade unions and professional associations – all of which compete with one another locally for funding and "customers". The *Kommission Montanregionen* (a commission set up by the *Land* in the late 1980s to assess the problems of the coal and steel regions) estimated that there were over 120 training providers in the Dortmund–Unna–Hamm region alone, and that most of these did not co-operate with one another even on an informal basis. Local training provision is often not co-ordinated even between the chamber of industry and commerce and the craft chamber; the two chambers in Aachen do co-operate with one another (the IHK providing business and service sector training, and the HWK manufacturing training) and are regarded very much as an exception. In an attempt to promote co-operation between training providers, several locally based model projects have been set up, for example in Essen, Hattingen and Rheinhausen. The *Berufsförderungszentrum* Essen (employment promotion centre – BFZ) set up the PTQ-Project on vocational training for complex manufacturing systems at the end of 1989 (Körfer & Latniak 1994b). The project received government funding for three years (75% from the Bund and 25% from the *Land*) and brought together around 50 companies, vocational training colleges and centres into 8 local networks. The networks examined four problems caused by changes in production technology, namely:

- the difficulties experienced by both trainers and trainees in mastering all aspects of technical change in all fields of production technology
- the recent German reorganization of vocational areas as a result of increasingly technological complexity
- the critical nature of skills and work organization in making the best use of modern production systems
- the lack of appropriate training materials that integrate technical, organizational and social competences

The project therefore aimed to improve training standards and use collaborative endeavour to recognize and address practical difficulties in this field. Although funding was only available for three years, most of the groups continue to meet, because this type of problem-solving activity is perceived as particularly successful. Nevertheless, certain constraints exist, particularly difficulties in finding the time and financial resources to maintain a high level of co-operation; a high level of commitment by at least one actor, who can act as co-ordinator, is regarded as necessary. It should, moreover, be noted that collaborative endeavour is more likely to be successful if it has a clear remit and well defined objectives.

Attempts are currently being made to improve networking between providers of training and business services in Wales. The Welsh Office's recent "Prospectus for Improving Business and Enterprise Support Services in Wales" (1994) called on local authorities, TECs and other bodies to set up "local business development consortia" based on TEC areas, which would provide companies with single access points into support service networks. A collaborative approach to enterprise support is becoming increasingly important in Wales, with the view that the most productive form of organization is a "network of networks". Certain networks aimed at improving the exchange of information and best-practice already exist in the sphere of training, for example the Council of Welsh TECs, the network of industrial liaison officers in Welsh HEIs, and the *Fforwm* (forum) of the principals of Welsh FE colleges. Nevertheless, contact at a local level

157

between different types of organizations appears to be more limited; for example, there appear to be few links between HEIs and FE colleges based in the same locality, or between colleges and other local actors such as TECs, schools and local authorities. Also, links with national level i.e. WDA, Welsh Office, FEFCW and HEFCW. Although this approach is still in its infancy, it could plan an increasingly important role in future (Begg 1990). TECs could play a key role in encouraging co-operation between bodies at a local level, possibly via the business services consortia, as well as in improving co-ordination between the local and national levels (including the Welsh Office, WDA and relevant NDPBs).

Decentralization

These local networking initiatives are part of a more general trend in both NRW and Wales towards decentralizing economic development strategies, and may be perceived as part of the rhetoric of "post-Fordism" (Hirst & Zeitlin 1990), which emphasizes endogenous potential for growth and "localities taking responsibility for their own destiny". One critical reason for such developments – in which the private sector often participates – is the decreasing amount of finance available from central governments in recent years. In the UK, such cuts are reinforced by the government's ideological withdrawal from many spheres of public life whereas in Germany lower levels of finance are based on a pragmatic reaction to difficulties caused by the pressures of reunification, global upheaval and cyclical change. As many training and job creation schemes in Germany are financed from the same local authority source as unemployment benefit, there is less funding for training programmes in times of increased unemployment. Moreover, as much of the *Bund's* funding has been redirected to the new *Bundesländer*, less finance is available to areas such as the Ruhr. For example, although NRW still receives subsidies from the *Bund* for improving regional economic infrastructure (via the *Gemeinschaftsaufgabe zur Verbesserung der regionalen Wirtschaftsstruktur*), it now has to contribute to the *Bund's* tax revenue sharing programme *(Länderfinanzausgleich)*, which assists structurally weak regions. Although this programme has favoured the *Ruhrgebiet* in the past, it will be devoted for the foreseeable future to restructuring the new *Bundesländer*. NRW will therefore be unable to continue to finance training projects at the level of the late 1980s.

Despite the fact that a major impulse for decentralizing training strategies has been the negative factor of financial difficulties, which has focused attention on cost-effectiveness, endogenous (or "bottom-up") initiatives are particularly important in areas such as the South Wales Valleys and the *Ruhrgebiet*. Both are characterized by their multipolar nature, that is, they have several equally important towns rather than a group of smaller towns around a large centre (although both areas stand in this kind of relationship to external cities, that is, Cardiff and Swansea, Cologne and Düsseldorf). Because of this, the Valleys and the *Ruhrgebiet* share the peculiarity of lacking a "ripple effect"; investments in infrastructure and economic development (including training measures) in one town or locality have few positive effects on neighbouring towns (for example, between Merthyr and Aberdare or between Dortmund and Essen). Economic development strategies at a local level, which include effective retraining and further training initiatives are, therefore, essential if all areas are to benefit from regeneration. This is particularly true of more problematic areas of training policy, including conversion training programmes for workers made redundant as a result of structural decline.

Conclusions

The German vocational training system is generally perceived as superior to the British system, because of a consensus of the importance of education and training, as well as to the fact that the system is employer-led and that all companies are legally obliged to participate. Far fewer firms in Wales, as compared with NRW, have effective training strategies. A report undertaken for South Glamorgan TEC by IFF Research Ltd in September 1991 (South Glamorgan TEC 1992) showed that 40 per cent of employers provided training, although the bulk of it was on-the-job; the figure was lower in SMEs, and extremely low in manufacturing (36%) compared with the public sector (76%). In March 1991, a study of Gelsenkirchen, a town with 200000 inhabitants in the *Ruhrgebiet's* Emscher–Lippe area indicated that, in the previous three years, 68 per cent of companies had implemented initial training programmes and 62.3 per cent had implemented further training programmes (Schönfeld & Stöbe 1992). It should be noted that South Glamorgan, which is concentrated on the city of Cardiff, has a higher grade of training than most parts of Wales, whereas Gelsenkirchen is situated within the northern part of the *Ruhrgebiet*, which has yet to experience significant regeneration. Ironically, however, the very efficiency of the German initial training system can exacerbate difficulties in creating effective retraining strategies. Firms' resources are bound up with initial training schemes, and the system's inflexibility means that it is often difficult for unskilled or semi-skilled workers to upgrade to achieve a recognized vocational qualification on the basis of work experience. However, initiatives by private bodies and employers such as *Ruhrkohle* AG assist in addressing the needs of a region suffering profound structural change. Moreover, in Germany, temporary increases in unemployment are met with government-funded employment creation schemes, rather than training courses, which can seem futile because they hold no guarantee of a job. The *Bund* and *Land* job creation schemes have, however, been criticized for insisting that any jobs that are created must be "extra". Although this condition ensures that these sources of finance are not used to pay existing workers, which would negate any impact on employment opportunities, it also tends to mean that any jobs created are peripheral and therefore tend not to be at high or intermediate skill levels.

Nevertheless, despite current austerity measures, considerable finance is available for training in NRW, partly because legislation compels employers, chambers (IHK and HWK) and government to invest in at least initial training. There is, moreover, a deep-rooted commitment in NRW to developing the labour-force and to continuing to "manage" structural decline in a socially responsible way, as well as the strong cultural commitment that exists throughout Germany to providing effective training, and a willingness to use co-operative endeavour as a means of drawing on new resources and exchanging information and ideas. A high level of private sector investment in training is complemented by government measures at *Bund, Land* and local authority levels. The public sector contributes by gathering, analysing and diffusing information on skill shortages and training needs; by formulating strategic responses; and by encouraging the formation of local training networks. Effective strategic action by both government and industry is particularly important in regions that suffer structural decline and thus need effective conversion and further training initiatives, as well as to assist SMEs, which are often unwilling or unable to formulate wide-ranging training strategies.

Far more fundamental difficulties face the provision of training in Wales, which is not high in quality at present, even by British standards. The low average qualification levels of school-leavers has dire consequences, not only on the skill levels of the Welsh workforce, but also on the capacity of employees to participate in further training and retraining programmes and, particularly, in continuous learning processes. Moreover, few school-leavers or adults in Wales receive high quality vocational training to medium/high skills levels, and any retraining offered to workers made redundant as a result of structural decline tends to be on a piecemeal basis. At the root of these weaknesses is the failure of either the private or public sector in Wales to invest significant resources in training programmes. British companies, unlike their German counterparts, have no legal obligation to undertake training and the British government does not believe it has a responsibility to address the consequent "free-rider" problem. Although there is a growing awareness in Wales of the need rapidly to improve training levels, it appears unlikely that the present shortcomings of the training system will be resolved until a means is found of boosting the commitment of both industry and government. In the meantime, attempts to form strategic responses to training difficulties on a collaborative basis, between both companies and institutions, contribute in some measure to transforming Wales from a low-skill and low-wage economy to one based upon high levels of skill and quality.

CHAPTER TEN

The industrial transformation of the Great Lakes Region

Richard Florida

Since the early 1980s, State, local and regional economic development strategies have faced an accelerating pace of technological change, new patterns of work and production organization. The globalization of technology and markets is transforming economic development as we know it. These strategies represented a considerable advance over traditional approaches to economic development, which were premised upon the core principles of the old mass-production economy and thus focused on the recruitment of industrial branch plants through the use of incentives such as tax breaks, industrial revenue bonds and so forth (Harrison & Kanter 1978, Blair & Premus 1987). The movement away from "smoke-stack chasing" involved a cluster of strategies designed to spur the development of locally based high technology, entrepreneurship and venture capital in an attempt to emulate California's Silicon Valley and Boston's Route 128 (Piore & Sabel 1984, Saxenian 1984, Birch 1987, Eisenger 1988, Osborne 1988, Rosenfeld 1992). A related set of strategies emphasized manufacturing through the development of policies and programs to encourage companies to adopt advanced manufacturing technology (Cohen & Zysman 1988, Shapira 1990, Rosenfeld 1992). In large part, these *second wave* strategies focused on providing technical assistance to firms in specific areas related to changing patterns of economic competition. Put simply, these approaches emphasized the use of specific government business services and in effect saw the role of government as providing direct "retail" economic development services to business.

Although producing some critical successes, these programs were unable to address the fundamental components of economic transformation and they failed to spur significant improvements in regional economic performance. Indeed, by the early 1990s, flagship programs that virtually defined the new wave, such as the Michigan Modernization Service, were abandoned. Others, such as the Ben Franklin Partnership, were substantially refocused and scaled back. And, in a discouraging turn of events, recent years have seen the resurgence of even more virulent rounds of smokestack chasing, as States continue their attempts to outbid one another to attract such companies as BMW, Daimler–Benz and United Airlines' Maintenance Center. These programs are limited by their failure to recognize that the heart of the economic change under way is a transformation in the nature of the production system itself. Pumping new technologies, new capital and new skills into an outmoded and vanishing production system, these approaches essentially boiled down to the use of new tools to fix an old economy.

The challenge for both development theory and practice is to move beyond the search for singular fixes such as technology development and export assistance, and to design strategies that effectively connect local and regional economies to the broader process of economic transformation.

In the following pages, we outline what we believe is an effective path for bringing economic development theory, practice and policy into tune with the demands of the new economy. Our strategy is based on a recognition of the fundamental transformation of our economy and of the need to reshape our regional economic infrastructures in ways that support this new economy. To make our ideas and concepts as concrete as possible, we focus on the experience of one region – the US Industrial Heartland – which is making the transition from traditional mass-production industrial organization to the new model of high-performance organization. We present the preliminary findings of a three-year research project conducted jointly by the Council of Great Lakes Governors, a consortium of the governors of the eight States bordering the Great Lakes and the Center for Economic Development at Carnegie–Mellon University, Pittsburgh. Once seen as a region of deindustrialization, disinvestment, despair and desolation, the Industrial Heartland provides a powerful lens from which to view the dynamics of the new economy and their potential to inform new regional economic development strategies and policies.

The transformation of the industrial Midwest

In the late 1970s and early 1980s, Midwest manufacturing appeared to be headed for near total collapse, and the region had the steepest decline in real income during the 1982 recession. However, by the early 1990s the Midwest was boasting rates of growth in productivity rivalling that of Japan, and rates of income and job growth outpacing the coastal regions of the USA. Moreover, a region that was once decimated by international competition had become the export belt of the USA. Although new technologies have played an important role in this transformation, the region's economic resurgence is the result of its ability to adapt to a more fundamental shift in the nature of production. New ways of organizing work, new relationships with suppliers and customers, and a focus on continuous improvement are the key elements of this new *high-performance* production system.

The Industrial Midwest is defined as the eight States that border the Great Lakes: Ohio, Michigan, Illinois, Indiana, Wisconsin, Minnesota, New York and Pennsylvania. The region is the historic centre of American heavy industry, and from the late nineteenth century to the mid-twentieth century was the dominant production region in the world (Meyer 1983). Its growth was informed by the system of scientific management and mass production (Hounshell 1984, Lazonick 1990, Womack et al. 1990) that provided an underlying logic for the region's economy and for government policy.

During the 1970s and early 1980s, the region experienced disinvestment and deindustrialization coincident with the decline of this mass-production model (Bluestone & Harrison 1982). Traditional manufacturing corporations moved plants to the Sunbelt and the developing nations in search of low costs, docile labour, and so-called "better business climates" (Crandall 1993). The region was rocked by plant closings. Many of the region's steel mills closed, as steel producers consolidated their operations or diversified into the energy sector or other business. The region's unemployment rate exceeded the national average, reaching 25 per cent in some industrial cities. The eight Great Lakes States had the highest rate of business failures and the steepest decline in real income in the nation.

By the late 1970s and early 1980s, a consensus view emerged: the Midwest region would face long-run, secular, and chronic disinvestment and deindustrialization (Bluestone & Harrison 1982) brought on by a shift of traditional industries to low-wage locations (Crandall 1993), the development of new high-technology complexes in California and New England (Saxenian 1994), and a broader shift to a post-industrial service economy (Bell 1973). The consensus among business leaders, policy-makers and

164

academics was that the region would never again be a centre for competitive manufacturing – its costs were too high, and its labour climate too adversarial. The manufacturing belt, it was argued, would be left behind in a broad and fundamental shift to a post-industrial economy of high technology, finance and services.

It is increasingly recognized that such predictions were premature and in many cases incorrect. The Industrial Midwest has not deindustrialized – nor has it become a post-industrial economy. Our fundamental hypothesis is that the region's industrial base is in the throes of a complex transformation and restructuring, catalyzed by an emerging core of high-performance companies such as Xerox, Motorola, Honda, Bosch and countless others. At the same time, too many of the region's manufacturers remain locked in the old mind-set of cost-cutting, downsizing, short-termism, disinvestment and management by stress. Thus, we suggest that the intersection of these two trends has produced a complex process of economic transformation, characterized by expanding clusters of propulsive growth alongside continued pockets of decline: a phenomenon of *reindustrialization within deindustrialization*.

A review of aggregate economic performance provides considerable support for this hypothesis. After a severe contraction from 1977 to 1987, manufacturing output from the Industrial Midwest grew at 7.8 per cent from 1987 to 1988, surpassing not only the 7.4 per cent rate of the USA as a whole, but also the 6.3 per cent rate for Japan and the 5.2 per cent rate for Germany. From 1980 to 1988, manufacturing productivity in the Industrial Midwest rose by 36 per cent, compared to 15 per cent for Germany, 32 per cent for the USA, and 52 per cent for Japan. Roughly 15 per cent of this gain for the region came from 1986 to 1988, a surge that not even the Japanese economy could match. A Federal Reserve Board study found Midwest manufacturers to be 20 per cent more efficient than their national counterparts. Meanwhile, the region's manufacturing employment has virtually stabilized, after shrinking 15 per cent from 1977 to 1982 and continuing to fall until the late 1980s. Despite having only 30 per cent of the nation's population, the region accounts for 36 per cent of all manufacturing output in the USA, 60 per cent of the steel, 55 per cent of its automobiles, and 50 per cent of its machine tools. Remarkably, the Industrial Midwest produced more automobiles and steel in 1992 than a decade before, even when counting the General Motors plant closings.

Explaining the economic turnaround

There are several potential explanations and hypotheses for the economic transformation of the Industrial Midwest.

INDUSTRIAL CLUSTERS

Research by Michael Porter (1990) suggests that regional economic performance depends upon local competition and the vitality of industrial clusters of related and supporting industries. According to this view, improved regional economic performance is attributable to increased levels of local competition and the development or revitalization of clusters of related and supporting industries in the automotive assembly, automotive parts production, steel and other related industrial sectors. Variants of this approach would suggest that improved regional performance is related to the adoption of new technology and the "downsizing" or disaggregation of large vertically integrated manufacturers and the emergence of networks of small and medium-size enterprises (Piore & Sabel 1984, Birch 1987).

GLOBALIZATION

A second hypothesis links the region's improved economic performance to its increasing integration into the world economy (Reich 1991, Dicken 1992, Council on Urban Economic Development 1993). According to this perspective, the region's turnaround is at least in part linked to its increasing integration to the global economy (Federal Reserve Bank of Chicago 1993). There is considerable support for this hypothesis. In 1991, for example, the region shipped over $100 billion dollars in manufactured goods to more than 80 countries, including $9.4 billion to Japan and $5.6 billion to Germany. The region's rate of increase in manufactured exports is double the national average, leading the *Wall Street Journal* (1993) to proclaim that the region "singlehandedly" returned the USA to the position of the world's largest exporter.

INTERNATIONAL INVESTMENT

A variant of the globalization hypothesis focuses on the relationship between international investment and improving regional performance. This perspective suggests that international investment, especially that

166

from Japan, has played a key role in rebuilding the region's traditional industries. More than half of all Japanese foreign direct investment in automobiles, steel and rubber is concentrated in four Great Lakes States: Ohio, Indiana, Michigan and Illinois (Florida & Kenney 1991). A recent report by the McKinsey Global Institute found that international investment increases national and regional productivity by facilitating the transfer of best-practice organizational and management techniques. Thus, Japanese inward investment has facilitated the transfer of world-class manufacturing technology and state-of-the-art management practices to the industrial Midwest, leading over time to higher rates of adoption and diffusion of these practices and techniques by domestic as well as international manufacturing establishments in the region (Kenney & Florida 1993, McKinsey Global Institute 1993).

LOW LEVELS OF DEFENCE DEPENDENCE

A fourth hypothesis is that the economic transformation of the Midwest industrial base is linked to the relatively low level of defence dependence of its major manufacturing sectors. Research by Swonk (1990) notes that the industrial Midwest never became as defence dependent as those in other parts of the country winning the region (on a per capita basis) only one third as much defence business as California and Massachusetts. In 1991, Michigan, Indiana and Wisconsin ranked 48th, 49th and 50th respectively in federal spending per person. The Midwest is less defence-dependent than any other region, with defence outlays per person of only 60 per cent of the national average. The region's $444 per person in defence spending compares to more than $1200 per capita for California and more than $1400 for Massachusetts. As a result, Midwest manufacturers have retained their commercial focus and are better positioned to weather proposed defence cuts.

SHIFT TO HIGH-PERFORMANCE ECONOMIC ORGANIZATION

A potentially integrative theory, and one that we have organized our continuing research around, suggests that the economic transformation of the industrial Midwest reflects a deeper shift in the nature of production organization and management. According to this perspective, the economic transformation of the industrial Midwest is tied to the shift from traditional forms of mass-production organization to a new model of high-performance organization. As defined in the literature, high-performance

167

organization refers to a cluster of best-practice organizational and managerial techniques that, when taken together, harness intellectual as well as physical resources at all levels of the firm and the broader production system in which individual firms are embedded (Zuboff 1989, Florida 1991, Nonaka 1991, Drucker 1993, Kenney & Florida 1993). Put somewhat differently, the improved economic performance of the industrial Midwest is tied to relatively high rates of adoption, diffusion and penetration of high-performance principles by manufacturers in the region.

According to this perspective, the transformation of the industrial Midwest thus reflects a deeper and more fundamental transformation in the nature of capitalism – a shift to a new knowledge-intensive economy, where the keys to success are harnessing the ideas and innovative capabilities of all workers from the R&D lab to the factory floor to turn out the high-quality, state-of-the-art products the world's consumers want to buy. Under this new form of organization, the factory itself is becoming more like a laboratory, with knowledge workers, advanced high-technology equipment, and clean-room conditions free of dirt and grime. Indeed, as Drucker (1993) and Nonaka (1991) suggest, capitalism may be entering into a new age of knowledge creation and continuous innovation. This new system of *knowledge-intensive capitalism* is based upon a synthesis of intellectual and physical labour: a melding of innovation and production (see also Florida 1991, Kenney & Florida 1993). This new system of economic organization, these scholars argue, represents a major advance over previous systems of Taylorist scientific management or the assembly-line system of Henry Ford, where the principal source of value and productivity growth was physical labour.

The shift to high-performance manufacturing can be understood at three interrelated levels. First, international investment has resulted in the transfer of best-practice technology and management. Secondly, domestic firms in the region have made substantial investments in organizational restructuring. Firms such as Xerox, Motorola and Steelcase responded to mounting global competition by restructuring themselves into better organizations than they were before. These companies invested heavily in new factories and production technology, instituted total-quality-management programs, and developed powerful partnerships with their suppliers, increasing their ability to compete globally and capture new overseas markets for their products.

Thirdly, high-performance organization is also diffusing into the broader manufacturing supplier base. Findings from a survey of roughly 2000 small and medium-size manufacturers in the industrial Heartland

168

indicate that many of these companies – more than half of all survey respondents – are implementing elements of high-performance organization, such as total-quality-management programs, self-direct work teams, and just-in-time inventory control. Research by MIT's Paul Osterman indicates that roughly one-third of this nation's manufacturing companies are engaged in the transition to high-performance.

Regional dimensions of economic transformation

The process of economic transformation has an important regional dimension. Indeed, we suggest that regions are inextricably connected to the process of economic transformation.

Until the late 1970s, the Midwest economy grew by extracting natural resources such as coal and iron ore, making materials such as steel and chemicals, and manufacturing durable goods such as cars, appliances and industrial machinery (Meyer 1983). The region prospered because it had natural comparative advantages that allowed it to be a mass producer of commodities competing largely on the basis of relatively low production costs. Public policies emphasized the financial incentives, reduction of the marginal costs of operation, and regulation of business externalities and, at the State level, the recruitment of branch plant firms. But, since the early 1970s, the economies of the Midwest, the nation and the world have changed fundamentally. Global competition has shifted the base of manufacturing activity, as foreign competitors have succeeded in making lower-cost commodities to challenge the region's companies in both domestic and international markets. Global markets are now demanding increasingly sophisticated, high-quality, high-value–added products and services, not just commodities (Dicken 1992, National Council for Urban Economic Development 1993).

In an important and provocative essay in *Foreign Affairs*, Ohmae (1993) suggests that regions or what he calls *region-States* are coming to replace the nation-State as the centrepiece of economic activity. In his words:

> The nation state has become an unnatural, even dysfunctional unit
> for organizing human activity and managing economic endeavor in
> a borderless world . . . On the global economic map the lines that
> now matter are those defining what may be called region states.

169

Region-States, Ohmae points out, are fundamentally tied to the global economy through mechanisms such as trade, export, and both inward and outward foreign investment – the most competitive region-States are not only home to domestic companies, but are attractive to the best companies from around the world.

We begin from the notion that regions must be defined by the same criteria and elements that comprise a high-performance firm: continuous improvement, knowledge creation, organizational learning, and integration into global markets. Regions must adopt the principles of high-performance economic organization and in effect become *learning, or knowledge-creating regions* (Cooke 1996).

Learning regions provide a series of related infrastructures that can facilitate the flow of knowledge, ideas and learning. In other words, learning regions provide the crucial inputs required for high-performance economic organization to flourish: a manufacturing infrastructure of interconnected vendors and suppliers; a human infrastructure that can produce knowledge workers, facilitate the development of a team-orientation, and which is organized around life-long learning; a physical infrastructure that facilitates and supports constant sharing of information, electronic exchange of data and information, just-in-time delivery of goods and services, and integration into the global economy; and a capital allocation and industrial governance system attuned to the needs of high-performance organizations (Table 10.1).

Major transformations are already occurring in the *manufacturing infrastructures* of regions. Mass-production organization was defined by a high degree of vertical integration and internalization of capabilities. External supplies tended to involve ancillary or non-essential elements, were generally purchased largely on price, and were stored in huge inventories in the plant. High-performance economic organization is characterized by a much higher degree of reliance on outside suppliers and the development of co-dependent complexes of end-users and suppliers. In heavy industries, such as automobile manufacturing, large assembly facilities play the role of a hub, surrounding themselves with a spoke network of customers and suppliers in order to harness innovative capabilities of the complex, enhance quality and continuously reduce costs. A learning region requires a manufacturing of infrastructure of globally orientated firms with R&D and innovative capabilities and dense, interactive and co-dependent supplier relations.

Regions have a *human infrastructure* – a labour market from which firms draw "smart" workers. Mass-production industrial organization was

170

Table 10.1 From mass production to learning regions.

	Mass production region	Learning/knowledge-creating region
Basis of competitiveness	Comparative advantage based upon: • natural resources • physical labour	Sustainable advantage based upon: • knowledge creation • continuous improvement
Production system	Mass production • physical labour as source of value • separation of innovation and production	Knowledge-based production • continuous creation • knowledge as source of value • synthesis of innovation and production
Manufacturing infrastructure	Arm's-length supplier relations	Supplier systems as a source of innovation
Human infrastructure	Low-skill low-cost labour Taylorist work force Taylorist education and training	Knowledge workers Continuous improvement of human resources Continuous education and training
Physical and communication infrastructure	Domestically orientated physical infrastructure	Globally orientated physical and communication infrastructure
Industrial governance system	Adversarial relationships Top-down control	Mutually dependent relationships Network organization
Policy system	Specific retail policies	Systems/infrastructure orientation

characterized by a schism between physical and intellectual labour: a large mass of relatively unskilled workers who could perform physical tasks but had little formal involvement in more managerial, technical or intellectual activities, and a relatively small group of managers and executives responsible for planning and technological development. The human infrastructure system of mass production – the system of public schools, vocational training, and college and university professional programs in business and engineering – evolved over time to meet the needs of this mass-production system, turning out a large mass of cogs-in-the-machine and a smaller technocratic elite of engineers and managers. The human infrastructure required for a learning region is quite different. As its name implies, a learning region requires a human infrastructure of knowledge workers who can apply their intelligence in production. The education and training system must be learning system that can facilitate life-long learning and provide the high levels of group-orientation and teaming required for high-performance economic organization.

All regions possess a physical and communications infrastructure upon which organizations deliver their goods and services and communicate

171

with one another. The physical infrastructure of mass production facilitated the flow of raw materials to factory complexes and the movement of goods and services to largely domestic markets. High-performance firms are global players. Thus, the physical infrastructure of the new economy must develop on a global basis links to, and facilitate the movement of, people, information, goods and services. Furthermore, high-performance organization draws a great portion of its power from the rapid and constant sharing of information and increasingly electronic exchange of key data between customers, end-users and their suppliers. For example, Johnson Control's factory, which manufacturers seats for Toyota's Kentucky assembly plant, receives a computerized order for seats as each new Camry begins its way down the assembly line. A learning region requires a physical and communication infrastructure that facilitates the movement of goods, people and information on a just-in-time basis.

To ensure growth of existing firms and birth of new ones, all regions have a capital allocation system and financial market. One of the existing weaknesses in the USA is that financial systems are creating impediments to high performance. For example, our interviews with executives, and surveys of high-performance firms, indicate that banks often require inventory to be held as collateral, creating a sizeable barrier to the just-in-time inventory and supply practices that define high-performance economic organization.

All regions provide mechanisms for industrial governance: formal modes and informal patterns of behaviour between and among firms, and between firms and government organizations. Mass-production regions were characterized by top-down relationships, vertical hierarchy, high degrees of functional or task specialization, and command-and-control methods of organizing. Learning regions must develop governance structures that reflect and mimic those of high-performance firms, that is co-dependent relations, network organization, flat or lean organization, and a focus on customer requirements. This goes for government and non-profit organizations, particularly economic development organizations, as well as for private enterprises.

Learning regions provide the crucial inputs required for high-performance economic organization to flourish: a manufacturing infrastructure of interconnected vendors and suppliers; a human infrastructure that can produce knowledge workers, facilitates the development of a team-orientation, and which is organized around life-long learning; a physical infrastructure that facilitates and supports constant sharing of information, electronic exchange of data and information, just-in-time delivery of goods and services, and integration into the global economy; and a capital allocation and industrial governance system attuned to the needs of high-performance organizations.

Implications for economic development strategy and policy

The processes of economic and regional transformation hold considerable implications for economic development policy.

The incredible strength of the US economic organization in the first half of the twentieth century was premised in large measure upon a close fit between mass-production industrial organization and government policy. The vitality of the nation's mass-production system was bolstered by a broader political economy that supported mass production – everything from roads, railways and ports to the land-grant post-secondary education system that grew up alongside and in support of mass-production industry. But, we suggest that government economic policy (regional economic development policy included), which once worked so well, may be thought of as being increasingly out of sync with the demands of the emerging high-performance model of economic organization. One way to think about this policy environment is as a large and increasingly unwieldy *layer-cake* of policies and programs that built up over time to meet the needs and requirements of a bygone industrial epoch. This mass-production policy system is not only costly and inefficient: it comprises a considerable obstacle to the emergence of the new economy.

According to this view, the US economy at the national and regional levels is caught between two business climates: an old one structured to accommodate the dynamics of mass production, and an emerging high-performance one. The nature of economic transformation thus entails completing the transition between business climates. The role of economic development policy is to develop an institutional framework that can facilitate the shift to this new production system and, just as importantly, to eliminate any remaining policy and regulatory barriers that inhibit its emer-gence. New policies and strategic investments are likely to be required to shape and leverage reindustrialization simultaneously, and to expand the evolution of the new system of production organization upon which it is based.

The lessons from the emergence of a new economy based upon high-performance principles hold two potential immediate implications for economic development policy.

First, high-performance economic organization requires policies that work at the systems level. The essence of high-performance organization is its systems orientation. We therefore hypothesize that public and regional interventions to improve competitiveness must also share this systems orientation. The high-performance revolution necessitates that policies and services shift from a focus on specific firms or sectors to the networks of companies that make up high-performance production systems. Indeed, our preliminary research and interviews with high-performance firms suggest that they are not inclined to support direct government intervention in the management of the enterprise of the sort provided by manufacturing extension centres.

The challenge for economic development policy is not to provide specific services, but to create the structure, rules of the game and incentives required for high performance. In essence, the issue is not to give firms, regions and communities specific information and assistance, but to provide a new economic framework and set of incentives. This further suggests that technical assistance to firms, workers and communities is likely to be more effective if linked to policies designed to transform the overall business climate. For example, public financing for manufacturing technologies will likely have only limited impact if regulations create a bias against private financing for low-inventory firms. Similarly, technical assistance to reduce pollution may have greater impact if environmental regulations do not create a bias towards installing end-of-pipe control equipment. And, customized training programs are likely to be more effective with a general education system orientated around problem-solving skills, team capabilities and outcome-based learning. In contrast with mass production, high-performance organization depends upon a fundamentally different infrastructure of education and transportation investments, and environmental, financial, and business regulations.

Secondly, high-performance economic organization has a significant regional dimension. Unlike the period since the early 1970s, when the decline of mass production encouraged dispersion, high-performance organization creates powerful centrifugal forces. Put simply, *place matters* to the high-performance economy. This dynamic is reflected in a changing industrial landscape. The mass-production economy was marked by large-scale production facilities served by many scattered and unrelated suppliers, for example, the global factory and the world car strategy. Conversely, high-performance production is marked by dense corporate complexes of end-users and key suppliers (Florida & Kenney 1991). Hence, although mass-production facilities became increasingly free of locational constraints,

174

high-performance production complexes are more firmly rooted in specific places. No production trend in recent times has offered as great an opportunity to establish an industrial stake in regional development.

Thus, once in place, high-performance production complexes tend to have a natural bias towards investment and improvement of the surrounding supplier base and economic area. The improved competitiveness of existing businesses and investment in advanced services and programs enhances the creation of the emergence of such clusters. In Battle Creek, Michigan, Nippondenso was a leading force in the restructuring of community college programmes and the creation of advanced industrial services to support its supplier base. In an inner-city neighbourhood of Columbus, Ohio, the LSE corporation has established a state-of-the-art steel facility based on high-performance principles. And Motorola has invested in transforming the entire educational program of the five school districts serving its major production facilities. High-performance economic organization thus creates considerable incentives for regional redevelopment by stimulating private investment in regional firms, workers and community institutions.

Summary

Since the early 1970s, experts have predicted a shift from manufacturing to a post-industrial service economy, or from basic industries to high technology. In the wake of the predictions, efforts were made to invest in new critical technologies and industries. But, the change under way in the USA and throughout the world is not one of old sectors giving way to new, but is more fundamental in terms of the way goods are produced and the economy itself is organized – from a mass-production economy to a new knowledge-based economy. This change holds sweeping implications for government. The critical need for government economic development policy is not to help invest in new technologies, but to help put in place the economic infrastructure required for the new economy to flourish. The challenge is to redesign the broad infrastructure of government economic policy and the incentive system it helps to set in place, in ways that can facilitate – not impede – the shift from mass production to high-performance economic organization.

The emergence of high-performance economic organization offers a unique opportunity to establish a unified framework for industrial and regional revitalization. This opportunity rests in the critical dependence of high-performance economic organization on new type of policy system and related regional infrastructure. Our findings and those of others have documented the emergence of high-performance economic organization in and around the industrial Midwest. Our findings further indicate that existing retail-led approaches to economic development policy are out of sync with their needs. This work suggests the need to move to systems-level or infrastructure approaches that can provide a broad climate in which high-performance economic organization can take root and flourish.

Given all of this, economic development policy must be reorientated to speed the development of a business climate and overall economic infrastructure that enables workers, firms and communities to make the transition to the new economy. Economic development policy-makers and professionals must help put in place the incentive structure and regional infrastructure. Long-run economic growth and development fundamentally depends upon it.

CHAPTER ELEVEN

The dash for gas –
consequences and opportunities

Richard Calverley Watson

Wales has for long been a net energy exporter because of its traditionally powerful coalfields. Typically, exploitation of these despoiled landscapes and coal-consumption polluted the environment. Despite the decline in deep-mined coal production, Wales is not taking advantage of opportunities to become a more responsibly "green" energy-producing and consuming economy, because *laissez-faire* government policies have encouraged a rapacious profit-maximizing approach to energy exploitation. There could be a more responsible harnessing of resources for more sustainable economic development, and some of these possibilities are prefigured in what follows. But the "dash for gas" typifies present-day policy and overshadows efforts to develop a new cleaner approach to energy management and use.

The dash for gas, a feature of electricity privatization, has affected the economy of South Wales, a formerly important coal producing area. It remains to be seen whether the effects of this and other changes in the energy market can be used to assist in the revitalization of the Welsh economy, particularly in South Wales. This chapter describes the features and results of electricity privatization, sets out two scenarios for the future of energy and the environment in the economy, and considers the consequences for Wales.

South Wales, a coal economy

The economic history of Wales has been shaped by its geography and natural resources. In particular, the economy of South Wales has been dominated until very recently by coal. It was coal that brought copper smelting to Swansea Bay and iron furnaces to the Heads of the Valleys in the eighteenth century. In the nineteenth century the mining of coal for sale, especially for steam raising, transformed the South Wales valleys, and Cardiff became the leading coal exporting port in the UK, and hence the world. By the end of the century, coal was the principal fuel for sea and land transport and was also used to produce secondary fuels, coke, gas and electricity.

After the First World War, coal, on which the economy of South Wales was by now excessively dependent, faced increasing competition from oil. However, the building of the national electricity grid in the 1930s gave coal an important role in power generation and it remained until the 1960s the principal feedstock for gas production. Nevertheless, the South Wales coalfield never again reached the levels of output achieved in the first quarter of this century.

By the 1950s coal held a declining market share in most markets as competition increased from nuclear power and oil in power generation, and from oil in most other sectors. Meanwhile, with the landing of natural gas from the North Sea, gas production ceased and a new successful rival in the heating and industrial process markets appeared.

The dash for gas

In 1990 the British government privatized the electricity supply industry. One of the consequences was a rush to build new power stations, in which natural gas was the most popular choice of fuel. This development became known as the dash for gas.

In England and Wales, privatization changed not only the industry's ownership but also the structure and operation of the market and the responsibility for security of supply. Similar changes were effected in the Scottish industry, although it largely retained its integrated structure. It was planned that the new electricity market in England and Wales would foster both competition in power generation and in local electricity supply among the privatized companies and would encourage new entrants.

During the privatization of the industry, new and more efficient methods of using natural gas to generate electricity were widely publicized, the increasing extent of the world's reserves of natural gas was becoming more widely known, and the Commission of the European Union (EU) relaxed its opposition to the use of natural gas for power generation. The privatized generating companies, however, had commitments to take large quantities of coal in the first four years after privatization, but would then be free to negotiate new deals. They were interested in diversifying their sources of fuel and both closed older coal-fired plant and planned to build new gas-fired power stations. Gas power stations are relatively quick to build and, on current prices, economical to run; soon all but one of the privatized companies and some new entrants had substantial stakes in plans for new gas-fired power stations.

At the same time gas supplies were being liberalized, as British Gas lost its right to be the sole purchaser of gas from UK Continental Shelf (UKCS) and agreed to make some of the gas in its existing contracts with suppliers available to its competitors.

The choice of gas was strengthened further by its being the least polluting of the fossil fuels, and gas was presented as a green solution to the demand for additional and more diversely owned generating capacity.

Thus, with a new wave of power stations, the supply liberalized and a new green image, the dash for gas was under way.

The energy market

MARKET SECTORS

The UK energy market can be divided into several sectors, reflecting different uses and patterns of demand.

Transport is the largest sector, with 33 per cent of energy consumption in 1993, and is the major user of oil in the UK. Electricity is either in use or planned for several railway lines and rapid transit systems, and it powers trains in and around London and beyond.

The domestic fuel and power market (29% in 1993) has been transformed by the spread of central heating. Gas and electricity dominate this sector, although oil and coal also have small shares. The gas and electricity utilities have monopolies for the supply of their fuels, both in this sector and to other smaller users. Their prices are published in tariffs and price changes are controlled by the appropriate regulator. The proposed loss of these monopolies will effect a further transformation of this sector.

The services sector (13% in 1993) includes almost any buildings or activities that are not domestic or industrial. Its range of demand is similar to the domestic sector for heating, cooking, lighting and power, although the pattern will vary for different types of premises; leisure centres and hospitals, for example, have provided opportunities for the installation of combined heat and power (CHP). Tariffs normally apply for small users, but contracts are agreed with large users. Gas and electricity predominate, although coal and oil have some market share.

In the industrial sector (25% in 1993), the demand for heating is often no different from the services sector's. However, in many cases the principal use will be in industrial processes where the specific qualities of the fuel supplied, particularly in control and ease of use, will be as important as economy and efficiency. Prices are either published in tariffs and or agreed by contracts, depending mainly on the level of consumption.

The last major user of primary fuels is the power generation market, where the nuclear and coal-fired stations provide the base load, supplemented by other fuels and sources.

In South Wales the demand of the non-domestic sectors has traditionally been relatively higher than in other UK regions, partly because of industrial character of the area and the small size of its settlements, but also because its milder climate results in a lower demand for heating.

DEMAND PATTERNS

Demand for energy varies throughout the year, the week or the day. Seasonal changes affect the demand for heat and light and can be predicted on the basis of average weather patterns, both for the country as a whole and for particular areas. Daily demand patterns, which will differ from sector to sector, and the differences between weekdays and working days, can also be predicted on the basis of past experience.

Although demand may vary, fuel production does not, since coalmines, oil wells and gas fields are normally operated at set levels of production throughout the year. The fuel suppliers have to balance a steady supply with a fluctuating demand. With oil and coal, storage and stockholding by the supplier or by the customer are the usual means of providing for seasonal changes in demand. Gas is more expensive and difficult to store, and although British Gas and other suppliers use British Gas's storage for most of the year, meeting the peak demand in winter is supported by the contracted interruption of supplies to customers with access to alternative fuels. However, electricity cannot be stored and the suppliers meet seasonal and daily peaks in demand by bringing additional generating capacity on stream in a planned sequence. It is therefore important that there is sufficient capacity to meet the expected peak demand in cold weather.

Energy demand is also affected by customers' expectations and their attitudes, to both the price of fuel and to the natural environment. Many customers have become more aware of the issues in the energy market and their expectations are more diverse, sometimes vociferous and in some cases conflicting. Energy suppliers will probably, therefore, need greater skill and sensitivity in identifying, predicting and meeting future demand.

PRODUCERS AND SUPPLIERS

The oil companies play a major part in the UK energy market, in exploring and producing on the UKCS, in the refining and processing of primary fuels and as suppliers to wholesale and retail customers. Their involvement in both gas and electricity ventures in Britain is likely to increase their influence further.

British Gas has dominated the UK gas sector as the major purchaser of natural gas and the owner of the natural gas transmission and local distribution systems. However, its hold on the market has been weakened by its agreement to reduce its share of larger customers to less than half. Furthermore, a report by the Monopolies and Mergers Commission in August 1993, recommended that British Gas should divest itself of its downstream gas supply business, where the market would be opened to free competition. The government made no immediate decision on the report, and the company has since abandoned its federal structure and has reorganized into several UK-wide business units. The Queen's speech in November 1994, however, included proposals to open the entire gas sector to competition by 1998.

British Coal, which owns almost all the mines in the UK is due to be sold, as five separate companies, to private bidders in 1995. Other suppliers include smaller private collieries and imports of coal, for which some electricity generating companies have built their own terminals.

The electricity generation and supply industry in England and Wales formerly consisted of the Central Electricity Generating Board, with responsibility for power generation, the national grid for security of supply throughout the system, and twelve area boards, with responsibility for local distribution and supply. The privatized industry includes power generators, the twelve regional electricity supply companies (RECs), and the National Grid Company (NGC), which runs the operations of the market. The generators are three of the companies formed from the CEGB, National Power, Powergen and Nuclear Electric, and several new entrants.

On vesting day, National Power had three coal-fired stations, two gas-turbine stations, two hydro stations and one oil-fired station in Wales. Powergen had one hydro station and Nuclear Electric two magnox nuclear stations. In addition, the NGC owned the pumped storage stations at Ffestiniog and Dinorwic in Snowdonia. The two RECs in Wales are MANWEB in North Wales and SWALEC in South Wales.

At present, although there have been several joint undertakings and co-operative ventures, there have been no major mergers or take-overs among the privatized energy companies. However, there is involvement, particularly in new ventures, by both foreign and domestic oil companies and other energy businesses. A further structural change is expected to occur in 1995, when the NGC, which is currently owned by the RECs, is to be floated on the Stock Exchange.

Four recent developments

OIL AND GAS IN THE UK CONTINENTAL SHELF

Hydrocarbons were discovered under the UKCS in the early 1960s, although the first major oil discoveries, which followed the licensing of· blocks in the central and northern North Sea did not occur until the early 1970s. Oil production began in 1975 and grew rapidly, reaching a peak of 127.6 million tonnes in 1985. Output and revenues have since declined and, although a recovery close to that level is expected in the mid-1990s, and in the next few years new areas of the UKCS will be brought into production, in the longer term output will fall.

However, gas had been discovered in the southern North Sea and production started earlier than oil, with the first pipelines bringing gas ashore in 1967. Although the discovery and drilling of new fields developed apace, the rate of extraction was slower and UK resources were supplemented by imported gas. British Gas converted its customers to the new fuel, gas production from coal and oil ceased, and natural gas became the leader in domestic energy supply. Until its privatization, British Gas ran its own depletion policy, which sought to restrict supplies to premium uses of the fuel.

Unfortunately, the government did not use the revenues arising from oil & gas production for investment in industry, where it has been estimated that productive capacity had been reduced by a third in the 1980/81 recession. These revenues were used to reduce the National Debt and to support programmes of cuts in personal taxation, which, with the deregulation of the financial markets, led directly to the unsustainable consumer boom of the late 1980s and so to the recent deep recession, the longest since the 1930s.

OPEC AND THE OIL PRICE

Since 1970, the oil-producing countries have tried with varying success to control the world oil market. There have been two major increases in oil prices, in 1973 and 1979. The effects of these rises in oil prices on the world economy were considerable and the UK energy market felt the effects. Oil became uncompetitive in many sectors where gas was the principal beneficiary. In power generation, reliance on largely imported oil was seen to make the country strategically vulnerable and the CEGB switched back to coal. There was also growth in the international trading of coal, with the development of "spot" and "futures" markets, and in the importance of the fuel in the growing economies of the Far East.

In Wales gas gained considerably, particularly in the domestic and industrial markets. Coal also benefited from the revival of the coal-fired generation market, where its strategic importance as an indigenous fuel seemed to assure it of a healthy future. It also managed to hold on to important shares in other sectors, including steel and domestic sales particularly in the mining valleys; in 1987 it still held 35 per cent of the domestic heating market in Wales.

THE MINERS AND THE CONSERVATIVE PARTY

The energy market is highly political and its operation is affected and often directed by government policies. In the early 1970s the miners' strikes and the consequent power shortages were seen by many in the Conservative party as instrumental in their election defeats in 1974. In contrast, the Labour governments of 1974–9 sponsored the Plan for Coal, which envisaged a key role for the fuel in the British energy market. However, the return of a Conservative government in 1979 committed to a free market ideology and with suspicion or outright hostility towards the miners, did not bode well for the Plan. In 1984, with predictions of massive pit

183

closures, the National Union of Mineworkers embarked on a national strike, in which the miners were defeated and split into two mutually hostile trades unions.

In 1989 Parliament passed the Conservative government's Electricity Act, which would privatize the electricity industry and introduce a new electricity market with a long-term bias against coal. In 1992 the government announced the closure of 35 pits, ostensibly as a market response to reduction in demand from the generators, but more probably as a preparation for privatization. In spite of spontaneous and widespread opposition, pit closures continued, and there are now two pits left in South Wales (Tower in the Cynon Valley and Bettws Drift in Dyfed) and one in North Wales (Point of Ayr in Clwyd).

PRIVATIZATION

The Conservative government began its major privatizations after its second election victory in 1983. As with oil and gas revenues, the proceeds of privatization were absorbed in cuts in personal taxation and the reduction of the National Debt. In many cases the proceeds were considerably reduced by the costs of the privatizations themselves and by the generally low and attractive offer prices. First gas and then electricity were floated on the London Stock Market. Both sales were aimed at the small investor, but, as with all of the other privatizations, the bulk of the shares ended up in the hands of institutions. In 1994 the government started privatizing British Coal by dividing the coalfield and inviting potential buyers to bid. The bidders included an employee buy-out at Tower Colliery in South Wales.

Claims were made at the time that privatization would improve the effectiveness of the businesses and benefit the customer through reduced prices and better service. However, there has been little concrete evidence that privatization has made any difference to the utilities' performance. Profits, dividends and share prices have increased, as have the rewards of the companies' directors. Although gas prices have been contained by the depressed oil price and by tight regulation since privatization, electricity prices have increased by some 25 per cent in South Wales. Privatization of gas, electricity and coal has done little for the Welsh economy, since it has generally reduced the businesses' level of employment and economic activity.

Privatized electricity in England and Wales

STRUCTURE

The privatization of the UK electricity industry was ambitious. A new market was established, changing the method by which electricity was traded within the industry and sold to the consumer.

The generators compete to supply electricity through a pool, operated by the NGC. They include not only generating companies but Scottish and French importers and any organization that has a licence to offer power to the grid. The generators also bypass the pool operation and enter into contracts with the RECs for agreed prices and supplies.

The market for supply within the area of each REC is also open to competition. From the start, generators and other competing suppliers were allowed to tender for customers with an annual consumption exceeding 1000Kw hours. By 31 March 1994, this limit was reduced to 100Kw hours and, by 31 March 1998, the entire market shall have been opened to competition. Regulation by OFFER (the Office of Electricity Regulation) aims to maintain fair competition in the market, and the price formulae for electricity have been less stringent than those for gas. In spite of competition in the generating market, there have been complaints, particularly from large users, that National Power and Powergen were exercising duopoly powers to control the market.

Faced with possible competition in their own sector of operation, both the generators and most of the RECs have made moves into the other sector. The generators have signed contracts with consumers and the RECs have planned several power stations, usually in joint ventures with other energy companies. These stations are all gas-fired, as current prices make gas an economical fuel. In order to remain competitive in their own field, National Power and Powergen also planned to build gas-fired power stations. Among these is Powergen's new station under construction at Connah's Quay, which will use gas from the Hamilton field off the North Wales coast. Ironically, this gas will be brought ashore close to the last North Wales deep mine at Point of Ayr.

As well as meeting competition in the generation field by building gas-fired power stations, the two generating companies are also diversifying the sources of their other fuel supplies away from an almost total reliance on British Coal.

SECURITY OF SUPPLY AND GRID OPERATION

When nationalized, the CEGB was responsible for ensuring that, within defined limits, supplies never failed, an obligation it met by building sufficient power station capacity to meet high expectations of demand. When privatized, the CEGB's stations (which were not nuclear) were predominantly coal-fired and provided a long-term commitment to British Coal.

The new market has changed the responsibility for security of supply from the generator to the supplier. The RECs have therefore taken over the obligations of the CEGB, and their new gas-fired stations could provide additional capacity to help meet peak demand.

In order to cope with fluctuations in demand, both during the day and in the winter, the CEGB brought power stations into action in order of operating cost, taking account also of a station's location, its fuel source and the needs of the grid. This was known as the merit order, and a similar system, based on bid prices, is operated by the NGC in the new market.

Under the CEGB's regime the nuclear stations were kept in continuous operation and were first in the merit order. They were followed by any hydro stations, imports from Scotland and France, and then by the coal stations. These met the base load, although not all the coal stations would be working to full capacity. Peak demand was met by additional power from the coal stations, bringing them closer to capacity, by some oil-and gas-fired stations that could be switched in quickly and by the pumped storage stations. In the pumped storage system, at periods of low demand water is pumped from a lake up into a storage cavern for release back into the lake at times of peak demand, in order to generate electricity.

The market also changed the acknowledged costs of power generation. The CEGB used the marginal operating costs in putting together its merit order, whereas under the new trading system the generators' revenues from bids and contracts needed to cover their total costs. This change made the nuclear stations more expensive, particularly when allowance was made for the cost of their eventual decommissioning.

The government imposed several conditions that were to give some sources of supply an advantage. The Non-Fossil Fuel Levy (NFFO) was imposed on supplies from fossil fuel stations. It was to be used to raise money both for the decommissioning of the nuclear stations and for research and development in renewable energy. The suppliers are required to take all the electricity generated by the nuclear stations and by 1998 to have contracted for 1500 megawatts from renewable generating capacity. The two privatized generators were also required to agree a contract with

British Coal to provide supplies for the first four years of the market's operation.

The results of operating the new market

Since privatization several developments have taken place. The most controversial has probably been the expected new roles for the different stations, with gas-fired stations dedicated to base load and coal stations to the peak. This proposal has been criticized for ignoring the best use and suitability of each fuel. Gas stations can be brought up to capacity more quickly than coal stations and are therefore more suitable for meeting peak demand. Coal firing by contrast requires longer to reach capacity.

Nuclear Electric has started to close some its older stations, including Trawsfynydd in North Wales. Both National Power and Powergen have closed some of their older coal-fired stations. Several gas-fired stations have been planned with the construction in some cases already completed and with most under way. The new coal contracts with British Coal have reduced demand from over 80 million tonnes per annum to less than 50 million tonnes. The use of electricity from France and Scotland continues, and imports of coal have increased. There has also been some use of orimulsion, a very bituminous form of heavy fuel oil, and there are proposals to burn it at the oil-fired station at Pembroke. Several renewable energy schemes, including wind farms and hydroelectricity projects, have been constructed and others are planned in Wales, although the appearance of windmills on hilltops in Mid-Wales and the prospect of flooded valleys has not met with universal approval.

CONSEQUENCES

The new market is different but not totally free. The intervention of the government has left the coal industry reduced in size and importance and its future plans in chaos, although British deep mines are considered to be among the most efficient and productive in the world. Although the NFFL is being used to subsidize renewable sources for power generation including wind farms, hydroelectricity, waste combustion and digestion and landfill schemes, it is mainly used to subsidize the cost of electricity from the nuclear power stations.

Although Britain could have reserves of as low as 20 years of oil and 30 of gas, compared with over two hundred years' reserves of coal, British deep mines are being prematurely closed down and indigenous coal is being replaced by imported coal and other primary fuels and electricity from France. The UK's increasing dependence on imports, particularly of coal and gas, will make the energy market, and in consequence the economy as a whole, vulnerable to external forces over which government and industry have little or no control. In particular, prices of internationally traded fuels, such as oil, coal and gas, bear little relation to the cost of production and far more to economic and political decisions. More vigorous growth in the world economy would probably allow the producers to make substantial increases in oil prices, which, since gas prices are tied to oil prices, could make the proposed gas-fired stations relatively expensive. By then, however, much of Britain's coal, which would have been economic to produce, would be flooded in the abandoned seams of prematurely closed mines.

In the pursuit of operational choice in the short term and by reliance on spurious market forces, British energy production capacity is drifting from robust strength to strategic vulnerability.

The new energy market

THE WORLD ENERGY MARKET

In world energy markets, OPEC is currently weak and has been unable to maintain its target price of US$21 per barrel. Recently, real oil prices have been lower than at any time in the past 20 years, with Brent crude at US$13 a barrel in December 1993. Furthermore, oil is proving more difficult to find outside the Middle East, although the recovery in the world economy should generate more exploration and production activity, as well as firmer prices.

However, known gas resources are increasing and there are still major reserves waiting to be fully exploited. Some commentators and experts believe that gas might replace oil as the international marker for energy prices in the next decade.

There is also a well established market and extensive trading in coal, which is widely used in the rapidly developing countries of the Far East.

THE ENERGY MARKET IN THE EU

The EU Commission is trying to develop an energy policy that supports the use of indigenous fuels and resources, supplemented by imported oil and gas, the latter coming mainly from the former USSR and North Africa. Extensive pipelines are already in existence to bring these supplies to the EU customer, and the Commission has an aim to move towards a single market in energy on the basis of publicized pricing and a clear distinction between common carriage facilities and suppliers. The UK is probably further down this road than most, but there is opposition from the large national utilities on the European mainland.

CHANGES IN THE ENERGY MARKET

UK oil production is expected to decrease by the end of the century, in spite of its current recovery. From its peak of 127.6 million tonnes in 1985, production in 1991 was 91.3 million tonnes. It is expected to exceed 120 million tonnes in 1995 and to decrease thereafter. However, gas production has increased from 37.1 million tonnes oil equivalent (MTOE) to 47.5 MTOE in the same period and is expected to continue to increase into the next century. Competition has been introduced in the gas market and is to be increased. The demand for transparency in pricing will lead to the inclusion of variable transmission costs in British Gas's transportation prices to gas suppliers, making gas in places such as South Wales, which are relatively far from the North Sea, more expensive, unless the regulatory framework can prevent it. Such changes to gas prices in Wales could encourage local exploration.

The electricity market has been transformed by new priorities, new technologies, new roles and new entrants, although many new entrants are old competitors, particularly oil, gas and electricity companies, wearing new hats.

ENERGY STRATEGY

At the time of writing, a free market approach governs what passes for current government energy policy and there is no long-term energy strategy. Competition is proclaimed and where there are currently no competitors in a particular sector, regulation, as a precursor to the eventual dissolution of monopolies, is intended to provide surrogate competition. However, competition is broadly confined to the choice of fuel and to

189

rivalry within each fuel sector. As a result of this concentration upon the product as opposed to its use, each company's interest lies in maximizing demand for its fuel. Moreover, with few integrated businesses in the market, it is difficult for companies to offset the cost of encouraging conservation against lower investment in new power generation or fuel storage capacity, a technique known as least-cost planning. It is possible, however, that the role of the regulators could be expanded to include the promotion of energy conservation.

The new markets do not encourage the development of businesses, which would seek a more comprehensive approach: to satisfy customers' needs for economical and effective processes or for comfort and support in the home, work-place or leisure activity by a combination of advanced fuel technology, energy management and energy-saving measures. Such an approach would not only reduce energy consumption but would also encourage the development of new industries to support conservation and energy management with higher added value products; with its traditions and resources, Wales could be a natural home for such developments. The fragmentation of energy suppliers within each fuel sector, however, helps to perpetuate the traditional suppliers' markets, where competition is concentrated on the commodity price of the basic fuel. With a choice between a high added value energy services market and several low added value commodity markets, the British government seems to have chosen the latter.

WALES IN THE NEW MARKET

Wales has a changed position in the new energy market. Coal production is now only a small part of regional GDP. There are two oil refineries at Milford Haven and one at Llandarcy, but the oil terminal at Amlwch has closed. Today Wales is far from most of the UK's sources of oil and gas in the North Sea fields, although further discoveries in the Irish and Celtic Seas would change the situation.

There are, however, opportunities for the further development of several renewable sources for power generation, and the Welsh, as fuel consumers with a large industrial base, are in a position to benefit from better energy management and conservation.

Challenges facing the energy market

THE ECONOMY

The recent recession reduced overall demand and kept energy prices depressed. Low prices benefit the consumer, but they are also likely to inhibit exploration and investment by energy companies and to discourage conservation by reducing the cost of wasting fuel.

The structural weakness of the UK economy adds to the difficulties of the market. The present recovery appears uneven and its sustainability is likely to be vulnerable on two fronts. On the one hand, where the recovery is consumer led, there is likely to be strong demand for imports, leading to an unacceptable trade deficit and thus to deflationary measures to reduce it. On the other hand, where the recovery is in exports, the UK is likely, even if it manages to invest quickly, to lack the necessary capacity and skills in the workforce, which will in turn either choke the recovery or lead to excessive wage inflation as companies bid for skilled workers.

The economics of the energy market will also be affected by its recent and still current structural changes, including increasing dominance by overseas companies, the rapid depletion, abandonment and closure of indigenous resources and the influence, which short-term profitability exercises over long-term strategy, security of supply and price stability.

THE ENVIRONMENT

The care of the environment and the maintenance of natural amenities represent probably the largest current challenge to the energy businesses and their customers. Global warming may still be the subject of debate, but the issue has led to increasing public awareness of the environmental effects of carbon dioxide, other greenhouse gasses and of the sources and effects of air pollution.

Other forms of pollution, to which there is growing opposition, include acid rain, which is damaging woodlands in Wales and elsewhere, and both ground and water pollution. In Wales there are many contaminated sites, the rivers in many areas are often dangerously contaminated and the seas polluted.

Because many of the causes of pollution have their roots in energy production and consumption and because the use of fuels affects the environment, the energy market may well have to adapt to a situation where there will be a demand for growth in the market to be subordinated to the wider

191

public interest. Increasing regulation may be expected, of not only competition, prices and customer service standards, but also business strategies and environmental objectives, albeit at a currently undetermined rate, to be regarded as the normal method of ensuring both economical energy use and the promotion of a cleaner environment.

The EU Commission has already proposed the introduction of energy taxation, both on consumption as a whole and more specifically on carbon emissions. Recent EU anti-pollution legislation and directives have also reinforced the principle that the polluter should pay. In the UK the growth of lead-free petrol sales, largely through the use of lower taxes, has illustrated the acceptance by the public of the use of taxation to achieve particular objectives. On the other hand, there is considerable opposition to the imposition of VAT on all gas and electricity bills, for the purpose of increasing government revenue and with no specific purpose or benefit, especially as the tax does not differentiate between the environmental effects of particular fuels.

Taxation and regulation can be expected not to be purely arbitrary, but to form part of EU governments' comprehensive energy and environmental policies as these evolve. The speed with which such policies are developed and implemented will depend upon the style and propensities of national and regional governments, the strength of public opinion and the competitive advantage to be derived from green policies.

Scenarios for the energy market

POSSIBLE DEVELOPMENTS

In an endeavour to assess the range of possible responses to these challenges, two short scenarios follow. They describe the economic and political situation in some 12–15 years time, if either *laissez-faire* economics or environmentalist ideas and beliefs were to hold absolute sway in Wales and the UK, with at least tacit support in the EC and the rest of the world. These scenarios are not forecasts and they may appear far fetched, but they are an attempt to set discussion of the future in a broad range of possibilities. Each scenario is written with a retrospective view from about 2010.

THE *LAISSEZ-FAIRE* SCENARIO

In this scenario the free market is allowed to dominate not only economics but also the domestic, social and leisure activities of the people.

The Conservatives won the general elections of 1997, 2002 and 2007, thanks to some luck with the economic cycle and to regular leadership changes, which have enabled the party to present itself to the electorate as a change from the past. Prime Minister Mark Thatcher is able to count on a divided and demoralized opposition at home, while his 36 fellow heads of government in the EU generally support the concept of a free trade area rather than political union.

In the rest of the world, China is emerging as a second superpower, and nuclear re-armament is an issue in the USA. Poverty, famine and civil war continue to embroil Third and Fourth World countries, which have become more than ever dependent upon the rich nations. Meanwhile, in the OECD countries, major cities are collapsing and some are beginning to reproduce the chaos of large urban conurbations in the Third World.

The UK is dominated by *laissez-faire* ideology, which has been applied in the social sphere as well as in business. There are few government ministries left and no publicly owned industries or services. The EU Commission is primarily active in supporting the Single Market and in the promotion and control of fair competition. The world economy is dominated by the East Asian countries and by protection, bilateral agreements and the re-emergence of a modern form of mercantilism, involving the exploitation of poor and dependent countries by the rich.

The social costs of *laissez-faire* policies have been marked and the divide between rich and poor has widened. Wales has few areas of prosperity and some impoverished towns and deserted settlements; its population is now possibly as low as 2.5 million.

Those technologies that have been developed successfully have been those that needed little infrastructure and which could be brought quickly to a mass market.

The preservation of the natural environment has been subordinated to the creation of a completely free market. The government has negotiated delays in its international commitments to environmental improvements or has secured exemption from them. The results have been increasing pollution and, where political opposition has been ineffective, the growth of countermeasures by activist groups.

Transport policy has continued to favour cars and lorries/trucks, and more roads have been built, mostly private toll motorways, including two

193

that compete with the former Ministry of Transport A55 and M4 in North and South Wales. Railways are now confined to profitable business lines and some busy commuter routes. There has however been an increase in air travel following EU deregulation, with cheaper fares and more internal and international air routes.

Telecommunications developments have been successful in those markets that offer a quick return. The growth of optical fibre networks has been uneven and Wales still has relatively few homes connected to them. The lack of common standards has inhibited the rapid growth of the technology world wide.

In the world of work, nearly all employment is now on short-term contracts with little job security. All pensions are now provided by pension firms, following the enforced demise of the State and occupational schemes. The pension companies ran a successful campaign to deal with the problem of providing for the post-war bulge babies with a proposal to raise the official retirement age to 75.

Wales has lost much of its high technology industry, and its assembly and packing plants are now threatened by automation and by the spread of factories with no people.

In the home the number of labour-saving but energy-consuming gadgets has increased, as has the number and sophistication of security devices.

Leisure and entertainment are dominated by low-quality, mass-produced activities and productions and there has been a decline in the public provision of the traditional arts.

In the energy market the country's indigenous resources have been rapidly depleted and both UKCS oil and gas are expected to be exhausted before 2020 and 2025 respectively. There has also been rapid exploitation of energy reserves throughout the world and many analysts believe that the end of the oil industry is in sight. Gas has become more expensive, with particular problems arising during Russia's civil war and its long dispute with the Ukraine. The UK energy market is now almost wholly dependent on imported fuel.

Energy policies, in so far as there are any, aim to secure the success and survival of the members of the international cartel of major energy suppliers and take little account of public need or private choice. The world market is dominated by these half-dozen energy companies, which control most of the world's energy resources and broadly determine global energy strategy.

In practice there has been a withdrawal from unprofitable areas by the successors to the energy utility companies. In South Wales, the Global

Energy Corporation of Shanghai and Osaka plan to purchase the gas transmission main that brings gas from England, in order to fire a power station at Llandarcy. They are then expected to cut off gas supplies to the area and substitute their own electricity. In homes, work and leisure activities, wasteful habits continue to increase.

The environmental position, however, has deteriorated to such an extent that it is widely considered that the damage caused to the planet will soon be acknowledged by world leaders and their advisers as unsustainable and that action will be needed, in order to alleviate the situation. A debate has begun between the relative merits of imposing severe restrictions, including rationing, or heavy taxation, or a combination of both.

THE GREEN SCENARIO

In the green scenario the long-term aim of political and economic policy is the achievement of sustainable growth to meet the needs of all the world's people and to ensure the survival of the planet.

Throughout the world, politics is increasingly dominated by radical movements, which have grown during the past 20 years out of opposition to the reactionary policies of the monetarist school, which had been in the ascendant in the late 1970s and 1980s but had declined in the 1990s. Key features of their approach are the control and regulation of markets in the public interest, care for the environment and appropriate local autonomy. Environmental and energy policies tend to be formulated and implemented at each level to achieve a common goal.

Economic policies throughout the world are aimed at sustainable development. These policies include investment in appropriate and often labour-intensive projects in developing countries in order to nurture the indigenous growth of their economies, trading systems, which allow the poorer countries to participate as partners in world trade and the rich countries to promote (by deficit financing) growth in trade and economic activity. Investment in renewable energy sources is encouraged in both rich and poor countries, and while reforestation and land reclamation are strongly supported.

Social trends in the developed world are moving towards a strengthening of communities with some countries learning from more traditional societies. The move towards greater community awareness has been strengthened by the need to reduce travel to work and to encourage home and village working. The use of local renewable sources to supply some of the demand for energy has been encouraged, and schemes have been

195

implemented to generate electricity, using water, wind and waste, both agricultural and urban.

Technologies that enable more sustainable development policies to be pursued have been successful, particularly in the areas of communications, pollution control, insulation and energy management.

Living and working in harmony with the natural world has been the aim of environmental policies. Emissions of pollutants are either banned or strictly controlled, both through regulation and taxation. Transport has been greatly affected by the changes of the past decade. Preference has been given to public transport wherever possible and the use of high-consumption cars and lorries has reduced. Air and sea transport are popular for pleasure and for freight. In the area of business travel, however, improvements in telecommunications and the decline of the office have reduced the need to travel. As well as containing the demand for conventional fuels, considerable research has been carried out into alternative energy sources, leading to several new ventures, including the introduction and development of road vehicles with low or zero emissions and the general use of fuel cells.

Telecommunication provides the means to reduce travel for work and shopping, not only for goods but also for professional services. The EU trunk fibre optic network, paid for largely from Community funds, provides both visual and aural access for all homes and other premises, to colleagues, business associates, family and friends, to sources of information and knowledge, and to the suppliers of goods and services. The network also brings political discussion and decision-making, entertainment and participatory leisure activities to the home.

The world of work has been transformed. Offices have disappeared in many occupations, and factories have to meet stringent environmental and health and safety standards. The tax and benefits system has been overhauled to provide both security through a citizen's income and incentives to employers to invest in both new technologies and people.

Homes are more energy efficient and are used both for living and working by many people. New vernacular styles are developing and in Wales these seek to take advantage of the relatively mild climate while providing shelter from the rain.

Leisure activities are varied and they take place both inside the home and in public centres. Wales is popular for outdoor activities and educational courses. Live performances by local and touring companies and groups are also popular.

The control of the use of energy has helped to maintain the stability of the climate and to produce a cleaner environment. Indigenous resources are exploited carefully and clean technology has been introduced where appropriate.

Energy policy is set out by the EU's elected parliament in compliance with or ahead of international agreements and it has been heavily influenced by the Scandinavians. The Welsh Sennedd (the regional parliament) has developed comprehensive energy and environmental policies, set its own targets for achieving environmental standards, and encourages both conservation measures and local energy schemes. In practice, energy consumption has been stabilized in Wales and renewable resources have been sensitively developed. Least-cost planning and similar techniques have been used to reduce energy demand.

In the long term the people of Wales can look forward to a future of sustainable development based upon the careful management of the environment and on the increasing use of renewable energy sources.

PROBABLE DEVELOPMENTS

These two scenarios represent possible extremes of particular approaches to energy use. The future will more probably develop somewhere in between. The EU Commission is keen to take initiatives in the area of energy and the environment, although there are current objections to the its proposed carbon and energy taxes. It is probable, however, that the accession of new member States, with strong environmentalist traditions, will encourage a greener approach in the EU and will strengthen moves to make polluters pay. The widespread belief that current energy use is not sustainable will also probably increase pressure for energy prices to reflect environmental costs.

The UK government, moreover, has agreed to strive to meet several targets in reducing emissions, cleaning the environment and in moving to more use of sustainable energy sources. There are currently heavier duties on unleaded petrol in the UK, an imposition that has been well received and a new tax on landfill activities. However, the proposal to tax gas and electricity has met fierce opposition. Its credentials as a green tax were attacked both by environmentalists, because it did not differentiate between energy sources, and by campaigners for the poor, on the grounds that it bore particularly hard on the most vulnerable.

Some further regulation of the energy market is bound to occur sooner rather than later, unless all the predictions on energy use, pollution and climate change are wrong. Similarly, we can expect a gradual move

197

towards green responses, including better energy management, modest support for conservation measures and a preference for sustainable energy sources. It is also probable that the move towards greater regional autonomy in Wales will enable it to take more independent initiatives. The election of a government with a greater commitment to the environment and to regional autonomy would accelerate these trends.

Issues for Wales

THE WELSH ECONOMY

Wales has weathered the recent recession, but not without casualties. Its manufacturing base, which is relatively larger than that of the UK as a whole, has stood the Principality in good stead. However, the Welsh economy has a tradition of dependence on external capital, and manufacturing in Wales has sustained its importance with the assistance of considerable inward investment. Maintaining the current level and increasing the development of high added value industries will require an increasing level of skills. The growth of indigenous businesses in Wales needs encouragement, in order that the economy may be sufficiently robust to withstand any departures by companies, possibly looking elsewhere for lower costs and faster access to European markets. Without the complementary and independent growth of local businesses, as well as the continued development of a skilled workforce and access to capital on reasonable terms, inward investment could be less of a solution and more of a problem in waiting.

SAFEGUARDING THE ENVIRONMENT

Wales has some environmental problems stemming both from its industrial past and from its present-day activities, which include important primary and secondary industries, well developed pastoral farming and forestry, and a wide range of services. Wales has the capacity to be a serious polluter of its own and neighbouring natural environments.

Its factories, offices, amenities, homes, vehicles, and even its cattle, are sources of greenhouse gases and the growth of the economy will increase these emissions, unless steps are taken to control them.

Wales has many types of ground, air and water pollution, both from

198

former industrial sites, including coal mines and iron works and from modern industries, farming and domestic waste. The growing body of environmental legislation, and the increasing acceptance of the principle that the polluter pays, need to be assimilated and acted upon by public authorities, businesses and households.

Action will also be needed to maintain, rehabilitate and improve the natural amenities of Wales, both directly and by reducing energy consumption or at least its growth.

ENERGY USE

It is being more widely recognized by those with responsibility for energy strategies and by commentators that conservation, far from being a brake on economic development, in fact offers opportunities for the development of new industries and activities. These often have the capability of producing higher added value products. However, the current market encourages energy suppliers to seek increasing growth in the sales of their fuels. Although the gas and electricity utilities have promoted and rewarded energy saving and the economical use of fuel by their larger customers, their future prosperity depends upon increasing fuel consumption in their sectors of the market, albeit against a background in Wales of lower than average incomes and higher than average temperatures.

The quality of housing and of other buildings in Wales is widely considered to be inefficient in conserving energy. There is, however, little incentive in current targeted grant schemes to promote the widespread adoption of energy-saving measures.

There is a great deal of lip-service paid to the need for sound environmental policies, but a shortage of practical and affordable means to implement them. The links between fuel consumption, energy use and the environment are recognized, but there is little evidence of overall co-ordination and partnership or of the kind of structural change that would be needed to produce comprehensive action. However, Wales does have examples of initiatives in the fields of renewable energy, conservation and recycling, which could provide a pattern for the development of a clear strategic direction for energy and the environment.

ENERGY PRODUCTION

The decline of the deep-mined coal industry in Wales has been a long and painful process, which has brought upheaval to many traditional communities. The closure of exhausted or uneconomic pits has been a feature of the Welsh coalfields for some years, but the present situation is aggravated by earlier plans for a continuing role for coal, based on investment and productivity and on the positive response of the miners to that challenge. The most recent closures have also lacked credibility, as they are based on a very short-term and probably unrealistic assessment of the relative costs of coal and gas stations.

Although nearly all its deep mines have disappeared, Wales still has the opportunity to develop other sources of energy. These include open-cast coal mining, the production of oil and gas in the Celtic Sea, new power station capacity, using fossil fuels, hydroelectricity, wind, tidal and wave power, waste processing and even nuclear energy. Nearly all of these sources, however, can create economic or environmental problems, even when they have environmental advantages.

Open-cast mining, which is effectively quarrying coal, defaces the landscape, puts strains on the local infrastructure and generates less employment than does deep mining; it is also unpopular with grass-roots movements in its neighbouring communities.

Oil and gas production is also not universally supported. Although there has been little environmental opposition to the Hamilton gasfield off the coast of North Wales, proposals for oil and gas prospecting in Cardigan Bay have raised some objections from those concerned with the marine life and ecology of the area.

The burning of any fossil fuel in power stations generates greenhouse gases, and the use of coal, oil, and especially orimulsion, produces polluting gases, particularly sulphur oxides, which contribute to acid rain. As Wales lies to windward of the rest of Great Britain and northern Europe, the fitting of flue-gas desulphurization equipment is a minimum necessity. Combined heat and power schemes for small communities, using fossil fuels, would run into similar problems on a smaller scale.

The renewable resources are also not without their opponents. Although small-scale hydroelectric projects for local supplies are generally unobtrusive and clean, the drowning of valleys for large-scale schemes is, at the very least, controversial. Wind power, which is being exploited in Wales and for which the mountainous westerly landscape is well suited, has also aroused opposition from local communities; although it is favoured by some environmentalists and green campaigners, others object to the visual impact of windmills on the mountain tops in remote and beautiful locations, and to the noise, where they are close to human settlements. There are some six proposals for tidal power generation in

Wales, including the Severn and Dee barrages. Although these schemes produce electricity cleanly, they are expected to cause damage to the ecological balance of the waters and wetlands around them; they are also expensive to build and they require long pay-back periods to achieve economic returns. Wave power is currently the least significant of the renewable sources in Wales; it has received very little support in government research funding or from the CEGB, and Welsh waters are, at any rate, well suited to tidal power.

The use of waste to generate electricity has environmental advantages in its disposal of unwanted products, although the consequent production and burning of gas does raise environmental issues. Objections are less likely to be made to anaerobic digestion and landfill gas reclamation schemes than to waste incineration, which could be seen as a more serious source of pollution.

A new nuclear power station, which is currently an unlikely event in Wales, would be met with hostile reactions, not only in the immediate vicinity of the station but throughout the country. Opposition to the proposed extension to Hinkley power station on the Somerset coast in the late 1980s was as strong on the Welsh side of the Severn as it was in the West Country, and it drew protests from all over the UK.

THE ENERGY MARKET

The privatized utilities, now with freedom to operate in any markets of their choosing and with access to investment capital, ought to be able to play an important part in revitalizing the Welsh economy. However, their ability to do so is limited by several constraints. The new investments by the electricity companies are mainly in gas-fired generating plant, which, with the exception of the stations at Deeside and Connah's Quay, and one in Cumbria, are sited close to the gasfields in the North Sea. The markets for electricity supply by the two RECs in Wales are saturated and new investment can only follow the development of residential, commercial and industrial property. The RECs are also likely to be wary of diversification outside their core businesses, following the experience of failed investments by several privatized utilities. Gas companies have similar problems of saturation and have avoided non-core diversification, although their prices are more stringently controlled by the regulator than are those of the RECs.

It is not easy to generalize about the effect of competition, particularly on the growth of the regional economy. Gas prices have reduced in real terms, in both the competitive and the regulated sectors, but how far this is attributable to competition and how far to tight regulation, the requirement on British Gas to publish its contract prices and the depression of oil and gas prices since 1988 is difficult to assess. In electricity, with its more relaxed price controls and a duopoly in power generation, competition seems to have done little to reduce prices. Competition in the retail appliance and service markets has changed little, but the separation of different businesses since privatization has eliminated most if not all cross-subsidies from the core business and has tended to reduce the number of retail outlets and to increase the price of service calls. In these two sectors there ought to be opportunities in Wales for some new businesses to replace or compete with the utilities and their successor companies.

Finally, all the privatized utilities operate within the constraints of the UK's financial system, with its emphasis on short-term profitability, quick returns, a steady stream of dividend increases, ever-increasing share prices, and on giving absolute priority to shareholders rather than to all the stakeholders in the enterprise. These constraints are likely to force them to make cuts in the only two areas open to them – employment and investment in the infrastructure – two areas that could benefit the Welsh economy.

MEETING CUSTOMERS' REAL NEEDS

The retail energy market has been dominated by the suppliers of fuel and has been characterized by vigorous competition between coal, oil, gas and electricity. A strong feature of fuel marketing has always been efficiency, and all suppliers, of both fuels and appliances, have sought to improve the performance of their products. The typical tariff customer is left to make a simple choice of fuel and, in the "white goods" and heating sectors, to choose between a limited number of similar functional products within each product range. It can be questioned whether this choice best meets the customer's real needs for comfortable surroundings or effective processes. A different approach has been adopted in selling to major users in the industrial and services sectors, where the design of the total system has been a significant part of the sale. However, it has not been extended to the market as a whole to include package deals combining heating or heating and power (CHP) with insulation or a choice of burners and elements on a cooker. In the present UK appliance market, products have a monotonous similarity that is not found in mainland western Europe, where fuel supplies have traditionally been in the hands of State-owned or government-controlled monopolies, with the retail and installation businesses run by the small firms, which are typical of the private sector on the European mainland. It could be of benefit to the Welsh economy if such a market-place were to be developed in the region, both to try to reconcile desires for comfort, effectiveness, efficiency and conservation, and to provide more opportunities for investment and employment, particularly in higher added value industries. The new structure, however, moves the focus of the market further back from an energy market into separate fuel sectors. This situation, by reinforcing the commodity element of the market, can deflect attention and therefore investment from the downstream higher added value end of the market.

Prospects

THE WAY FORWARD FOR WALES

These problems do militate against the possibility of the energy industry playing a strong role in the revitalizing of the Welsh economy. Nevertheless, there are reasons for optimism.

Wales is a small country with variety in its geography and development, and where towns are in reasonable balance with the rural hinterland. There is an industrial tradition, which includes fuel production and a large reserve of labour with a variety of skills, many of which could be adapted to new industries and activities. Wales has a high proportion of poorly insulated and poorly heated housing in the older industrial areas, and the per capita income is below that of any other region of Great Britain, so there is both the opportunity and the incentive to achieve improvements in energy use and efficiency. It is therefore possible that Wales could prove an ideal region, in which to develop ideas in energy conservation and the use of renewable resources, and to become a centre for the study and practice of sustainable energy use and economic development.

SELF-HELP IN WALES

The energy utilities have a tradition of promoting energy efficiency. The conservation and efficient management of energy are also promoted through planning regulations, architectural practice and improvements in building standards, as well as by housing energy action and energy-saving trusts in the local community.

203

Local authorities, although not able to use receipts from the sale of council houses to build new homes, have been able to carry out many renewal schemes among their older dwellings, which have improved the insulation and comfort of much of their remaining housing stock. They have also been able to build leisure centres and other public buildings, which have used combined heat and power and other modern energy technologies.

Cardiff was made the first Energy Action City in 1985 and was recently designated the UK's second recycling city. The City Council continues to develop the ideas that were launched during the scheme. The Council has set up several recycling depots and collection points throughout the city, extended the use of green bags for residents to collect recyclable household waste, and is constructing an anaerobic digester to provide local energy from the city's rubbish.

Wales is also represented in the renewable energy business. Several schemes are in operation, under construction or planned, involving both Welsh businesses and others. In addition to the companies involved in renewable energy and insulation products, Wales has several university departments with interests in the environment and energy, including the University of Wales, Cardiff. The Centre for Alternative Technology at Corris in Mid-Wales is a combination of a community dedicated to sustainable self-sufficiency, a thriving tourist attraction, an information centre on sustainability, and a source of new enterprises in renewable sources of energy and sustainable development.

The Welsh Development Agency (WDA) has promoted the study of issues in environmental and energy matters, recently commissioning a comprehensive review of energy in Wales: the Welsh Energy Project. The Agency has been also been active in land reclamation, a consequence of the industrial development of Wales, which left many contaminated sites, often associated with the production of primary and secondary fuels.

THE WELSH ENERGY PROJECT

The Welsh Energy Project, which was a major review of energy in Wales, was carried out over a two-year period by the Welsh Development Agency and the Mandix consultancy of Cardiff, with wide consultation throughout and beyond Wales. The project team reported in March 1993 and received widespread support, including the endorsement of its action plan by the Environmental Group of the Prince of Wales' Committee.

Their conclusions for the energy market were that it was necessary to maintain the long-term trend of lowering energy use per unit of GDP, to arrest the decline of energy production as a proportion of GDP, to reduce Welsh emissions of greenhouse gases, and to preserve the amenities and where possible improve the quality of the environment in Wales. They also suggested priorities for action to reconcile economic development and the protection of the rural and urban environment, and proposed initiatives to improve energy and waste management.

The project team examined rural and urban energy management on a broad front. In the countryside they recommended both diversification in the rural economy and the growth of a renewable energy industry, as well as the means to achieve these aims. Their priorities for urban areas were to reduce the need to travel and to decrease services infrastructure costs, to reduce the environmental effects of energy supply and to encourage energy efficiency in buildings. They also made recommendations on the use of statutory local plans, public investment, and the ready availability of information to increase energy efficiency, and on the use of environmental improvement targets in new plans and developments.

The project team also proposed targets, exceeding those for the UK as a whole, for improving energy efficiency and environmental quality in Wales and the means by which these improvements might be achieved. They suggested that energy and environmental research bodies in Wales should increase their share of the market for research contracts. They drew attention to the need both for information to be widely and readily available and for local initiatives and collaborative action.

Having drawn up their conclusions, the project team proposed a five-point action plan, a major regional initiative in a business community not renowned for its green credentials. It is now promoted and monitored on a continuing basis by the WDA.

The first action point was the establishment of seven sustainable economic development areas, one in each of the WDA's regions and one in the area of the Development Board for Rural Wales. In each area, an energy management initiative was proposed, in some cases, building on existing work. Progress has been made on all seven.

The establishment of a network of local information centres was proposed, including two existing centres in Mid-Glamorgan and at the Centre for Alternative Technology in Mid-Wales. As well as the WDA, Cardiff Bay Development Corporation, the Energy Saving Trust and energy suppliers agreed to support this initiative. New centres have since been established in Cardiff, Swansea and Newport.

Several business development initiatives were included in the plan, in the areas of training, research, environmental databases and in specific sectors of the energy market. Some progress has been made, including several sector initiatives covering coal, renewable energy, the property market and an environmental strategy for buildings.

Ways were sought of supporting planning authorities in the preparation, implementation and monitoring of the energy and environmental aspects of local development plans. In particular it was proposed that targets should be used for environmental improvement, that energy-monitoring computer-based systems should be developed and that planning staff should be provided with the necessary training, information and advice.

The last action point was the encouragement of public investment in energy efficiency and thus in the growing world market in environmental protection. This would be achieved through a review and updating of existing plans with waste and energy management targets, and the establishment of an "eco-fund" to support appropriate business loans.

Opportunities for Wales

Although Wales is a part of the UK and is therefore dependent to a great extent on policies agreed in London, there are steps that could be taken to put Wales in the forefront of the development of a sustainable and sensible approach to energy and the environment.

In the first instance the Welsh Office (or a Welsh Sennedd) could adopt the proposal of the Welsh Energy Project and set more demanding targets than those to which the government has agreed, and take steps, including the promotion of appropriate businesses, to meet them. Such businesses could market, use and export the skills, experience and products developed in the process.

The industrial development of Wales is supported by the Welsh Office and its agencies, principally the Welsh Development Agency and the Development Board for Rural Wales. It is therefore possible for Wales to develop and pursue its own industrial policies, which can be designed to meet its economic and environmental priorities.

In encouraging the growth of indigenous businesses and in the pursuit of inward investment, the Welsh Office or Sennedd and its agencies can promote business activities in energy and the environment, which would develop synergy rather than conflict. New controls on environmental pollution and on energy use and emissions would be seen not as constraints on economic development but as opportunities to develop new industries, skills and jobs. Thus, the support and promotion, by development and enterprise agencies, of local initiatives in the integration of energy use, conservation and the maintenance of the environment, could contribute to revitalizing the older and less prosperous areas of Wales.

The pursuit of research projects to improve conservation and efficiency in the use of energy should be expanded, and links between the researchers and industry established, both to develop research as a service to the energy and environmental industries and to ensure the rapid development of new ideas, projects and products.

Above all, Wales needs an energy strategy that will promote a clear vision and direction to organizations, both commercial and non-commercial, towards the sustainable use of energy in a sound and healthy natural environment. Such a strategy, by concentrating on the real needs of customers and society as a whole, could also encourage the growth of higher added value businesses in Wales. Many people in Wales, not least the young, recognize the need and would be ready to respond enthusiastically to a challenging lead.

Sources and acknowledgements

Most of the information quoted in the chapter is taken from the UK government's 1994 *Digest of UK energy statistics* (the "Brown Book"), Wood Mackenzie's May 1994 *European energy report*, the BP *Statistical Review of World Energy,* June 1994 and from the Electricity Act 1989.

I am also indebted to British Gas plc and to the Mandix consultancy in Cardiff for providing assistance and access to information.

CHAPTER 12

Restructuring policies: the Emscher Park International Building Exhibition

Heiderose Kilper & Gerald Wood

Socio-economic character of Emscher[1]

The Emscher subdistrict is not an administrative unit, nor is it in any sense an important historical region. Such regional homogeneity as it displays arises from its origins in the second half of the nineteenth century in a few bursts of development attributable to the South–North movement of the coal industry in the Ruhr district. The Emscher subdistrict forms the "middle layer" of the industrial core of the Ruhr. It is roughly 800 m^2 in area and is inhabited by 2 million people (Figs 12.1, 12.2).

The boundaries are formed by motorways, canals and rivers. The southern boundary is the M40, the northern border the M2. To the west, is the Rhine and to the East the M1. The central axes are the Rhine–Herne canal and the River Emscher, which has not only given the subregion its name but also serves as an open sewer for the entire Ruhr. The primary role of the River Ruhr, on the other hand, is to supply the Ruhr district with fresh water.

Large collieries and iron & steel works dominate the spatial and economic structures of the Emscher subregion, whereas other branches of industry are almost completely absent. This is attributable to the fact that the industrial take-off of the Emscher took place much later than that of the southern part of the Ruhr district (known as the Hellweg subdistrict) and also because, despite the large numbers in population, this subregion does

---

1. We would like to thank Rainer Danielzyk for his helpful advice on sections of this chapter, which were written by G. Wood.

—·— Federal boundaries · · · · State boundaries ▨ Emscher subdistrict

Figure 12.1 The Emscher subdistrict within the Federal Republic of Germany.

not have any (traditional) urban centres. In the International Building Exhibition (IBA) memorandum the area is characterized as "the most densely built-up industrial landscape in Central Europe with the highest levels of environmental pollution and the most intensely carved-up open spaces." (IBA 1989: 10). The old industries not only dominate the appear-

209

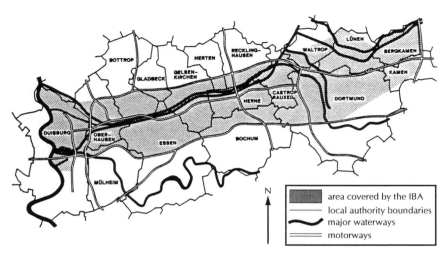

Figure 12.2 The Emscher Park International Building Exhibition (IBA): participating local authorities (*Source:* IBA 1988: 6).

ance of the area and the economy, they also dominate the labour market as well as the sociocultural identity of the Emscher subdistrict – despite a massive decline in the past.

These processes of economic and social restructuring started in the late 1950s when the coal industry was increasingly pressurized by competing fuels and foreign competitors on the one hand and by the progression of the south–north shift in coal-mining on the other. The situation was aggravated by the steel-crisis that began in the 1970s and which led to further cuts in output and colliery manpower (Schlieper 1986). At present, the economic problems of the Emscher subdistrict are far from being resolved. On the contrary, as a result of the forseeable rise in international competition as a consequence of the expanding European economy (particularly to the East), the economic predicament of the Emscher is likely to continue or even to become worse (Ache/Kunzmann 1992).

The present socio-economic situation can be identified as follows:

- Coal still dominates the spatial structures of the Emscher subdistrict (particularly the layout of settlements) but, equally, sociocultural patterns such as the attitudes and qualifications of people, or the frame of mind of local politicians, and so on.
- On the economic side, there are many structural shortcomings, particularly in "high technology" branches and in the professional and scientific services (Ache & Kunzmann 1992).
- There are high rates of unemployment (and long-term).

- High levels of unemployment will most likely be "solved" by demographic trends rather than by economic progress (Ache et al. 1988).
- However, as a result of their socially selective nature, these demographic trends will exacerbate social and economic problems because many young, qualified and economically integrated persons go away, leaving behind the older and socially weaker ones whose proportion will rise as a consequence.
- Economic decline on the one hand and the processes of social erosion on the other constitute a twin grip on the local authorities in the area, because not only does their revenue in local taxes decrease but at the same time they are confronted with having to foot an ever-growing supplementary benefit bill. This is why local authorities have virtually become unable to act, let alone effect any structural economic changes. Therefore, their legally entrenched rights (for which they are sometimes envied by their UK counterparts), may not be such an asset after all.

Structurally induced economic and social decline first surfaced in the late 1950s. There were several measures that both the federal government and the government of North-Rhine–Westphalia introduced to combat the problems (for an overview, see Danielzyk & Wood 1993). Typical of the "coping strategies" of the past was the underlying belief in a "classical" form of modernization and in the ability of the State government to effect structural change by means of a comprehensive and integrated procedure. The International Building Exhibition (IBA), which we are now going to discuss, is one of several policy measures introduced in the 1980s that can all be seen as constituting a clear break with these past arrangements. However, before embarking upon a discussion of the divergences we think it is necessary to briefly outline the essentials of the Building Exhibition.

A theoretical debate of the IBA

THE IBA: AN OUTLINE OF THE ESSENTIALS

The driving force behind the idea of the Building Exhibition was the Ministry of Urban Development, Housing and Transport for the State of North-Rhine–Westphalia, especially the former minister Christoph Zöpel. He was known for his ambitious visions of an academically informed public policy. Also, he and the ministry were particularly engaged in urban renewal programmes for the industrialized towns of the State. Thus, the stimulus for the IBA idea largely resulted from urban development and housing policies rather than from the Department of Spatial Planning, which is part of the Ministry of Environment and Agriculture (MURL) or from the Ministry of economic affairs, which is responsible for structural policies and which was the driving force behind the other decentralization measures in the 1980s.

In May 1988 the State government of North-Rhine–Westphalia resolved to stage the IBA and it called upon towns, companies, architects, citizen's pressure groups, and so on. To make single project proposals. Thus, this step was taken before the Berlin Wall came down and well before unification of the two German States. This point is important, because not only has there been a massive drain of finances towards the East after unification, but also the political weight of the Ruhr and of the Emscher sub-district has been substantially curtailed. In other words, in the light of the grave economic difficulties of almost all of the new German *Länder*, the Ruhr is no longer in the centre of political interest. Therefore, the IBA was given the go-ahead just in time.

Since spring 1989 the Emscher Park Planning Company plc has been in operation. Up to now well over 80 proposals have been chosen as projects, most of which are in the stage of being implemented (around 60).

In essence, the Building Exhibition has two aims (IBA 1989: 7). First, it is meant to challenge the above mentioned complex problems of economic and social decline, as well as the poor ecological situation of the area (IBA 1989: 7). Secondly, the Building Exhibition ambitiously endeavours to give an internationally recognized example of State-led economic, social and ecological restructuring of old industrial areas. To do so, the Building Exhibition "is intended to bring together the international know-how available on this issue" (IBA 1989: 7). This is why the official subtitle of the IBA is "Workshop for the Future of Old Industrial Areas".

Thus, the IBA is more than just an environmental policy. It is a comprehensive strategy intended to meet the challenge of renewing OIAs. What is more, this is to be accomplished "by the comprehensive, long-term co-operation of government, business and professional organizations." (IBA 1989: 6). As Sieverts (1991: 9) points out, the Building Exhibition is "a strategy intended to bring together structural policies of the *Land* government and the manifold local initiatives".

When setting up the IBA the aim of the *Land* government was to decentralize State policies on the one hand and to retain the power to determine the guidelines within which the IBA and its projects are expected to operate on the other (Danielzyk 1992a). To make sure this set-up works, IBA projects are given funding priority within the mainstream State programmes so that the different actors are stimulated to co-operate and also to accept the State's role of controlling the restructuring processes and, in particular, of securing that certain ecological, social and other standards are met. Because of the integration of IBA projects into the mainstream State programmes, the Building Exhibition proves to be astonishingly crisis-proof – despite the dire financial situation of the State in the wake of unification.

By 1994, around 83 projects were either planned or implemented, and roughly DM1.4 billion (£461 million) of public money had been levered into the area.

The organizational set-up and the contents of the Building Exhibition suggests that we are dealing with a policy approach that can be labelled "renewal from within". Essentially, this means that restructuring processes are not primarily to be effected from the outside but rather by tapping the (creative) potential on the spot.

In order to understand why the government chose to set up the Building Exhibition, which can be characterized as a policy approach that "backs the strong players"[1], we would now like to turn to what we believe are the reasons for staging the IBA.

THE IBA – AN EXERCISE IN DECENTRALIZING STATE POLICIES:
THE MOTIVES

The functionalist argument   The functionalist argument behind decentralizing strategies of the *Land* government, of which the Building Exhibition forms an integral part, comprises two elements. First, there is the opinion that economic–ecological structural change necessitates new organizational economic structures. According to this view, structural economic change leads to an increased international integration on the one hand and to the necessity of building up decentralized regulatory structures on the other, the latter preferably being realized on a regional level (Danielzyk 1992b). At present, there are, of course, regulatory structures in operation below the State level. It is neither the intention of the State government, nor would it have the political clout to abolish them. Rather, the aim is to effect political and cultural innovations in order to change existing politi-

---

1.Cf. Heinze & Voelzkow (1991) who have labelled the government's decentralization of structural economic policies "stage-managed corporatism".

cal and cultural structures that are seen to be part of the present problem. However, this constitutes one of the paradoxes that the new approach entails: change is to be and needs to be effected by the same people whose attitudes and ways of handling or ignoring structural change is to be blamed for the current situation. We will come back to this issue later.

The second functionalist motive for decentralization is the fact that in the 1980s the State government realized that, as a result of the global economic restructuring processes, the scope of action of any government continuously decreases. As one high-ranking civil-servant of the day put it:

> In view of the growing economic and political interdependencies the scope of action of a national economic policy and an autonomous State policy is declining. The thrust of State policy must therefore lie in helping to adapt to the changed global economic frame of reference on the one hand and in fully utilizing the remaining scope of action with a view to safeguard a socially and environmentally tolerable process of adjustment on the other. (Schlieper 1989: 160; our translation)

Therefore, the government refrained from imposing centralized and standardized forms of intervention in the process of (economic) restructuring. Instead, it embarked upon a policy of involving the "creative potential" close to the existing problems in search for solutions.

The argument of political legitimacy   The argument of political legitimacy also consists of two elements. First, by regionalizing State policies, the government wants to show that it tries to handle structural change by means of new, unconventional and promising approaches. It is hoped that, if successful, these new ways of coping with change will help to legitimize the (continued) existence of the State and, of course, of the government. One could, however, also argue that these policies do not necessarily have to be "successful" in a limited sense of the word in order to boost the esteem of the government. The very act of decentralizing State policies is a way of showing that the State is indeed taking the initiative and not only reacting to change, and therefore not to be reproached with idleness. Secondly, the fact that the government emphasizes the responsibility of the regions without considering the transfer of administrative powers or financial resources can be seen as a case of discharging political responsibility to the regions, particularly if things go wrong. Therefore, although the government holds sway over development processes, it cannot be made directly responsible.

The IBA contrasted with British and American strategies of handling the renewal of OIAs   The Building Exhibition was devised against the background of the developments taking place in other countries in areas with problems similar to the ones of the Emscher subdistrict. Particularly important for the formulation of the aims of the IBA are the British and the American models of coping with structural change in OIAs. The following considerations are meant to highlight the differences in approach between the IBA on the one hand and the British and American political strategies on the other, as they are pointed out by the IBA (cf. IBA 1991: 23). The discussion centres on a critical appraisal of the British Urban Development Corporations and the various (other) public–private partnerships that exist in both countries.

To begin with, UDCs are regarded as bypassing initiatives because they generally do not benefit the local population, and because they also take planning powers away from democratically elected bodies. What is more, they represent a centrally prescribed formula for regeneration that negates the uniqueness of place and which denies the regions a renewal from within, or even a self-determined path of development.

The overriding economic aim of this "central State localism" is to attract footloose, preferably international, capital. This strategy necessitates the breaking up of the traditional modes of regulation, and, in particular, the redefinition of the role of the trade unions.

By contrast, the private sector is given a much greater say. The reason for doing so lies in the simplistic assumption that regional problems would not exist or be less severe had the private sector only been given more political clout in the past. However, economic problems are the result of the investment and disinvestment decisions of the private sector, which is now being heralded to be the saviour of the problem-ridden areas.

But even if the private sector were the solution to the problems besetting OIAs, could this be a reason good enough to authorize the shift of decision-making processes away from the public arena to exclusive roundtables and the concurrent exclusion of many other interests in a democratic society?

Another central point of criticism levelled against the British and the American ways of coping with decline in OIAs is the objection that a strategy that aims at the long-term economic, social and cultural renewal of a region in crisis cannot do with authorities who claim they know all the solutions. Because of the complex and the comprehensive nature of structural change, there is no single group learned enough to be able to implant a process of regeneration. What is more, such a top-down approach dis-

215

misses a process of social mobilization that, according to the IBA, is a prerequisite for new developments. This process is an open one of experimenting and learning, and it is also a process that needs to include all economic and social actors of a region. It is a key feature of the Building Exhibition.

The IBA as a plc wishes to set processes of economic, social, ecological and cultural renewal in motion, but at the same time it refrains from putting them into effect itself. It uses the expertise of its staff to check whether project proposals are likely to renew or to maintain old and obsolete structures. The decision of choosing project proposals is then taken by a guiding committee. The chairman of this committee is the Minister of Urban Development; members represent other ministries, public bodies (chambers of commerce, etc.), the trade-unions, towns, companies, federations of architects, environmental protection associations, and so on. Thus, there is a wide social spectrum involved when crucial decisions have to be made.

Emscher Park planning and regulation model

We would now like to develop further two of the points made earlier on. To recapitulate:
- Since social restructuring is a highly complex process, there can be no individual elitist actors or groups of actors who would be able to determine and to realize the aims, ways and instruments of regional revitalization. What's called for is quite the opposite: an open process of experimenting and learning that embraces all political, economic and social actors of the region.
- This leads to a paradox situation in which the process of regional restructuring has to be both shaped and carried out by – or at least together with – those institutions and actors whose attitudes, habits and views of life, whose patterns of thought and behaviour, have shaped the existing political and social structures of the region and who have caused the recent situation with all its interlinkages, ossified structures, crises and stagnations in the first place.

In our view, two observations are important in characterizing the political and social situation of the Ruhr Area in general and of the Emscher subregion in particular:
- The Ruhr Area's mining industry has created specific patriarchal

216

forms of both housing and social policies during the 150 years of its history. Likewise, since the Second World War, codetermination in the coal, iron and steel industry has led to special business policies and special industrial relations.

- Since the war, town halls have been ruled by the same political party, which in local elections usually obtains absolute majority by capturing between 52 and 65 per cent of the votes.

It is a polemic simplification, but it contains at least a grain of truth when our colleague Schmals at Dortmund University describes the political and social conditions of the Ruhr Area and the Emscher subregion as "a ruling coalition of mining capital, trade unions, local Social Democrats and local bureaucracies". This leads us to the questions at the heart of this section:

- How can one set in motion a "colossus" like the Emscher region with all its inert and ossified political structures in such a way that it in itself will become the innovative "workshop for the future of old industrial regions", as the subtitle of the IBA memorandum has it?
- Which methods and instruments are necessary to bring about the vision – also in the IBA memorandum – "to re-erect landscape along the River Emscher between Duisburg and Dortmund in an especially densely populated and highly polluted industrial landscape and to create new urban qualities in order to open up new opportunities for work, culture and housing"?

The remainder of this section is subdivided into three parts.

First, we will point out what in our view distinguishes the Emscher Park IBA as an innovative approach to regional development and structural policies in Germany. Secondly, we will outline the guiding principles and functional mechanisms of the IBA model of planning and regulation. And, finally, we will specify what we regard to be the essential prerequisites for the policy model Emscher Park IBA to work.

THE IBA AS AN INNOVATIVE APPROACH TO REGIONAL DEVELOPMENT AND STRUCTURAL POLICIES IN THE FEDERAL REPUBLIC OF GERMANY.

For four reasons the Emscher Park International Building Exhibition is remarkable as an experiment in restructuring and modernizing an old industrial region:

- With its programme and its projects – which currently number 83 – it points out that, in mining areas mining as well as the coal, iron and steel industries have created a material heritage that has to be rehabilitated and repaired, which, although it needs to be pulled down in parts, must at the same time be kept up and maintained. This is the case for areas of natural landscape, as well as for residential areas and municipal districts, for partially listed industrial monuments and for the huge industrial wastelands.

Thus, for the Emscher Park IBA, the structural policy of the region is not just to locate new businesses, to designate new industrial sites or to improve the transport infrastructure. On the contrary, it defines regional structural policy as an integrative comprehensive concept transcending policy areas.

- The Emscher Park IBA isn't dead set on external large-scale investors for prestigious mega-projects in the communities. Rather, its "philosophy" maintains that the region's renewal should be developed and carried out by the region itself. At the same time it is to mobilize existing potentials, institutions and actors for new orientations and contents, for new methods and ways of co-operation, and for the creation of new interlinkages and network structures. Danielzyk (1992a) has remarked very aptly that the Emscher Park IBA "experiments very carefully with a new political model without attempting a radical break with the past".

- Although the Emscher Park IBA was initiated by the North-Rhine–Westphalian *Land* government, it is not a traditional government-sponsored development programme allocating certain sums over fixed periods. The main regulatory instruments of the programme are the social, ecological and architectural standards, as well as the quality standards of town planning and design the projects have to meet if they want to qualify for inclusion in the IBA. Those projects complying with the quality standards receive priority support from the North-Rhine–Westphalian government. However, this support remains within the limits of the various development programmes already existing on the levels of the EC, the Bund and the Länder.

- With the start of the Emscher Park IBA, the North-Rhine–Westphalian government shows that it has learned its lesson in structural policy. This lesson is that the restructuring of an old industrial area is a long-term process and not a matter of just a few years. Accordingly, in contrast to other development programmes for the Ruhr Area, the Emscher Park IBA has a duration of ten years, from 1989 to 1999.

THE EMSCHER PARK PLANNING AND REGULATION MODEL

First component: guideline projects   The Emscher Park IBA gives a thematic definition of its project activities in five guideline projects – which we have compiled in Figure 12.3.

First: Emscher Landscape Park

- Its aim is the gradual creation of a continuous green area and land-scape park crossing the northern Ruhr Area from east to west. Nineteen projects are affiliated to this guideline project.
- *Second: the ecological improvement of the Emscher system*
- Its aim is to redevelop the river Emscher and its tributaries as well as to decentralize the Emscher's sewage system. Ten projects are affiliated to this guideline project.
- *Third: new utilization of industrial buildings*
- Here, the aim is to maintain industrial monuments in the region, to rehabilitate and put them to new use. Six projects are affiliated to this guideline project.
- *Fourth: working in the park*
- The aim of this guideline project is to clear the industrial wastelands and to redevelop them by building new housing stock and locating

First component

Guideline projects (and affiliated projects)

> 1. The Emscher Landscape Park (19)
>
> 2. The ecological improvement of the Emscher system (10)
>
> 3. New utilization of industrial buildings (6)
>
> 4. Working in the Park (21)
>
> 5. Housing/integrative development of municipal districts (27)

quality standards

position papers

quality agreements

Figure 12.3   The Emscher Park planning model.

219

new manufacturing and service industries in their place. It is planned to set aside at least 50 per cent of the redeveloped space as green areas. Twenty-one projects are affiliated to this guideline project.

- *Fifth: housing/integrated development of municipal districts*
- Here the aim is to rehabilitate old workers' housing estates in a way befitting listed buildings and to test new methods of tenant participation. The project also provides for experimenting with ecologically orientated housing, dwellings for joint families and flats that meet the special demands of women. Twenty-seven projects are affiliated to this guideline project.

The IBA sees itself as a "comprehensive regional development programme" (IBA Document 1991: para. 3) and a "complex renewal strategy" (Ganser 1991: 14) for the Emscher subregion. With its five guideline projects it defines structural change in this subregion as a political task that has to combine the reclamation of industrial wastelands, ecology, cultural policy, social policy, housing and urban development with the promotion of economic development.

With their quality standards, position papers and quality agreements between project agencies and the IBA Planning Company, these five guideline projects are the first component of the Emscher Park model of planning and regulation.

Second component: new planning principles   The second component consists of new methods of both planning and project management, which we have listed in Figure 12.4.

The Emscher Park IBA calls itself a "workshop for the future of old industrial areas". The "workshop" metaphor encompasses a variety of different messages:

- something new is supposed to be produced
- experiments are both allowed and welcomed
- everyone in the workshop has to contribute his skills and ideas
- co-operation and division of labour are basic functional mechanisms.

The IBA memorandum translates these associations from everyday language into that of planners. Here, new brainstorming methods are required, integrative thinking and planning is to be promoted, new methods of co-operation and co-ordination are to be tested, and new methods of participation for citizens' initiatives are to be developed. But it is also required that such innovations are to be tested in the planning phase, which promise to concentrate, intensify and shorten both planning and implementation processes.

Second component

New planning principles

e.g.

- new brainstorming methods

- architectural competitions

- advancement of integrative thinking and planning

- new forms of co-opertion and co-ordination

- new methods of participation by citizen's initiatives

- new public relations activities

Figure 12.4   Emscher Park planning principles.

In other words, the new planning principles, as formulated by the Emscher Park IBA, aim at two different models of planning and policy: on one hand, there is increased efficiency of administrative planning; on the other, new ways of decentralized planning "from below" are to be tested – which means citizen participation and mobilization of the region's population. In the past, this second component has created confusion among observers. Not without justification have they asked what precisely is so innovative about this planning practice; after all of this has been state of the art for the longest time in other places. What the critics hint at here is one of the central problems of the IBA – which is the "problem of invisibility". This means that "the value of the new housing development, et cetera, does not lay in its architectural quality in itself, which can be found just as well in Graz, Berlin or elsewhere – but in the fact that it could occur here, at this very place, in the Emscher subregion. The real feat is that the real estate could be mobilized at all, that a solution to the problem of reclaiming industrial wastelands could be found, that landowners and housing associations have been prepared to carry out experiments with new ways of building as well as with workshops, competitions and participation, that all of this could develop in an environment that has been almost completely hostile towards innovations up to a few years ago" (Selle 1993).

2.2.3 Third component: the IBA planning company as a new actor in the region
The IBA Planning Company plays a crucial part in initiating these "invisible", procedural innovations. Therefore, we regard it as the third component of the Emscher Park model of planning and regulation.

The company is the only new actor that has evolved in the context of the Emscher Park IBA. It was founded by the North-Rhine–Westphalian government as a plc and it started work on 12 May 1989 at Gelsenkirchen. It is the operative unit of the *Land* government in the Emscher region without being directly integrated into the decision-making structures of that government as determined by hierarchy and budget law.

In Figure 12.5 we have listed the organizational structure of the Emscher Park IBA with its four subdivisions.

- The Board of Trustees, which is headed by the Prime Minister of NRW. Its function is to secure political legitimacy.
- The Supervisory Board: its chairman is the Permanent Secretary of the Ministry of Urban Development, and it controls the Managing Director of the IBA Planning Company.
- The Steering Committee is headed by the Minister for Urban Development and has advisory functions and decision-making powers.
- The IBA Planning Company proper, which carries out the executive functions.

Each subdivision works as a separate small network with its own specific contacts in society and the region, the economy, politics and sciences.

The main business is carried out by and shared between the "Steering Committee" and the "IBA Planning Company".

Third component

The IBA Planning Company as a new actor in the region

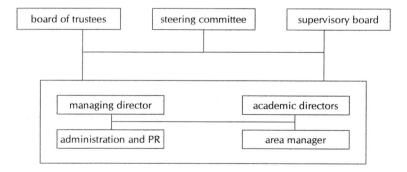

Figure 12.5 IBA Planning Company.

The Steering Committee, which meets two to three times a year, is the central decision-making body of the Emscher Park IBA. Its two main tasks are the following:

- it decides on the inclusion of projects in the Emscher Park IBA
- it makes policy decisions on contents, strategies and quality standards.

Its composition represents the dominant political powers and institutions of the region: *Land* government ministries, local authorities, the social partners, the Kommunalverband Ruhrgebiet, which is the working association of local authorities in the Ruhr Area, federations of architects, housing associations, and environmental protection associations. With every justification Walter Siebel, one of the Academic Directors of the IBA Planning Company, points out the political "burden" of the Steering Committee, which results from the fact that "a decision-making body that is composed in such a way can represent just the ossified structures and the inertia of the region, which it is supposed to force open" (Siebel 1992: 227).

Those bringing a "fresh breeze" into the region are, first of all, the full-time staff of the IBA Planning Company who, incidentally, generally do not originate from the Emscher subregion. They are the ones who mobilize ideas and know-how from outside for the benefit of the Emscher sub-region, organize international conferences and workshop talks, initiate architectural competitions, lay down the quality standards of the Emscher Park IBA in position papers, develop quality agreements, and so on. By defining standards in co-operation with a professional elite and by mediating them with a decentralized, open planning "from below" they are in effect trying to square the circle.

This leads us to the fourth component of the Emscher Park model of planning and regulation, to the horizontal self-co-ordination affected by the decentralized project groups (Fig. 12.6).

Fourth component: horizontal self-co-ordination "from below" in decentralized project planning groups　Let us first recall the objectives that serve as guidelines for the IBA project groups:

- the groups act within an integrated structural and development programme whose principles are laid down in the IBA memorandum and the Emscher park position papers
- they have to stipulate quality targets specific to each project
- through optimal project management they have to realize these by a certain pre-arranged date.

The project groups are many-membered and widely ramified bodies.

Fourth component

Horizontal self-co-ordination "from below" in decentralized project planning groups

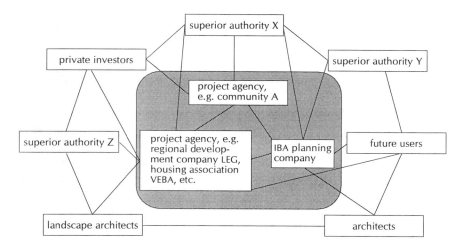

Figure 12.6 Emscher Park project planning groups.

Their internal structure is the combination of a constant and consistent core group with around 15–20 persons with wider and more open sub-groups surrounding the core group like satellites.

Membership in the core group is obligatory. Institutions acting as agencies of IBA projects delegate members into the project group. So does the IBA Planning Company. Although the company itself, being a "decentralized system" in accordance with the Emscher Park IBA definition, cannot be a project agency, it is a member of the core group via its area managers.

Depending on the function of subgroups, membership in them is partially obligatory and partially voluntary. All members of the project subgroups have in common that they are responsible for certain tasks that are parts as the project as a whole. This can be to rehabilitate old but not necessarily listed buildings or to reclaim industrial wasteland, or it can be landscaping or architectural design, to name but a few examples.

IBA project groups work according to the logic of multilateral negotiating systems. Horizontal self-co-ordination procedures dominate, following the principle of "deliberation–negotiation–stipulation". The IBA project groups are characterized fundamentally by the symmetry of relations between their members. Anybody who wants to contribute something is allowed to do so. Unclear points and discrepancies can be voiced, regardless of hierarchical status.

The Emscher Park's quality and project competition gives this logic a specific IBA character. From the outset the negotiating system is subject to external discipline since quality criteria are stipulated and projects have to deliver results by a certain date because of the IBA interim presentation arranged for the years 1994/5.

In composition and internal structure, the IBA project groups are an expression of a technocratic and politically disinterested project management. Agencies of the project groups are mainly composed of members of middle management. Remarkably often they are committed administrative experts who have been open to new ideas for a long time and who are prepared to tread new ground in administration.

This background makes it plausible that the innovative potential of the IBA project groups develops throughout in three directions:

- The extreme complexity of the IBA projects matches the IBA programme's claim to be a comprehensive renewal strategy. Therefore, each core group is characterized by a composition that transcends special fields and government agencies. Communities and public as well as private agencies send two, three or four delegates in different special fields and different spheres of responsibility into the IBA project group. In these groups, urban planners, promoters of economic development and architects share one table with members of the local buildings administration and the local parks administration – and this is indeed a new experience for many local governments.

- Here and there, new constellations of actors develop in the IBA project groups. Deliberate introduction of external expertise for the benefit of the region can break up established routines of institutional co-operation. New co-operation partners are discovered and become into the project management.

- Despite – or even because of – their technocratic and politically disinterested approach, the IBA project groups can experiment with new forms of participation, especially in the housing projects. This allows new actors to shape policy.

In parts and with differing intensity, the IBA project groups develop network relations because they are supported by four factors:

- the intensive interaction of different actors is their lifeblood
- the main interest of all concerned is joint constructive problem-solving
- the project groups live on the willingness of all concerned to enter into a common learning process
- to a high degree they live on mutual trust and common values.

The evolution and stabilization of such network relations advances the synergetic effects within the project groups as well as their efficiency.

We see two approaches to a new political mode in the Emscher Park IBA: one in the structure and method of the decentralized project groups, the other in the combination of procedures of the horizontal self-co-ordination "from below" (within the project groups), with continuous supervision and intervention in points "from above" (mainly by the area managers and directors of the IBA Planning Company).

With this, the Emscher Park model of planning and regulation comes very close to realizing the vision of the State as a partner of autonomously acting and interacting actors on the regional level.

SOME SPECIFIC CONDITIONS OF THE EMSCHER PARK IBA

Here we shall dwell on some specific conditions of the Emscher Park IBA.

The first condition is the political system of the Federal Republic of Germany. With its federal structures, this offers the *Land* government of North-Rhine–Westphalia the opportunity to initiate such a development programme on its territory. The German financial system and its political intertwinements enable the North-Rhine–Westphalian government to utilize and combine different financial resources on all levels of the political system for IBA projects.

The second condition is the strong lobby the Ruhr Area had with the political decision-makers of the "old" Federal Republic before reunification. The Ruhr Area has been undergoing a process of structural change since the end of the 1950s. Accordingly, the State has almost continuously issued regional development and structural programmes. Therefore, of all the *Länder*, North-Rhine–Westphalia can boast the most highly developed concepts and strategies for regional structural policy.

Following the crisis in the steel industry and the confrontations about the preservation of steel-industry locations in the mid-1980s there was a strong political will in the *Land*, the federal government and the EC to earmark considerable sums for this region. This is why the IBA projects could, and still can, receive priority access to State funds.

The third condition the specific party politics of North-Rhine–Westphalia and the Emscher subregion. For more than 20 years the Social Democrats have been the only party to form the North-Rhine–Westphalian government. They have been in power in the communities of the Emscher subregion since the end of the war, capturing absolute majorities of 50 to 60 per cent of local votes. This political homogeneity at both local and *Land* level has created a strong loyalty among the Emscher subregion's communities towards the *Land* government. In the Emscher subregion, regional actors show a strong identification with the political objectives of the *Land* government. A high-ranking official told us in a recent experts' survey that there was an "amazing raison d'état" throughout the subregion, a kind of belief in the ability of the State. It would not be wrong to talk about an uncritical attitude towards the Regierungspräsident (Regional Commissioner), who as the chief official in the administrative district of the *Land* has an intermediate position in the State administration. This, of course, gives the members of the IBA Planning Company the best reputation in the region and makes them even more capable of asserting themselves.

On the other hand, facing the accumulation of problems resulting from the sectoral restructuring of the Ruhr Area, the actors in the Emscher subregion show a certain insecurity and, as a consequence, a certain openness towards new ideas and those from outside. As one of our interlocutors put it, "the local politicians do have to think a little about what they are really doing and how they are doing it. They aren't as smug any more."

The fourth condition is the polycentric space. With its 17 large communities, which are comparatively autonomous, the Emscher subregion is a polycentric area that facilitates innovative action because there are so many centres of action. In the words of one IBA actor, "there's always someone doing something." At the moment, this condition coincides with a generational change that is to be noticed on both the administrative and the work levels of local authorities, as well as in other social institutions. This again makes it easier for the Emscher Park IBA to find allies inside established institutions.

Let us now briefly sum up our reflections on the contribution of the Emscher Park IBA to the restructuring of the northern part of the Ruhr district. The IBA Planning Company acts as an autonomous agent and as an initiator and mediator of experts' networks in the region. With its new strategy of initiating competitions and improved quality standards, it brings new resources into the region, and it opens exclusive access to State financing for the projects it accepts.

With their methods of horizontal self-co-ordination, integrated problem-solving and their careful shaping of new constellations of agents and co-operative relations, the IBA project groups are a "workshop" for experimenting with new forms of politics. With this, the Emscher Park IBA creates important prerequisites for the development of innovative social environments, as well as for the mobilization of endogenous potentials that should help in the restructuring of the region.

227

A preliminary assessment of the IBA

We would now like to try and tentatively assess the Building Exhibition. This discussion will take into account the role of local authorities, the question of whether the IBA can be regarded as an adequate response to structural change in OIAs, and, lastly, the paradoxes arising from the IBA experiment.

THE ROLE OF LOCAL AUTHORITIES

Although it was the State government of North-Rhine–Westphalia that instituted the Building Exhibition, it is the local authorities of the Emscher subregion that play a dominant role in the process of putting IBA projects into effect. This is the result of the specific constitutional context in which local authorities operate and which grants them legally entrenched planning rights that cannot be infringed or altered by a State government. Therefore, the implementation of IBA projects is impossible without the approval of the respective local authorities. This entails two things; first, a local perspective of renewal strategies. Secondly, because most councils of the Ruhr district are led by traditional Social Democrats – who are usually rather conservative and hence not committed to innovative strategies and ideas such as those devised by citizen's pressure groups – many projects are severely impeded because they do not fit into the mainstream political thinking of councillors.

However, there are certain mechanisms that can counterbalance these impediments. For instance, there are many examples of direct co-operation between the Ministry of Urban Development and citizen's initiatives that redress the traditionalism of local authority leaders. The Building Exhibition can be regarded as an example of this mechanism, which local authorities are under pressure to accept because they have a twofold interest in securing projects with the "IBA seal of quality": prestige and finance. Because of their dire financial situation (as was pointed out above) local authorities have a particular interest in the money accessible through projects with IBA priority because it gives them back some scope of action.

THE SPATIAL FRAME OF REFERENCE

Any evaluation of the IBA has to address the question of whether the IBA can be regarded as an adequate response to structural change. We will discuss this question now by concentrating on two aspects of the Building Exhibition: the spatial frame of reference and the contents.

228

The spatial frame of reference of the Building Exhibition is criticized by some experts who argue that the Emscher subdistrict is part of a larger region, namely the entire Rhine–Ruhr agglomeration, which displays specific spatial divisions of labour. Consequently, these experts call for a regional development strategy that covers the whole Rhine–Ruhr agglomeration, including Düsseldorf and Cologne, with their international linkages in banking, trading, the media, and so on (Voss 1989). However, other critics have reproached the State government for a long time with having ignored the desperate situation of the Emscher subregion and, especially, the growth of social problems there. One could say that the IBA managed to bring the problems of the Emscher subregion to the attention of the general public and to those responsible for regional policy.

THE SUBSTANTIVE CONTENT OF THE IBA

The substantive adequacy of the Building Exhibition needs to be discussed on a broader basis. The IBA neither comprises any regional economic strategy defined in a more narrow sense, nor even an analysis of the economy of the area, which could be used as a basis for action. On the other hand, it is in any case very questionable whether the problems of the Ruhr district could be solved with the limited instrument of a regional economic policy devised by the State government, particularly in view of the fact that the Federal Ministry of Economic Affairs had a very strong commitment to a "liberal market economy" in the 1980s and obviously no interest in complex regional development strategies. These considerations refer to the fundamental question of how far federal or State policies can intervene directly in a market economy with any hope of success. This is why confining State intervention to a broadly defined location policy – as the IBA does – may be the best choice from a pragmatic point of view.

Another important achievement that can be attributed to the Building Exhibition is that it has broadened the spectrum of interest of regional policy. As was outlined above, the IBA's conception of regional renewal not only involves the improvement of the physical infrastructure and the restoration of building facades but also ecological regeneration; the IBA is not only about the re-employment and retraining of redundant workers but also about their encouragement and sociocultural innovations. We think that through the IBA's activities the awareness of the importance of such aspects for a successful regional development will be enhanced.

A SUMMARY CRITIQUE OF THE IBA

On a very general level we think that the Building Exhibition is a remarkable experiment in creative restructuring processes. However, there are several inherent discrepancies and paradoxes, some of which to our minds cannot be or are not likely to be solved. Because of their continued importance, we would like to briefly outline these paradoxes:

- As was pointed out above, change is to be, and needs to be, effected by the same people whose attitudes and ways of handling or ignoring structural change are to be blamed for the current situation.
- Furthermore, what is typical of a strategy of renewal from within, such as the IBA is the so-called pedagogical paradox: the teacher's role is to teach the students independence and maturity. Along similar lines, activities "from below" are to be stimulated "from above".

Also, because the IBA backs the strong players and is therefore very much a corporatist form of intervention, a bias exists towards professionally organized planning, whereas projects devised by citizen's pressure groups can hardly manage to meet the standards set by the IBA and the regular planning procedures. Neither do these groups have enough time or sufficient funds or expert knowledge to be able to draw up plans that would stand a chance of becoming a prestigious IBA project.

Nevertheless, despite these paradoxes, problems and other shortcomings of the Building Exhibition, the IBA is rapidly becoming an exceptional example of a public sector-led approach towards the restructuring of old industrial areas. This is why we think the Building Exhibition is setting new standards of renewing old industrial areas by which others elsewhere could be measured.

CHAPTER THIRTEEN

Keeping to the high road: learning, reflexivity and associative governance in regional economic development
Phil Cooke

Introduction

Today, the Rustbelt regions of Europe and North America are at the forefront of a global competitive struggle to retain jobs and investment in the face of an economic challenge the like of which Western economies have never before experienced. In the 1970s, energy-poor Japan and the lesser economies of the East Asian Pacific Rim launched an export-drive of monumental proportions to earn the foreign exchange to buy the fuel needed to keep their economies functioning. Although it did not directly cause the demise of the heavy industries such as coal, steel and heavy manufacturing the Rustbelt regions specialized in, this global burst of competitive power helped undermine the structures of production, eased into place over the previous century, and engendered a perception in the West that things could never be the same again. Markets for heavy industry could not be recovered at their former scale, labour markets could never be so full of secure and well paid jobs, the future lay in developing or attracting new jobs in new industries.

To a very large extent, these perceptions and effects are realized concretely in the cases reported in this book. The sense of an economic watershed having been passed is strong, the perception of a loss of older certainties is pervasive, the experiences of social and economic dislocation are vividly reported. But amid the confusion, as the dust settles, the outlines of renewal are increasingly clearly perceptible. At the outset of this

231

book, the fear that Rustbelt regions were finished was reiterated as an echo of a common response to evidence of the early deindustrializations of places such as Pennsylvania–Ohio and South Wales in the late 1970s and early 1980s. Gratifyingly, this fear is shown to be in substantial ways misplaced, at least for the Rustbelts described in these accounts.

The resilience shown is a quite remarkable testimony to the ingenuity and determination of, in some cases, business enterprise itself, but overwhelmingly the diverse representative and other civic institutions active in the regions themselves. Of course, the scars of large-scale deindustrialization have not completely healed in any of the regional economies and societies discussed. Older male workers are the most obvious direct casualty, many of whom have become permanently detached from the labour market long before retirement age. Indirectly, their family members, and particularly younger males, have found their economic aspirations and prospects negatively affected by the changing demands of the labour market. Some whole communities, such as the guestworkers in Germany, former coalmining communities in all cases and, particularly, African-American communities attracted north to the US manufacturing belt, have suffered disproportionately.

However, this book has the aim of identifying seeds of hope as well as despair and there is much in the experiences reported to give grounds for believing that seriously devastated heavy-industry economies can be rejuvenated, albeit slowly and, inevitably, unevenly. Clearly, such areas are a real test of the capacity of development authorities because, unlike industrial areas that are relatively undeveloped, they bring the sociocultural and political *mentalités* associated with the heyday of management, worker and governance practices under a previous, conceivably now anachronistic, production regime. Stimulating enterprise and innovation in such conditions is, on the face of it, likely to be less propitious than doing so in a small farm or peasant economy where there are, albeit simple, enterprise management expertise, payroll administration skills and widespread engagement with market modes of exchange. However, partly for reasons having to do with some of the issues raised in the introduction to this book, partly because of more global less regional imperatives, the Rustbelts that are the focus here can be said, with much justification, to be on the rise again. In what follows, the main reasons for this are teased out, summarized and, on that basis, recommendations are drawn.

Regions, clusters and innovation networks reconsidered

The introduction to this book invited readers to reflect on three frame conditions that much of the economic, geographic and business management literature presently finds enticing as explanations for economic success. It is said by writers such as Porter (1990) and Ohmae (1993) that a *regional* sensibility is an important factor in helping us understand how, on the one hand, the global competitive process actually operates on the ground, while, on the other, industries successfully cope with the demise of the nation-State as an economic guarantor of survival (e.g. through its past capacity for subsidy, protection or promotion of "national champions").

Little that has been reported in the foregoing chapters would lead to serious disagreement with the proposition that regional government assists the process of adjustment, even where such government is not regionally accountable, as prevails in Wales, entwined in the parliamentary centralism typical of the UK system. Even there it is evident that the role of the Welsh Office and Welsh Development Agency has been important in helping encourage foreign firms attracted to the UK to settle in or near to devastated older industrial areas, then building supply-chain links, albeit often of modest proportions, between them and the inward investors. In the cases of North-Rhine–Westphalia (NRW), Ontario and Pennsylvania, definable policies had evidently been adopted at subcentral level, mainly to assist the establishment or expansion of small medium enterprises (SMEs). In NRW, though, this enterprise support is set within the frame of major *Land*-level investment in higher education, basic and applied research facilities, technology transfer centres and *associative* conferences at subregional level. Moreover, the financial power of the West LB, the NRW State bank, is available not only for individual SME investments but to support, for example, a mechatronics institute, in partnership. Although such financial powers are less evident in the public sector State and provincial systems of North America, regional policies in support of partnership-based restructuring of devastated economies are also prevalent.

So, this book adds to the confidence of those observers, whether professional regional scientists, or economists and other social scientists, who perceive the administrative region to be potentially – and in many cases actually – a key force in supporting competitive advantage among its industries, especially in smaller firm enterprise support through financing, training and technology transfer. There is also mild support for the thesis advanced by de Vet (1993) that such activity enhances regional eco-

233

nomic specialization with a discernible shuffling of foreign investment, especially in engineering industries, towards these Rustbelt locations. This is partly a function of upgraded inputs, such as steel, present in such regions and an undoubted attraction factor, and partly the existence or new development of supplier firms in sufficient quantity to constitute the "critical mass" that inward investor firms usually prefer to have within reasonable trucking distance.

Clusters of interacting industry branches, linking buyers and suppliers, customers and vendors in intricate supply-chains of subcontracted value-adding economic activity, are perceived by many, from policy protagonists to business gurus as the fount and origin of competitive advantage (Porter 1990). The case has been made extremely strongly in Rehfeld's chapter that the industrial might of the Ruhr was founded on the cluster-like character of the coal, steel and even chemicals industries centred in that district. Moreover, it is shown, convincingly, that as that cluster aged, a new one based on environmental technologies has already emerged from the ashes to give a new competitive advantage to firms engaged in pollution control. Elsewhere, it is a less pronounced but nevertheless emergent, or perhaps re-emergent feature of the industrial landscape.

In the Great Lakes region, engineering (especially automotive) and its heavier inputs such as steel, and lighter components-supply revolved around an epicentre in Detroit, the heartland of the American car economy. Serious damage was done to this traditional cluster by the twin-pronged challenge of Japanese and European competition in the 1980s. Yet, the Japanese, in particular, have been among the key forces assisting in the revitalization of the Mid-West auto cluster, which, although regionally less tight-knit, is in economic terms incomparably more competitive that it was. In Ontario each of the US main producers (Chrysler, Ford and General Motors) has a plant, to which Honda, Toyota and Suzuki are more recent additions. Evidence of the emergence of a world-class supplier base can also be found, giving the Ontario automotive cluster a substantial export surplus. Much the same can be said for Wales, until recently an unlikely candidate as a serious automotive industry location. However, the arrival of Ford's main family-car engine plant in the 1970s and Toyota's in the 1980s has stimulated some upgrading of indigenous suppliers and the filling of gaps with welcome inward investors such as Robert Bosch, to augment the likes of Lucas and Valeo, giving South Wales in particular some of the characteristics of a Porterian cluster while retaining the overall character of a supplier region to the UK and, increasingly, European automotive industry more generally. By contrast, in Wales the electronics

234

industry is mainly assembly plants, but with such firms as Sony, Aiwa, Panasonic and Hitachi increasingly sourcing componentry locally, if quality, price and delivery are acceptable.

Hence, as well as displaying regional neomercantilist strengths in the field of enterprise support, these Rustbelt regions possess, albeit in variably developed and uncompleted form, cluster-like characteristics in their mode of economic co-ordination. In the German case this has been reproduced through a process described at the outset of this book as *internal diversification,* by firms moving from one dominant branch to a new one. In the Welsh and Ontario cases, upgrading or *external diversification* by foreign-owned companies has been responsible for the contemporary regional economic profile. While in the US manufacturing belt around the Great Lakes, development has occurred by a mix of newly arrived transplants from Japan and Europe and upgrading by global companies such as Xerox and Motorola, Ford and General Motors, as Florida makes clear.

What, then, about the third ingredient thought to be, perhaps the key element to "the new regional growth theory" (Romer 1990), the development of endogenous growth capacity through the elaboration of technologically advanced *innovation networks*? Here, the story is more mixed. Deitrick & Beauregard have shown in detail how the State of Pennsylvania embarked on an innovative enterprise support scheme aimed at linking funding (the Ben Franklin Partnership) to advanced technology commercialization through building strong links between firms and research-based institutions, many in the universities. Moreover, support funding became dependent on proposals demonstrating the existence of local innovation networks. Yet despite the apparent success of such initiatives at the level of the single firm, Federal expenditure constraints and fiscal stress, caused partly by deindustrialization, mean the programmes remain small in size and effect. Florida, too, indicates scaling back over the years for the Ben Franklin Partnership and abandonment of another celebrated programme, the Michigan Modernization Service in the 1990s. In the case of Ontario, Gertler describes sophisticated policy inputs but as yet few networked innovation outcomes.

In Wales, such initiatives have yet to emerge. Innovation is the subject of innumerable initiatives from government, business associations and research councils, and is the focus of attention of policy advisers awakening from the equivalent of a Rip Van Winkle sojourn. But in Wales, as in the UK more generally, it may well be a case of too little, too late, as competitor economies move into second- and third-wave innovation programmes, sometimes, as in Japan, with distinctively regionalized delivery mechanisms to the forefront (JICST 1992). The most exciting innovation support ideas emanate from the European Commission, and Welsh institutions have been astute in accessing EU support early in the form of feasibility studies for the DG16 funded Regional Technology Plan and the DGl3 supported Regional Industrial Innovation and Technology Transfer Strategy for South Wales. Together, these both audit and make recommendations regarding needed improvements to the innovation infrastructure. They act as an important first step in encouraging the development of regionalized technology information and assessment services, especially for SMEs. Business Connect, a network of service providers based in eight subregions and including "Innovation Counselling" and "Innovation Credits" (in the same way Business Link does in England) is a new arrival on the scene. But even economic development professionals are critical of the bureaucratic nature of the application process, one that is virtually guaranteed to mean it will miss its main target audience, innovation-seeking SMEs.

The region of regions that, on the face of it, has it all in terms of growing, successfully functioning networked innovation services, is North-Rhine–Westphalia. As Huggins & Thomalla make clear, NRW industrial policy is based on creating increased workforce skills: to manage the complexities of closer supply-chain interactions; to capitalize on closer innovation links between industry and research institutions; and because the NRW government does not anticipate growth in opportunities for the manufacture of standard products. Like other German *Länder* with a high manufacturing density, NRW has embarked fully on a *"high-road strategy"* for its industrial future. The *"low road"* of low skills, low value added and low wages is, correctly, perceived as not a sustainable option. To that end it has invested hugely in technology-led regional industrial policy that networks R&D centres, technology transfer, innovative SMEs and technology support institutions both locally and throughout the region. It is claimed that, during the period 1984–94, when the policy gathered momentum, some 100000 new jobs, many of them in the environmental engineering industries, were created (NRW Ministry of Economics 1994).

So, at present, the construction of an innovation network architecture, capable of transforming Rustbelt regions into *learning regions* can only be said to have been approached in NRW. It has been the subject of political rhetoric and some modest State or provincial funding in the American Mid-West and Ontario. In Wales, as in the rest of the UK, such thinking is very new, politically contentious and culturally at odds with the "rugged individualism" that has supposedly been cultivated among British entrepreneurs as a consequence of the neoliberal market experiment most

236

closely associated with the governments of Margaret Thatcher. However, European Union initiatives have been important in stimulating early awareness of the importance of co-operation on innovation to the competitiveness of industry in Wales.

Institutional learning

It seems that one of the more difficult accomplishments Rustbelt regional economies face is developing the kind of interactive, even transparent, high-trust business culture that is associated with the (often hidden) co-operative dimension of competitive industrial clusters. Even in NRW, the network solution developed only after earlier policy failures at both Federal and *Land* levels in "picking winners" through subsidization of R&D and, in particular, supporting the computer industry. Networking represented a shift from "State-regulation" to "self-regulation" based on the idea of public–private partnership. Because of the relatively lengthy time-span of the policies in support of co-operative self-regulation, the networks themselves tend to have absorbed a learning disposition expressed as a determination to resolve problems rather than walk away from them (Latniak & Simonis 1994).

NRW's innovative SoTech (socially orientated technology) programme is analyzed by Latniak & Simonis (ibid.) in terms of its learning effects. Although it did not achieve the ambitious aims that many of its proponents hoped for – equipping workers and businesses involved in information technology with the skills fully to take advantage of the technology without being dominated by it – it inculcated a widespread and well embedded technocultural understanding in NRW society that affected future developments in technology policy. Among the more important of these were: the acceptance by the NRW government of the notion of a rolling rather than a finite policy; the establishment of a unique Commission for Man and Technology by the NRW parliament and the founding of a research institute (Institute for Work & Technology, Gelsenkirchen) in 1988 in support of it; establishing continuity of research groups around the issue; implementation of shopfloor-level projects for socially acceptable use of technology; development of a model of socially compatible work organization embodying information technology; and developing projects to assist learning transfer between firms and among occupations.

This experience draws attention to the theory of institutional learning

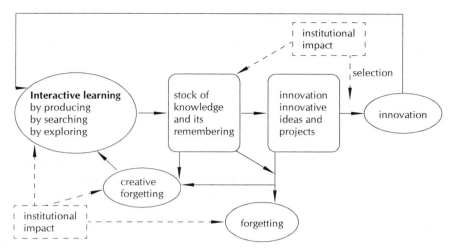

Figure 13.1 The relations between learning, growth of knowledge and innovation.

as developed by Johnson (1992) in his conceptualization of the learning processes embodied in interactive innovation (Fig. 13.1). It starts from an analysis of different kinds of learning such as learning-by-doing and learning-by-using, as performed by individuals. He then transfers this thinking to institutions. These include firms, governance organizations and para-State agencies that are the repositories, as all are, of "habits" and "routines" that constitute the "social regularities" of an organization and "signposts" for interactions between people. They provide the basis for both stability and change. Change usually requires getting new, but also forgetting old, knowledge. Innovation involves assessing such knowledge and translating what is usable into projects with innovative intent.

Of crucial importance to the whole process is the interactive learning function, which, as Johnson presents it takes several forms: learning-by-producing (including learning-by-doing and learning-by-using), learning-by-searching and learning-by-exploring. The search function has become of especial importance to the capacity of organizations to cope with change of the kind we have been discussing in this book. One of the key problems regional authorities have is in searching and sifting out new ways of doing things, or new things to do, that are of relevance to them. Discussions in the preceding chapters point not infrequently to "institutional borrowing" from European practices perceived to be innovative and competitive, as represented in regional systems such as those of Baden–Württemberg and others in what began as the Four Motors for Europe agreement with Catalonia, Lombardy and Rhône–Alpes. This is a kind of institutional "short-cutting" to gain new knowledge. But the extent to which it results in implementable learning and innovation gains remains open to question.

The case of NRW is instructive in this respect in that while there has for long been a domestic economic and political rivalry with Baden–Württemberg (Esser 1989) the "learning" that goes on between them is more in the vein of "doing the opposite" rather than institutional borrowing. To the extent NRW regional industrial policy can be said to have shown success, it can be traced to a, perhaps 20-year, period of learning by doing, seeking ways forward from within the framework of innovative opportunities offered within the declining industries themselves. This demands a tremendous capacity for association, concertation, discourse and willingness to engage with other interests. It is slow, painstaking but inclusive and thus less likely to generate opposition from "excluded others". Its weakness is that, sometimes, drastic remedies are called for, because of the unexpected, and it may be too inflexible; it can also be costly, as, for example, Germany's long-term "coal-tax" showed on employee's wage slips as they continued to subsidize an uncompetitive industry that market forces would have consigned to oblivion years previously.

Institutional reflexivity

A learning predisposition among institutions engaged in conducting or supporting regional economic development implies more than search and exploration. Attention has recently been drawn, not least by Ulrich Beck (Beck 1992) to the breakdown of established certainties, ranging from the demise of communism and the ending of the Cold War to the onset of a post-industrial type of society in former heavy industry regions. This, he argues, bears witness to the emergence of what he calls a "risk society". It is a condition in which political turbulence, economic uncertainty, dangers from new viruses, environmental catastrophes, the breakdown of the social fabric, increased criminality and several other social pathologies are all symptoms.

How does society, or rather in this context, its institutions respond to risk of this pervasive kind? Here Beck introduces the concept of *reflexivity*. However, the concept has a double meaning. What Beck claims to see happening is an increase in reflexivity of the "knee-jerk reaction" kind.

239

Businesses have competitiveness problems, the reflex is to sack workers, to "downsize" or "rightsize", to use the corporate graffiti. Crime is seen to be on the increase, so . . . build more prisons. Communism is dead, so . . . give the former communist countries a large dose of market neoliberalism. This is the kind of *unreflective* reflexivity that Beck argues typifies responses to problems, particularly as advocated by the master-institutions of modern society, the large corporations and the governmental agencies of the State.

But, interesting and persuasive as Beck's argument is, there is another kind of reflexivity that is of much more relevance, especially for regional economic development, and about this he has less to say (cf. Cooke 1994, Lash & Urry 1994). This is *institutional reflexivity* of the kind practised in what have elsewhere been called "intelligent regions" (Cooke & Morgan 1991). Because of both the cyclical and unexpected downturns occasioned by competitiveness, confidence and credit-related crises to which regional economies at the leading edge have become more prone, especially where systematically integrated through clustering, such systems require exceptional antennae to cope.

In regional systems such as Baden–Württemberg and Emilia–Romagna "intelligence" is captured through several different mechanisms; as well as learning by interacting with firms, other agencies, other regions they learn by monitoring their own policy performance (as NRW has with SoTech); they are intelligent in their retrieval and accessing of data; they demonstrate intelligence in realizing when it is time to let go of a facility or function they may have developed but which may be better run by an outside agency or firm; and they seek to anticipate future needs of the regional economy by having periodic commissions to engage in policy or technology foresight, for example. The *Land* government of NRW has its Standing Commission on Man & Technology, in Wales the Institute of Welsh Affairs' Commission 2010 performed that foresight function, in Ontario the Premiers Commission, in Baden–Württemberg it was the 1994 Future Commission, which followed the Büllinger Commission ten years earlier. And in Emilia–Romagna the Regional Presidents' Commission was responsible for reviewing the whole panoply of enterprise support, again reporting in 1994. Interestingly, all the regions involved in studies reported in this book have been subject to commissions, whether the Great Lakes Region Governors' Commission or the State-wide examples such as the Michigan or Pennsylvania initiatives. All these regions display *reflexivity* in the sense of demonstrating concern about regional performance and competitiveness threats for the future. The key question concerns the nature and extent of

240

the action that follows. As we have seen this can be variable, sometimes shallow and often short-lived or underfunded. There is clearly little point in having *institutional reflexivity* of the second kind without having the will to follow through in a thoroughgoing manner.

Regional associationalism

Where institutional learning and institutional reflexivity are strong at regional level it is common to find *associative* relationships between diverse political and economic interests underpinning them. Recent writing on "the culture of the economy" (see, for example Casson 1993, 1995, Albert 1993) has stressed the apparent superiority as a cultural base for modern economic co-ordination of an *associative* ethos. The idea has recently been expounded at length also in the field of political philosophy (see, for example, Hirst 1994). The basic idea has much in common with that noted as defining the policy shift in NRW industry policy from State-regulation to self-regulation.

Hirst advocates three principles of associative political organization. First, the concepts of voluntary self-governing associations in civil society being ceded functions of democratic economic and social governance by the State, supported by appropriate financial mechanisms. Secondly, the proposal that authority should be divided into the largest feasible number of territorial or functional domains, preferably as localized as possible but subject to a (possibly supranational) framework of regulatory rules. Third, a conception of democracy as effective governance based on communication, transparency, adequate information flow and consultation as a prelude to the implementation of policy.

Networking, learning, reflexivity and self-regulation are practices that are being groped towards in the Welsh and North American instances, as is evidenced in many of these contributions, indeed encapsulates the title of Gertler's Ontario chapter. But as is made clear over and again in the chapters reporting the diverse experiences of restructuring in the German case, they are much more clearly within reach, if not in large measure already grasped, in NRW. Nowhere is this clearer than in Kilper & Wood's discussion of the IBA-Emscher Park experience. Here, not only were diverse interests brought together to determine the desired course of action on environmental recovery, but community sentiment was incorporated through the associative method of discursive problem resolution. Moreover, when

241

environmental upgrading measures were agreed, they integrated socio-cultural, environmental and economic actions in a seamless web.

Now it could be said that this approach is relatively easy to adopt in NRW because it is an archetypally German cultural characteristic so to operate. Certain baleful episodes in German history give ground for querying such an assertion, but nevertheless Albert (1993) freely argues that it is a predilection for associative cultural exchange that gives a present advantage to what he refers to as "the Rhine model of economic development":

> The assertion that there can be a "culture of the economy" may seem suspiciously vague to some, while to others it is a tautology. But if there is one word that designates a body of individual behaviour patterns shared by a whole population, enshrined within institutions, subject to agreed rules and forming a common heritage, then it is indeed culture. And in the Rhine model there is every indication that a specific "economy culture" operates at every level, with its own distinctive traits.   (Albert 1993)

Among the imputed characteristics of this "economy culture" are: an inclination to high savings; diminished income disparities; community interests take precedence over individual interests; industrial investment is more highly valued than that in finance; education and training are seen as priorities not luxuries; and civilian rather than military research is prioritized.

This list reads like a mirror-image of the Anglo-American "economy culture" with its preference for low savings, high income disparities, individualism, addiction to financial investment, weak attachment to the virtues of training and emphasis on military research. It is easy to see why such economies have difficulty in really taking the plunge on associationalism, but that they must break away from many of those characteristics is written into the contemporary logic of the foundations of contemporary economic success and failure. Whether in the "dash for gas" or the less than impressive results of reforms in the vocational training system, not to mention the distortions wreaked by an over-emphasis on military investment in a post-Cold War era, the weaknesses of reactive reflexivity in the "knee-jerk" sense are now glaringly evident.

Conclusions and recommendations

Rustbelt regions are hard to turn round. All the regions reported on here have done relatively well, some substantially better than others, in reducing unemployment, finding or generating new jobs, and healing many of the scars of heavy industrialization. The generic reasons why they have been successful where they have are threefold.

First, all the regions examined have more or less powerful institutions capable of intervening in support of vocational training, small medium enterprise expansion and innovation promotion, including some degree of technology transfer and encouragement of interaction between research institutes and industry. Noticeably, the four main regions studied, NRW, Ontario, Pennsylvania and Wales had all had some kind of Commission of Inquiry, organized regionally, to look into the nature of the regional economy's problems and set the tone for policy channels to be pursued, more or less vigorously, by the appropriate, responsible authorities. In each case, the emphasis on innovation, skills and supporting small business is quite strikingly present in both policy rhetoric, and, to varying degrees, policy action. Of course, in the North American and Welsh cases the role of foreign direct investment is appreciated and efforts made to attract it, with considerable success. But whether in relation to foreign or domestic larger firm investment, there is a recognition of the importance of enabling indigenous firms to become competitive as *suppliers* to larger industry. This is true of NRW also, even though the emphasis on attracting foreign investment has been less pronounced.

Secondly, and less equally the case in generic terms, these Rustbelt regions all had, historically, integrated industrial complexes of varying degrees of elaboration and sophistication. These clusters, as they are now called, consisted of coal–steel–chemicals–heavy-engineering in NRW, coal–steel–automotive–electrical-engineering in the Great Lakes manufacturing belt (including Ontario) and coal–steel–metal-processing in Wales. Remnants of the most primary elements of these input–output chains persist in most cases, but new clusters have emerged or are prefigured further down stream in the production chain. Thus, in every case, whether because of internal or external diversification of the regional economy, the key activities cluster towards what Florida calls *high performance engineering production*. This is especially true of automotive, electronic and, in NRW, environmental engineering, where higher value-added, higher-skill and higher-wage labour is in demand. There is, thus, the aspiration to pursue generically a *"high road"* manufacturing development path, with all that

243

entails for intensifying research, design and innovation in the regional economy, even though in some instances *"low-road"* semi-skilled employment in branch plants has been the regional inheritance from the imposition of outdated, top-down regional industrial policies.

The third generic conclusion regarding the relative success of these Rustbelt regions in revitalizing their economic base lies in the recognition that there is substantial scope for inter-institutional interaction or networking in helping new or existing firms benefit from or become more innovative in their products, services or processes. Moreover, most had adopted a set of policies with support funding to encourage precisely such network-building between firms, intermediary agencies and research or higher education institutions, although, with the exception of NRW, this approach was visibly experimental and vulnerable to changes in political whim. In the case of NRW the networking approach to innovation extends beyond inter-firm or firm–institution levels to encompass whole strategies, notably for the environmental recovery of the highly polluted Emscher valley, where integrated civic development planning has proved successful. That approach has been extended in the concept of *"regional conferences"* within NRW, which are seen as an important means of generating further innovative ideas and approaches for economic development policy.

Such achievements as these signify the fruition of a new move towards self-regulatory, civic-minded mobilization of what Putnam (1994) calls "social capital". In his book he explains regional economic success in Italy in terms of the mobilization of social capital through civic consciousness and politically sensitive, decentralist policy-formulation. The key problem with Putnam's analysis is his emphasis on the thousand-year *durée* necessary to achieve this happy State. This is unnecessary, learning involves borrowing as well as introspection or search activities. Rustbelt regions have moved a long way in 10–20 year periods.

However, there is still some distance to go, and the key to the next phase of recovery is the implantation as permanent features of the landscape of regional governance the three following features.

First, it is clear that there remains great variability even between these reasonably successful, institutionalized, clustered (or part-clustered) and networked (or at least network-conscious) regions in the degree to which they have absorbed the practices of innovative learning. Intelligent regions have already reached the stage, at least periodically, of what Stiglitz (1987) calls *"learning-by-learning"*. That is, they habitually, al-though not necessarily permanently, evaluate their performance in terms of the strengths and weaknesses of their own implementation, incorporating what Argyris & Schon (1978) refer to as "double feedback loops" where they also compare with others as well (on this in, for example, Baden–Württemberg, see Naschold 1994).

Secondly, this leads into the requirement to improve not only learning capacity but also *reflexivity* in the implementation sphere. This is often difficult for administrative authorities to do; for example, having developed a service, as happened in Emilia–Romagna, with *"servizi reali"* (Bianchi & Gualtieri 1993), i.e. innovation services to firms that the market had failed to supply. But in a period of reflexivity occasioned by political change in Italy, the decision to allow the private sector in to compete as providers of those same services was reached after a prolonged, wide-ranging discourse exercise. NRW's SoTech and other innovation development strategies, rolling forward but not necessarily being controlled by the *Land*, but rather shifting towards self-regulation, would also be a case in point. Market failure is predictable; if an activity has no apparent, predictable, short-term return on investment, no investment comes forth. But, as Johnson (1992) notes, *government failure* can only too easily occur too when the ambition to demonstrate relevance clouds the recognition that continued government policy-domination may be inappropriate.

Finally, both *institutional learning* and *institutional reflexivity* require the existence of a civil society capable of responsible self-management. The US and German experience suggests that, experimentally, there are strong signs of a willingness on the part of communities to engage in this kind of *associative* activity, to make a contribution and take initiative, provided it is backed with appropriate financial mechanisms or guarantees. Nevertheless, Rustbelt regions often inherit a culture of defensiveness and dependence from long years of class-based solidaristic struggle. Cultural change in the mentalities of members of civil society, their elected representatives and managers of business enterprises is a prerequisite for securing the gains that have been made in the recent past. It is the reflexive, associative, learning regions that are highly likely to make the economic running in future, and the challenge is to emulate them.

References

Abromeit, H. 1986. *British Steel*. Leamington Spa, England: Berg.

Ache, P., H-J. Bremm, A. Mertens 1988. Emscherzone im Umbruch – Entwicklungslinien des räumlichen Strukturwandels. *RaumPlanung* **42**, 197–204.

Ache, P. & K. R. Kunzmann 1992. Bleibt die Emscherzone als Verlierer(in) zurück? In *Die Emscherzone: Strukturwandel, Disparitäten und eine Bauausstellung*, P. Ache, H-J. Bremm, K. R. Kunzmann, M. Wegener (eds), 7–19 [Dortmunder Beiträge zur Raumplanung]. Dortmund: Institut für Raumplanung, IRPUD.

Albert, M. 1993. *Capitalism versus capitalism*. London: Whurr.

Alemann, U. 1990. Sozialverträgliche Technikgestaltung, ein NRW-Modell für Europa? In *Die Kraft der Region: Nordrhein–Westfalen in Europa*, U. Alemann, R. Heinze, B. Hombach (eds), 547–60. Bonn: Dietz.

Amin, A. & J. Tomaney 1993. Turning the tide? The impact of urban and regional regeneration initiatives in North East England. In *Community economic development*, David Fasenfast (ed.), 65–89. London: Macmillan.

— 1994. The regional dilemma in a neo-liberal Europe. Paper presented at "The evolution of rules for a single European market" conference, Exeter, September.

Argyris, C. & D. Schon 1978. *Organizational learning: a theory of action perspective*. Reading, Mass.: Addison–Wesley.

Avis, R. 1990. British Steel: a case of the decentralization of collective bargaining. *Human Resource Management Journal* **1**(1), 90–99.

Bacon, N., P. Blyton, J. Morris 1994. Steel, state and industrial relations: restructuring work and employment relations in the steel industry. In *International privatisation: strategies and practice*, T. Clarke (ed.), 98–119. Berlin: de Gruyter.

Bagnall, J. 1991. Why Nortel is retreating from Canada. *Financial Times of Canada*, 15 June.

Bakker, I. 1992. Taking the high road to economic change. In *Empowering workers in the global economy: a labour agenda for the 1990s* [background papers and proceedings from a conference]. Toronto: United Steelworkers of America.

Beauregard, R. A. 1989. *Atop the urban hierarchy*. Totowa, NJ: Rowman & Littlefield.

— 1993. Industrial diversification as economic policy. In *Community economic development*, David Fasenfast (ed.), 109–121. London: Macmillan.

— (forthcoming). Institutional constraints and subnational planning: economic development in the USA. *Evaluation and Program Planning*.

Beauregard, R. A., P. Lawless, S. Deitrick. 1992. Collaborative strategies for reindustrialization: Sheffield and Pittsburgh. *Economic Development Quarterly* **6**(4), 418–30.

Becattini, G. 1990. The Marshallian industrial district as a socio-economic notion. In *Industrial districts and interfirm co-operation in Italy*, F. Pyke, G. Becattini, W. Sengenberger (eds), 37–51. Geneva: International Institute for Labour Studies.

Beck, U. 1992. *Risk society*. London: Sage.

Begg, I. & D. Mayes 1993. Cohesion, convergence and economic and monetary union in Europe. *Regional Studies* **27**, 29–38.

Bell, D. 1973. *The coming of post-industrial society*. New York: Basic Books.

Bericht der Kommission Montanregionen des Landes Nordrhein-Westfalen 1989. Düsseldorf: Ministry of Economic Affairs (NRW).

Bertin, O. 1990. Campbell shrinks under free trade. *The Globe and Mail*, 29 November.

Bertin, O. 1991. Campbell to buy back Canadian shares. *The Globe and Mail*, 29 March.

Best, M. 1990. *The new competition: institutions of industrial restructuring*. Cambridge: Polity Press.

Bianchi, P. & M. Gualtieri 1993. Innovation policy at the local and national levels: the case of Emilia–Romagna. *European Planning Studies* **1**, 25–42.

Birch, D. 1987. *Job creation in America*. New York: Free Press.

Blair, J. & R. Premus 1987. Major factors in industrial location. *Economic Development Quarterly* **1**(1), 72–85.

Bluestone, B. & B. Harrison 1982. *The deindustrialization of America*. New York: Basic Books.

Blyton, P. 1992. Steel: a classic case of industrial relations change in Britain. *Journal of Management Studies* **29**(5), 635–50.

— 1993. Steel. In *Public enterprise in transition: industrial relations in state and privatized corporations*, A. Pendleton & J. Winterton (eds), 42–58. London: Routledge.

Blyton, P., H. W. Franz, J. Morris, N. Bacon, R. Lichte 1993. *Changes in work organisation in the UK and German steel industries: implications for trade unions and industrial relations*. Report for the Anglo–German Foundation for the Study of Industrial Society, University of Wales, Cardiff, and SFS Dortmund.

Boekholt, P. 1994. Methodology to Identify Regional Clusters of Firms and their Needs. Paper to SPRINT–RITTS Workshop, Luxembourg, May.

Bosch G. 1992. *Retraining not redundancy: innovative approaches to industrial restructuring*. Geneva: International Institute for Labour Studies.

Bosch G. 1993. Regionale Entwicklung und Weiterbildung. In *Akademie für Raumforschung und Landeskunde, Forschungs- und Sitzungsberichte*. Hannover: Band 191.

Braun-Henze, G., S. Heizelmann, H. Rieger 1986. *Die Bedeutung der beruflichen Weiterbildung im Rahmen der technischen und wirtschaftlichen Innovation in Nordrhein–Westfalen*. Landesverband NW für Weiterbildung in Technik und Wirtschaft e. V., Düsseldorf.

— *Auswertung der Umfrage zum Qualifikationsbedarf in der Industrie*. Landesarbeitsamt Nordrhein–Westfalen, Düsseldorf.

Braun, J. U. A. 1984. Bedarfsorientierte Beratung in der Weiterbildung. Technologische Entwicklung und Arbeitslosigkeit als Herausforderung für die Weiterbildungsberatung, München

Brusco, S. 1982. The Emilian model: productive decentralisation and social integration. *Cambridge Journal of Economics* **6**, 167–84.

Brusco, S. 1992. Small firms and the provision of real services. In *Industrial districts and local economic development*, F. Pyke & W. Sengenberger (eds), 177–196. Geneva: International Institute for Labour Studies.

Carnesale, A. 1991. *America and the new economy.* San Francisco: Jossey–Bass.

Casson, M. 1993. Cultural determinants of economic performance, *Journal of Comparative Economics* **17**, 418–42.

— 1995. *Essays in the economics of trust.* London: Routledge.

Castells, M. 1989. *The informational city.* Oxford: Basil Blackwell.

CEC (Commission of the European Communities) 1992. *Treaty on European Union.* London: HMSO.

Chandler, A. 1990. *Scale and scope.* Harvard: Harvard University Press (Belknap).

Chesnais, F. 1988. Technical co-operation agreements between firms. *STI Review* **4**, 52–115.

CLES 1990. *First Year Report on UDCs.* Manchester: Centre for Local Economic Strategies.

Cochran, T. C. 1978. *Pennsylvania: a bicentennial history.* New York: Norton.

Cockerill, A. & S. Cole 1986. Restructuring British Steel. In *Ailing steel,* W. H. Goldberg (ed.), 149–63. Aldershot: Gower.

Cohen, S. & J. Zysman 1987. *Manufacturing matters.* New York: Basic Books.

Cooke, P. 1992. Regional innovation systems: competitive regulation in the new Europe. *Geoforum* **23**, 365–82.

— 1993. The experiences of German engineering firms in applying lean production methods. In *Lean production and beyond: labour aspects of a new production concept,* W. Sengenberger & D. Campbell (eds), 77–94. Forum Series on Labour in a Changing World Economy 2, International Institute for Labour Studies, Geneva.

— 1994. Institutional reflexivity and the rise of the region State. In *Space and social theory: geographic interpretations of postmodernity,* G. Benko & U. Strohmeyer (eds), 101–116. Oxford, Basil Blackwell.

— 1996. The new wave of regional innovation networks. *Small Business Economics* **9**, (in press).

Cooke, P. & K. Morgan 1991. The intelligent region: industrial and institutional innovation in Emilia–Romagna. Regional Industrial Research Report 7, Centre for Advanced Studies, University of Wales, Cardiff.

Cooke, P., F. Moulaert, E. Swyngedouw, O. Weinstein, P. Wells 1992. *Towards global localization: the computing and communication industries in Britain and France.* London: UCL Press.

Cooke, P. & S. Davies 1993. *An economic profile of North-Rhine–Westphalia.* Report commissioned by the Welsh Development Agency, Cardiff.

Cooke, P. & G. Jones 1993. Local development strategies: Cardiff and Rhondda. In *Local development in economically disintegrated areas: a proactive strategy against poverty in the European Community,* F. Moulaert et al. (eds), 103–140. Lille: IFRESI.

Cooke, P. & K. Morgan 1993. The network paradigm: new departures in corporate and regional development. *Environment & Planning D: Society & Space* **11**, 543–64.

Cooke, P., J. Morgan, A. Price 1993. *The challenge of lean production in German industry.* Regional Industrial Research Report 12, Centre for Advanced Studies, University of Wales, Cardiff.

— 1993. *The future of the Mittelstand: collaboration versus competition.* Regional Industrial Research Report 13, University of Wales, Cardiff.

Cookson, C. 1994. UK advance promises quicker computers. *Financial Times* (26 October), 16.

Council of Europe 1986. *Role of the regions in building Europe.* Strasbourg: The Council.

Coy, R. 1992. Cooperation networks and innovative roles for employers' and workers' organisations. Paper presented to an International Conference: "Regional development: the roles of technical service institutes and co-operation networks", Valencia, November.

Crandall, R. 1993. *Manufacturing on the move*. Washington DC: Brookings Institution.

Danielzyk, R. 1992a. Gibt es im Ruhrgebiet eine "postfordistische Regionalpolitik"? *Geographische Zeitschrift* **80**(2), 84–105.

— 1992b. Niedersachsen im Umbruch – Probleme und Perspektiven der Regionen und der Regionalpolitik. Verein Eigenständige Regionalentwicklung Niedersachsen. In *Wer entwickelt die Region?*, 9–30. Hannover: Stiftung.

Danielzyk, R. & G. Wood 1993. Restructuring old industrial and inner urban areas: a contrastive analysis of State policies in Great Britain and Germany. *European Planning Studies* **1**(2), 123–47.

Davies, S. 1994. Interfacing universities and SMEs in North-Rhine–Westphalia. Proceedings of an international conference, "Co-operation & competitiveness: interfirm co-operation – a means towards SME competitiveness", 401–47. Lisbon: PEDIP.

Davis, L. E., J. R. T. Hughes, D. M. McDougall 1972. *American economic history: the development of the national economy*. New York: Harper & Row.

Dawkins, W. 1990. Rhône–Alpes: a spirit of independence. *Financial Times* (27 March), 18.

Dei Ottati, G. 1994. Co-operation and competition in the industrial district as an organisation model. *European Planning Studies* **2**, 463–83.

Department of Education and Science 1991. *Education and training for the 21st century*. London: HMSO.

Derenbach, R. 1984. Berufliche Kompetenzen für eine selbsttragende regional-wirtschaftliche Entwicklung, Plädoyer für eine qualitative Regionalpolitik auf der Grundlage von Qualifikation und Innovation, Informationen zur Raumentwicklung, Heft 1/2 1984, S.84.

Dertouzos, M., R. Lester, R. Solow 1989. *Made in America*. Cambridge, Mass.: MIT Press.

Deubner, C., U. Rehfeldt, F. Schlupp, G. Ziebura 1979. *Die Internationalisierung des Kapitals: neue Theorien in der internationalen Diskussion*. Frankfurt: Campus.

Dicken, P. 1992. *Global shift*. London: Paul Chapman; New York: Guilford.

Drache, D. 1992. *Getting on track: social democratic strategies for Ontario*. Montreal: McGill–Queen's University Press.

Drache, D. & M. Gertler 1991. *The new era of global competition*. Montreal: McGill–Queen's University Press.

Drucker, P. 1993. *Postcapitalist society*. New York: Harper Business.

Eisinger, P. 1988. *The rise of the entrepreneurial State*. Madison: University of Wisconsin Press.

Esser, J. 1989. Does industrial policy matter? *Land* governments in research and technology policy in Federal Germany. In *The new centralism: Britain out of step in Europe?*, C. Crouch & D. Marquand (eds), 84–96. London: Political Quarterly Books.

European, The 1994. How Wales manages to keep its customers satisfied (14 April).

Fainstein, S. S. & N. I. Fainstein 1989. The ambivalent State: economic development policy in the US federal system under the Reagan administration. *Urban Affairs Quarterly* **25**, 41–62.

Federal Reserve Bank of Chicago 1993. *Regional economies in global markets*. Chicago: Federal Reserve Bank of Chicago.

Florida, R. 1991. The new industrial revolution. *Futures* **23**(July-August), 559–76.

Florida, R. & M. Kenney 1990. *The breakthrough illusion*. New York: Basic Books.

—1991. The Japanese transplants, production organization and regional development. *American Planning Association, Journal* **57**(Winter), 21–38.

—1993. The new age of capitalism: innovation-mediated production. *Futures* **25**(July-August).

Franz, H-W. & R. Lichte 1991. *Challenges facing the steel industry: the challenge facing the unions*. Dortmund: SFS.

Fromhold-Eisebith, M. 1992. *Wissenschaft und Forschung als Regionalwirtschaftliches Potential?* Working Paper 4, Maas–Rhine Institute, Aachen.

Fürst, D. & H. Kilper 1995. The innovative power of regional policy networks: a comparison of two approaches to political modernization in North-Rhine–Westphalia. *European Planning Studies* **3**, 287–302.

Ganser, K. 1991. Die Strategie der IBA Emscher Park. *Garten und Landschaft* **10**, 13–15.

Garofoli, G. 1992. *Endogenous development & southern Europe*. Aldershot, England: Avebury.

Gertler, M. 1991. *Toronto: the state of the regional economy*. Working paper 6, Royal Commission on the Future of the Toronto Waterfront, Toronto.

Giarratani, F. & D. Houston 1989. Structural change and economic policy in a declining metropolitan region. *Urban Studies* **26**, 549–58.

The Globe and Mail 1994a. Doors close at NorTel plant. 27 May.

The Globe and Mail 1994b. Northern Telecom targets growth in Asia. 27 May.

Gorzelak, G. & A. Kuklinski 1992. *Dilemmas of regional policy in eastern & central Europe*. Warsaw: University of Warsaw Press.

Gorzelak, G. & B. Jalowiecki 1993. *Regional question in Europe*. Warsaw: University of Warsaw Press.

Grabher, G. 1990. *On the weakness of strong ties: the ambivalent role of inter-firm relations in the decline and reorganization of the Ruhr*. Discussion Paper FsI 90-4, Science Centre, Berlin.

— 1991. Rebuilding cathedrals in the desert: new patterns of co-operation between large and small firms in the coal, iron and steel complex of the German Ruhr area. In *Regions reconsidered: economic networks, innovation and local development in industrialized countries*, E. Bergman, G. Maier, F. Tödtling (eds), 59–78. London: Mansell.

— 1993a. The weakness of strong ties: the lock-in of regional development in the Ruhr area. In Grabher (1993b), 255–77.

— (ed.) 1993b. *The embedded firm: on the socio-economics of industrial networks*. London: Routledge.

Graham, O. 1976. *Toward a planned society*. New York: Oxford University Press.

Hahne, U. 1984. Endogenes Potential: Stand der Diskussion. In *Arbeitsmaterial Akademie für Raumforschung und Landesplanung* 76, Endogene Entwicklung. Theoretische Begründung und Strategiediskussion, Hannover, S.27–39.

Hamm, R. & H. Wienert 1990. *Strukturelle Anpassung altindustrieller Regionen im internationalen Vergleich*. Berlin: Duncker & Humboldt.

Harrison, B. 1994. *Lean and mean: the changing landscape of corporate power in the age of flexibility*. New York: Basic Books.

Harrison, B. & S. Kanter 1978. The political economy of States' job creation business incentives. *American Institute of Planners, Journal* **44**, 424–35.

Harvie, C. 1994. *The rise of regional Europe*. London: Routledge.

Hassink, R. 1992. *Regional innovation policy: case studies from the Ruhr area, Baden–Württemberg and the North East of England*. Utrecht: NGS.

Heinze, R. & H. Voelzkow 1991. Kommunalverbände und Verbände. Inszenierter Korporatismus auf lokaler und regionaler Ebene? In *Brennpunkt Stadt: Stadtpolitik und lokale Politikforschung in den 80er und 90er Jahren*, H. Heinelt & H. Wollmann (eds), 187–206. Basel: Birkhäuser.

Held, D. 1991. Democracy, the nation State, and the global system. *Economy & Society* **20**, 138–72.

Herrigel, G. 1993. Power and the redefinition of industrial districts: the case of Baden–Württemberg. In Grabher (1993b), 227–51.

Hirst, P. 1994. *Associative democracy: new forms of economic and social governance*. Amherst: University of Massachusetts Press.

Hirst, P. & J. Zeitlin 1990. *Flexible specialisation and post-Fordism; theory, evidence and policy implications*. Working paper, Birkbeck Policy Centre, University of London.

Hounshell, D. 1984. *From American system to mass production, 1800–1932*. Baltimore: Johns Hopkins University Press.

Huggins, R. 1992. *Regional training development within national and European systems*. MSc dissertation, Department of City and Regional Planning, University of Wales College of Cardiff.

IBA (Internationale Bauausstellung Emscher Park) 1989: Internationale Bauausstellung Emscher Park – Workshop for the Future of Old Industrial Areas. Memorandum on Content and Organization. (Gelsenkirchen)

— 1991: Strategien für alte Industrieregionen. (= Emscher Park Tagungsberichte, 5) (Gelsenkirchen)

— (ed.) 1993. *Katalog zum Stand der Projekte. Frühjahr 1993*. Gelsenkirchen: International Building Exhibition.

— Dokument 1991: Zur strukturpolitischen Bedeutung der Internationalen Bauausstellung Emscher Park. In: IBA Emscher Park (Hrsg.): Arbeiten im Park. Kurzdokumentation der Projekte der Internationalen Bauausstellung Emscher Park (Gelsenkirchen).

— Memorandum 1998: Internationale Bauausstellung Emscher-Park. Werkstatt für die Zukunft alter Industriegebiete. Memorandum zu Inhalt und Organisation, edited by Minister für Stadtentwicklung, Wohnen und Verkehr des Landes Nordrhein-Westfalen (Düsseldorf).

IHK Siegen 1990. Info-Stelle Weiterbildung. Baustein einer dynamischen Qualifizierungsgesellschaft-Bilanz einer Pilotphase, Siegen MWTM (1985), Moderne Technologien in der beruflichen Bildung, Materialien zum Berufsbildungsbericht 1985, der Minister für Wirtschaft, Mittelstand und Verkehr des Landes Nordrhein-Westfalen, Düsseldorf 1985.

ILO 1992. *Recent developments in the iron & steel industry*. Geneva: International Labour Organisation.

JICST 1992. *White Paper on science & technology: regional development of science and technology*. Tokyo: Japan Information Centre of Science & Technology.

Jochimsen, R. 1990. The Länder role in local economic development. In *Local economic development in Britain and Germany*, R. Bennett, G. Krebs, H. Zimmermann (eds), 75–83. London: Anglo–German Foundation.

Johanson, J. 1991. Interfirm networks in Swedish industry. Department of Business Economics, University of Uppsala, Sweden.

Johnson, B. 1992. Institutional learning. In *National systems of innovation: towards a theory of innovation and interactive learning*, B. Lundvall (ed.), 23–42. London: Pinter.

Kelly, J. 1984. Management strategy and the reform of collective bargaining: cases from the British Steel Corporation. *British Journal of Industrial Relations* **22**, 135–53.

Kiesewetter, H. 1989. *Industrielle Revolution in Deutschland 1815–1914*. Frankfurt: Suhrkamp.

Kilper, H. 1992: Das Politikmodell IBA Emscher Park. Erfahrungen bei der Implementation der "Arbeiten im Park"-Projekte, Gelsenkirchen, IAT-PS 04.

Kilper, H. & D. Rehfeld 1992. *Vom Konzept der Agglomerationsvorteile zum Industrial District. Überlegungen zur Bedeutung innerregionaler Verflechtungen und Kooperationsbeziehungen für die Stabilität von Regionen*. Discussion Paper IAT-PS O3, Institute of Work and Technology, Gelsenkirchen.

Kooistra, D. 1991. *Regenerating urban economies through science and technology in Germany: the cities of Braunschweig and Aachen*. Delft: TNO.

Körfer, H. & E. Latniak 1994a. Approaches to technology policy and regional milieux – experiences of programmes and projects in North Rhine–Westphalia. *European Planning Studies* **2**, 303–320.

Körfer, H. R. & E. Latniak 1994b. *New perspectives in policies of economic modernisation in North-Rhine–Westphalia*. Report, Institut Arbeit und Technik, Gelsenkirchen.

Krugman, P. 1991. Increasing returns and economic geography. *Journal of Political Economy* **99**, 483–99.

KVR 1992. *Kommunalverband Ruhrgebiet: Umweltbezogene Kleinunternehmen im Ruhrgebiet – Bestand und Perspektiven*. Discussion Paper, KVR, Essen.

Land NRW 1992. *Landesentwicklungsbericht Nordrhein–Westfalen*. Düsseldorf: Ministry of Economic Affairs.

Lash, S. & Urry, J. 1994. *Economies of signs and space*. London: Sage.

Latniak, E. & G. Simonis 1994. Socially oriented technology policy in Germany: experiences of a North-Rhine–Westphalian programme. In *Technology policy: towards an integration of social and ecological concerns*, G. Aichholzer & G. Schienstock (eds), 223–48. Berlin: de Gruyter.

Lawless, P. 1991. Urban policy in the Thatcher decade: English inner-city policy, 1979–1990. *Environment and Planning C* **9**, 15–30.

Lazonick, W. 1990. *Competitive advantage on the shopfloor*. Cambridge, Mass.: Harvard University Press.

Lazonick, W. 1992. *Industry clusters versus global webs*. Unpublished MS, Department of Economics, Columbia University, New York.

Le Grand, J. 1990. *Quasi-markets and social policy*. Research Briefing 9, Economic and Social Research Council, Swindon.

Lipietz, A. 1987. *Mirages and miracles: the crises of global Fordism*. London: Verso.

Little, B. 1994. Ontario's "secret" boom belt: Hamilton to London – businesses roar ahead. *The Globe and Mail*, 5 December.

Loewe, W. & K. Wand 1987. Krisenbranchen – Produktionen und Regionen ohne Zukunft? *Gewerkschaftliche Monatshefte* **38**, 553–64.

Lorenz, C. 1994. The real face of Japanese R&D in Europe. *Financial Times* (17 October), 22.

Mahood, C. 1991. The Golden Horseshoe's getting rusty. *The Globe and Mail*, 7 June.

Mahood, C. 1994. Ontario wins $600-million plant: Toyota to expand at Cambridge site to produce 200,000 cars a year. *The Globe and Mail*, 4 November.

Maillat, D. 1991. Local dynamism, milieu and innovative enterprises. In *Cities of the 21st century*, J. Brotchie, M. Batty, P. Hall, P. Newton (eds), 265–74. London: Longman.

Marin, B. & R. Mayntz (eds) 1991. *Policy networks*. Frankfurt: Campus.

Massey, D. 1984. *Spatial divisions of labour*. London: Macmillan.

McKinsey Global Institute 1993. *Manufacturing productivity*. Washington DC: McKinsey Global Institute.

Meegan, R. 1994. A "Europe of the Regions"? A view from Liverpool on the Atlantic Arc periphery. *European Planning Studies* **2**, 59–80.

Markusen, A. 1987. *Regions: the economics and politics of territory*. Totowa, NJ: Rowman & Littlefield.

Markusen, A. & V. Carlson 1989. Deindustrialization in the American Midwest: causes and responses. In *Deindustrialization and regional economic transformation: the experience of the United States*, L. Rodwin & H. Sazanami (eds), 29–59. Boston: Unwin Hyman.

Markusen, A., P. Hall, S. Campbell, S. Deitrick 1991. *The rise of the Gunbelt: the military remapping of industrial America*. New York: Oxford University Press.

Marshall, A. 1927. *Industry & trade*. London: Macmillan.

Metropolitan Toronto 1994. *Year-end economic review, 1993*. Toronto: Economic Development Division, Office of the Chairman.

Meyer, D. 1983. The emergence of the American manufacturing belt: an interpretation. *Journal of Historical Geography* **9**(2), 145–74.

Mid Glamorgan TEC 1992. *Survey of employers' attitudes to training and skill shortages in Mid Glamorgan*. Report, Mid Glamorgan TEC, Treforest.

Ministry of Finance 1995. *Ontario economic outlook 1994–1998*. Toronto: Queen's Printer for Ontario.

MITT (Ministry of Industry, Trade and Technology) 1992. *An industrial policy framework for Ontario*. Toronto: Queen's Printer for Ontario.

Montankommission 1989. *Bericht der Kommission Montanregionen des Landes Nordrhein–Westfalen*. Düsseldorf: Ministry of Economic Affairs (NRW).

Morris, J., N. Bacon, P. Blyton, H-W. Franz 1992. Beyond survival: the implementation of new forms of work organisation in the UK and German steel industries. *International Journal of Human Resource Management* **3**, 307–29.

Nairn, T. 1977. *The break-up of Britain*. London: Verso.

Naschold, F. 1994. Jenseits des Baden–Württembergischen "Exceptionalism". Report 38, Akademie für Technikfolgenabschätzung, Stuttgart.

National Audit Office 1989. *Regenerating the inner cities*. London: HMSO.

National Council for Urban Economic Development 1993. *Forces in the new economy: implications for economic development*. Washington DC: National Council for Urban Economic Development.

NIEC 1994. *The implications of peripherality for Northern Ireland*. Report 111, Northern Ireland Economic Council, Belfast.

Nonaka, I. 1991. The knowledge creating company. *Harvard Business Review* **69** (November–December), 69–104.

NRW (North Rhine-Westphalia) 1990. NRW. *Spitzenland in Umwelttechnik*. Düsseldorf: Bonner Energie-Report.

— Ministry of Economics 1994. *Technologie-Handbuch Nordrhein–Westfalen*. Düsseldorf: Ministerium.

Ohmae, K. 1985. *Triad power: the coming shape of global competition*. New York: Harper & Row.

— 1990. *The borderless world*. New York: Harper & Row.

— 1993. The rise of the region State. *Foreign Affairs* **72**, 78–87.

Osborne, D. 1988. *Laboratories of democracy: a new breed of governor creates models for national growth*. Boston: Harvard Business School Press.

Osborne, D. & T. Gaebler 1992. *Reinventing government*. Reading: Addison–Wesley.

Perry, D. C. 1987. The politics of dependency in deindustrializing America: the case of Buffalo, New York. In *The capitalist city*, M. P. Smith & J. R. Feagin (eds), 113–37. Oxford: Basil Blackwell.

Perry, D. C. & Watkins, A. 1978. *The rise of the Sunbelt cities*. London, Sage.

Petzina, D. 1987. Wirtschaftliche Ungleichgewichte in Deutschland. In *Nord–Süd in Deutschland? Vorurteile und Tatsachen*, H. G. Wehling (ed.), 59–81. Stuttgart: Kohlhammer.

Petzina, D., W. Plumpe, S. Unger 1990. *Diversifizierungsprozesse im Ruhrgebiet in wirtschaftstheoretischer Perspektive*. Arbeitspapier 1/90, Zentrums für Interdisziplinäre Ruhrgebietsforschung, Ruhr Univeristät, Bochum.

Piore, M. & C. Sabel 1984. *The second industrial divide*. New York: Basic Books.

Piore, M. J. & C. F. Sabel 1985. *Das Ende der Massenproduktion*. Berlin: Wagenbuch.

Pittsburgh High Technology Council and Southwestern Pennsylvania Industrial Resource Center 1994. *Thinking differently about the region: Southwestern Pennsylvania's manufacturing and technology assets*. Pittsburgh: Pittsburgh High Technology Center.

Porter, M. 1990. *The competitive advantage of nations*. New York: The Free Press.

Powell, W. 1990. Neither market nor hierarchy: network forms of organization. In *Research in organizational behaviour* (vol. 12), B. Straw & L. Cummings (eds), 74–96 Greenwich, Connecticut: JAI Press.

Premier's Council 1988. *Competing in the new global economy*. Toronto: Queen's Printer for Ontario.

Pritchard, T. 1993a. Magna beefing up in Europe. *The Globe and Mail*. 21 October.

— 1993b. Magna continues acquisitions in Germany. *The Globe and Mail*. 30 November.

Prowse, M. 1995. Midwest toasts dollar's decline. *Financial Times*, 23 March.

Pujol, J. 1994. Between regional autonomy and European integration – the course of Catalonia. Paper presented at conference on "Regiovision: Roads to Sustainability", Oberhausen, Germany, October.

Putnam, R. 1993. *Making democracy work*. Princeton, NJ: Princeton University Press.

Radkau, J. 1989. *Technik in Deutschland, Vom 18: Jahrhundert bis zur Gegenwart*. Frankfurt: Suhrkamp.

Reich, R. 1991. *The work of nations*. New York: Knopf.

Rehfeld, D. 1992a. *Industrieller Wandel und Netzwerkstrukturen im Ruhrgebiet – das Beispiel der Umweltschutzindustrie*. Arbeitspapier für das Verbundprojekt "Alte Industrieregionen im Vergleich", Gelsenkirchen.

— 1992b. *Fragestellungen zur Diskussion um Produktionsketten und Produktionscluster*. Arbeitspapier für das Verbundprojekt "Alte Industrieregionen im Vergleich", Gelsenkirchen.

— 1993a. *Patterns of economic restructuring in an area of industrial decline: industrial development, change factors and regional policy in the Ruhrgebiet*. Future of Industry Papers 20 (FPO 373, final report), Brussels.

— 1993b. Produktionscluster und räumliche Entwicklung – Beispiele und Konsequenzen. In *Ökonomische und politische Netzwerke in der Region*, W. Krumbein (ed.), 187–206. Münster: LIT.

Rodwin, L. & H. Sazanami (eds) 1989. *Deindustrialization and regional economic transformation: the experience of the United States*. Boston: Unwin Hyman.

Romer, P. 1990. Endogenous technical change. *Journal of Political Economy* **98**, 338–54.

Rosenfeld, S. 1992. *Competitive manufacturing*. New Brunswick NJ: Center for Urban Policy Research.

Rusk, D. 1993. *Cities without suburbs*. Washington DC: The Woodrow Wilson Center Press.

Sabel, C. 1992. Studied trust: building new forms of co-operation in a volatile economy. In *Industrial districts and local economic regeneration*, F. Pyke & W. Sengenberger (eds), 215–50. Geneva: International Institute for Labour Studies.

Sauter E. 1993. Handlungsebenen der Weiterbildung. Überregionale Ordnungselemente für eine regionale Gestaltung der beruflichen Weiterbildung. In *Akademie für Raumforschung und Landeskunde, Forschungs- und Sitzungsberichte*. Hannover: Band 191.

Sauter E. & E. Fink 1980. *Planung, Organization und Durchführung von Weiterbildung in den Bildungswerken der Wirtschaft*. Ergebnisse einer Befragung in 11 Bildungswerken der Wirtschaft, Berichte zur beruflichen Bildung Heft 23, Bundesinstitut für Berufsbildung, Berlin.

Sawers, L. & W. Tabb 1984. *Sunbelt/Snowbelt*. Oxford: Oxford University Press.

Sayer, A. & R. Walker 1992. *The new social economy: reworking the division of labour*. Oxford: Basil Blackwell.

Saxenian, A. 1994. *Regional advantage: culture and competition in Silicon Valley and Route 128*. Cambridge, Mass.: Harvard University Press.

Schlieper, A. 1986. *150 Jahre Ruhrgebiet: ein Kapitel deutscher Wirtschaftsgeschichte*. Düsseldorf: Schwann.

—1989. Strukturelle Herausforderung für die Wirtschaftspolitik: Probleme, Chancen, Lösungen. In *Technik–Wandel–Steuerung: Planen und Gestalten heute*, J. Calliess (ed.), 157–65. Loccum: Evangelische Akademie.

Schmals, K. M. 1991. Modernisierungspolitik für ein starkes Stück Deutschland? In *Internationale Bauausstellung Emscherpark – Balanceakt zwischen internationaler Kapitalverwertung und lokaler Verbesserung der Lebensverhältnisse*, S. Müller & K. M. Schmals (eds), 48–60. Arbeitspapier 6, Fachgebietes soziologische Grundlagen der Raumplanung, Universität Dortmund.

Scholz D. 1991. Anregungen für eine Entwicklungs- und Beschäftigungspolitik in Frankfurt/Oder. In *Beschäftigungsplan und Beschäftigungsgesellschaft*, G. Bosch & H. Neumann (eds), 143–59. Cologne: Bund.

Schönfeld, M. & S. Stöbe 1992. *Personalpolitik, Ausbildung und Weiterbildung im Raum Gelsenkirchen*. Report, Institut Arbeit und Technik, Gelsenkirchen.

Schumpeter, J. 1943. *Capitalism, socialism & democracy*. London: George Allen & Unwin.

Selle, K. 1993. Unsichtbar in Spannungsfeldern. Anmerkungen zur Arbeit der IBA. In *Effektivität intermediärer Organisationen für den regionalen Strukturwandel*, D. Fürst & H. Kilper (eds), 293–315. Dokumentation der Tagung vom 18 Juni 1993 am Institut Arbeit und Technik, Gelsenkirchen.

Semlinger K. (1989), Vorauschauende Personalwirtschaft – Betriebliche Verbreitung und infrastrukturelle Ausstattung, in: Mitteilungen aus der Arbeitsmarkt- und Berufsforschung Heft 3.

Sengenberger, W. 1987. *Struktur und Funktionsweise von Arbeitsmärkten: der bundesdeutsche Arbeitsmarkt im internationalen Vergleich*. Frankfurt/New York: Campus.

Shapira, P. 1990. *Modernizing manufacturing: new policies to build industrial extension services*. Washington DC: Economic Policy Institute.

Shapley, D. 1994. Globalisation prompts exodus, *Financial Times* (17 March), 15.

Siebel, W. 1992. Die Internationale Bauausstellung Emscher Park: eine Strategie zur ökonomischen, ökologischen und sozialen Erneuerung alter Industrieregionen. In *Ökonomie und Politik in alten Industrieregionen Europas: Probleme der Stadt- und Regionalentwicklung in Deutschland, Frankreich, Großbritannien und Italien*, H. Häußermann (ed.), 214–31. Berlin: Birkhäuser.

Sieverts, T. 1991: Die Internationale Bauausstellung Emscher Park. Werkstatt zur Erneuerung alter Industriegebiete. Eine strukturpolitische Initiative des Landes Nordrhein-Westfalen. In *Internationale Bauausstellung Emscher Park – Zukunftswerkstatt für Industrieregionen*, T. Sieverts (ed.), 4–11. Cologne: R. Müller.

Staudt, E. U. A. 1985. Innovation und Qualifikation. *Frankfurter Allgemeine Zeitung: Blick durch die Wirtschaft* vom 9 September 1985.

Staudt, E., J. Bock, P. Mühlemeyer 1994. Technology centres and science parks: agents or competence centres for small businesses? *International Journal of Technology Management* 9(2), 196–212.

Stiglitz, J. 1987. Learning to learn, localized learning and technological progress. In *Economic policy and technological performance*, P. Dasgupta & P. Stoneman (eds), 125–53. Cambridge: Cambridge University Press.

Storey, D. & S. Johnson 1987. Regional variations in entrepreneurship in the UK. *Scottish Journal of Political Economy* 34, 161–73.

Storper, M. & B. Harrison 1991. Flexibility, hierarchy and regional development: the changing structure of industrial production systems and their forms of governance in the 1990s. *Research Policy* **20**, 407–422.

Storper, M. & R. Walker 1989. *The capitalist imperative*. Oxford: Basil Blackwell.

Stull, W. J. & J. F. Madden (eds) 1990. *Post-industrial Philadelphia*. Philadelphia: University of Pennsylvania Press.

Surtees, L. 1991. Unions unite forces against Northern Telecom. *The Globe and Mail*, 18 October.

Swonk, D. 1990. Regional winners and losers. *First Chicago Backgrounder* (May) [bank newsletter].

Thomalla, R. 1993. Structural change under joint responsibility: the technology network in North-Rhine–Westphalia. Paper presented at conference: "Revitalizing older industrial regions: North-Rhine–Westphalia and Wales contrasted", Cardiff, 29 September to 1 October.

US Congress, Office of Technology Assessment 1990. *Making things better: competing in manufacturing*. Washington DC: US Government Printing Office.

Vaizey, J. 1974. *The history of British Steel*. London: Weidenfeld & Nicholson.

Vanselow A. 1995. Qualifizierungskonferenzen als Faktor der regionalen Arbeitsmarkt-und Strukturpolitik, to be published by Institut Arbeit und Technik, Gelsenkirchen.

de Vet, J. 1993. Globalisation and local & regional competitiveness. *STI Review* **13**, 89–121.

Voss, A. 1989. Kritische Anmerkungen zur Internationalen Bauausstellung Emscher-Park. In *Emscher-Raum im Umbruch – Wohin führt die Strategie des IBA-Memorandums?*, 30–35. Arbeitspapier 3, Fachgebietes soziologische Grundlagen der Raumplanung, Universität Dortmund.

Wackerbauer, J. 1992. Der Umweltschutzmarkt: Zunehmender regionaler Wettbewerb um Marktanteile. *IFO-schnelldienst* **45**, 5–13.

Walker, R. 1989. Requiem for corporate geography. *Geografiska Annaler* **71B**, 1–65.

Weber, W. 1990. Entfaltung der Industriewirtschaft. In *Das Ruhrgebiet im Industriezeitalter* (2 Bde), W. Köllmann, H. Korte, W. Weber (eds), 200–319. Düsseldorf: Patmos.

Weißbach, H-J. 1990. *Zur Bedeutung der Kategorie "Branche" als analytischer Mesoebene*. Überarbeitete Fassung eines Vortrags anläßlich des Colloquiums im IAT Gelsenkirchen am 4 Dezember 1990, Dortmund.

Wolfe, D. 1994. Harnessing the region: new perspectives on Canadian industrial policy. Paper presented at the conference "Regions, institutions, and technology: reorganizing economic geography in Canada and the Anglo-American world", University of Toronto, September 23–25.

Womack, J., D. Jones, D. Roos 1990. *The machine that changed the world*. New York: Rawson Associates.

Zander I. 1995. Steuerungsansätze im Bereich Weiterbildung auf lokaler und regionaler Ebene, to be published by Institut Arbeit und Technik, Gelsenkirchen.

Zuboff, S. 1989. *In the age of the smart machine*. New York: Basic Books.

Index